For Us and for Our Salvation

For Us and for Our Salvation

A Pastoral Theology to Cope with These Strange Times

ROBERT E. SCHMITZ

WIPF & STOCK · Eugene, Oregon

FOR US AND FOR OUR SALVATION
A Pastoral Theology to Cope with These Strange Times

Copyright © 2025 Robert E. Schmitz. All rights reserved. Except for brief quotations in critical publications or reviews, no part of this book may be reproduced in any manner without prior written permission from the publisher. Write: Permissions, Wipf and Stock Publishers, 199 W. 8th Ave., Suite 3, Eugene, OR 97401.

Wipf & Stock
An Imprint of Wipf and Stock Publishers
199 W. 8th Ave., Suite 3
Eugene, OR 97401

www.wipfandstock.com

PAPERBACK ISBN: 979-8-3852-3240-6
HARDCOVER ISBN: 979-8-3852-3241-3
EBOOK ISBN: 979-8-3852-3242-0

04/30/25

Scripture texts in this work are taken from the *New American Bible, Revised Edition* © 2010, 1991, 1986, 1970, Confraternity of Christian Doctrine, Washington D.C. and are used with permission of the copyright owner. All rights reserved. No part of the *New American Bible* may be reprinted in any form without permission in writing from the copyright owner.

Excerpts from the English translation of the *Catechism of the Catholic Church* for use in the United States of America © 1994, United States Catholic Conference, Inc.— Liberia Editrice Vaticana, Used with permission. English translation of the *Catechism of the Catholic Church:* Modification from the Editio Typica © 1997, United States Conference of Catholic Bishops—Liberia Editrice Vaticana.

Excerpts from the documents of the Second Vatican Council are from *Vatican II: The Conciliar and Post Conciliar Documents,* edited by Austin Flannery, OP, 1992, used with permission of Liturgical Press, Collegeville, Minnesota.

Excerpts from the English translation of *Order of Christian Funerals* © 1985, 1989, International Commission on English in the Liturgy Corporation (ICEL); excerpts from the English translation of *The Roman Missal* © 2010, ICEL. All rights reserved.

For those who communicated to me
a love of learning.

Contents

Acknowledgments   ix

Introduction   xi

PART 1. A METHOD FOR A PASTORAL THEOLOGY

1. A Pastoral Dimension to Truth   3
2. What Faith Does to Us, in Us, and for Us   15

PART 2. A PERFORMATORY READING OF THE NICENE CREED

3. I Believe   41
4. In One God   51
5. Father Almighty   61
6. Maker of Heaven and Earth, of All Things Visible and Invisible   71
7. Lord Jesus Christ   88
8. Incarnate   99
9. Crucified   109
10. Rose Again and Ascended   122
11. Come Again in Glory   135
12. In the Holy Spirit, the Lord, the Giver of Life   152
13. Who Proceeds from the Father and the Son, Adored and Glorified   161
14. In One, Holy, Catholic, and Apostolic Church   173

PART 3. CONCLUDING THOUGHTS

15 Amen — 189

Bibliography — 197
Index — 203

Acknowledgments

THE FEEDBACK I HAVE received as a preacher or teacher is of two kinds: Most of it has been kind, even supportive. Most of it is also *pro forma*. I have also received more in-depth feedback. It has been provocative and challenging. Some believers and students want *more* from the faith. They need to know whether any of it makes a difference. Such feedback has stimulated my studies. Their thoughts jump into my head in meditative moments and have awakened me from standard explanations of the faith. I have been fortunate to encounter such people from the beginning of my ministry. I thank the searchers and seekers of St. Antoninus, St. Catharine of Siena, and the Community of the Good Shepherd. Now freed from administrative duties and in happy retirement, I have enjoyed encounters with such believers at St. Gabriel's, St. John's, and St. Michael's parishes. I am also glad to have taught part time at Xavier University; there is nothing like sparring with undergrads about religion. The most revelatory time in my long journey was my time in graduate studies at Columbia University. I owe Dr. Gillian Lindt an eternal debt.

Thanks to all those who have made me stop and think.

This book has evolved through many iterations. My friend Jim Johnston has suffered through a few of them. Many thanks! This current text was also critiqued by Rev. John Civille, Tom Giordano, Rev. Norm Langenbrunner, Linda Miller, Rita Mary Minghetti, Rev. Ken Overberg, SJ, and Mary Wlodarski. An earlier draft was critiqued by Jack Peltz. Each of these friends have made this book better. Many, many thanks!

Introduction

CHRISTIANITY'S VISION REMAINS ATTRACTIVE—EVEN in these times. Jesus said, "I have come that they may have life and have it more abundantly" (John 10:10). This book reflects on the communication of the Lord's vision. I am trying to imagine how to convey its original vitality. The goal is achievable because Jesus Christ lives to inspire a way of life. If I reach my goal, this work may contribute to pastoral theology for our strange times.

The situation is obvious to any perceptive believer. There is a disconnect between the attractive vision and today's proclamation. An even greater disconnect exists between the proclamation and its reception. A friend of mine, a brilliant historian, once asked me whether the church has reached a point of no return. He thought the church had become so out of touch with the contemporary world that it had permanently lost its ability to dialog with it. I thought then, as I do now, that he was far too pessimistic. Something crucial is missing, however. Here are some hints:

- Systematic theology records what humans think about divinity. But the Lord's way of life is more than cognition. Pastoral theology longs to know how believers are moved by self-giving love or how anyone bows before God in prayer. My seminary preparation never touched on the pastoral dimension—the life-creating potential—of faith.

- Scripture scholars can parse every word of the good samaritan parable. The formation leader tries to exchange complacency with compassion. But nowhere in the theological literature have I found a source that teaches a minister how to replace self-centeredness with charity.

- The creed confesses the one God. Teaching the unifying truth to people frightened by increasing pluralism may perplex pastors. The Other—those who differ from me and mine—are children of the one God. How to overcome fear of the Other is not taught along with the creedal proposition.

Pastoral theology needs to engage with the truth of Jesus Christ from its own vantage point. The challenge for pastoral ministry is the articulation of the life-constructing dimension of the truth. To support the ministry, pastoral theology needs to focus on the contemporary struggle to shape Christian lives.

The one truth has many dimensions. Both Popes Benedict and Francis acknowledge a dimension called *performative truth*. Benedict says this dimension "makes things happen and is life changing."[1] In an address at The Catholic University of America, he called for an incarnate truth that impacts the whole of one's being, that is creative and life-giving.[2] In the third section of *Veritatis gaudium*, Francis calls for a "performative interpretation of the reality brought about by the Christ event." In the previous sections, he quotes his predecessors to remind us they also called for a dimension of truth that inspires action to shape personal and collective life. Paul VI asked for an interpretation of the faith that "permeates thought patterns, standards of judgment, and norms of behavior." It is a truth that contributes to the development of the whole person, one that allows "[human persons] to find themselves."[3] Pundits sometimes use the term *performative* in a derogatory fashion to designate a false veneer, a fraud, hidden by some insincere statement or action. This is not the term's meaning when the popes use it. Instead, it is a perspective on the truth that shapes faith-filled action. A *performative* dimension of the truth helps us construct the Christian self and reengage with our world.

The faith was lived before it was articulated in Scripture and creedal propositions. As a living reality, it informed the composition of Scripture and creed. Over time, the articulation of the faith bent the church's reflection toward cognition. Even so, it remains a way of life. The pastoral theologian must glean life lessons from the revelation, from Scripture and creed, in a manner that allows contemporary believers to live the authentic faith. The lessons must remain true to the founder's vision and must also move believers in these times to form a Christian self and participate in a Christian community. Chapter 1 expands on this dimension of Christian truth.

1. Benedict XVI, *Spe salvi*, sec. 2.
2. Benedict XVI, "Diakonia of Truth."
3. Francis, *Veritatis gaudium*, sec. 3.

This development is urgent. Choices of lifestyle and life orientation are expanding at an extraordinary pace.[4] The claim that we live in a value-less society is mistaken. The challenge is the opposite. Our culture provides each person with a vast array of value choices. It produces multiple value systems offering many paths to a good life. Not all the value sets reflect Christian values. Without sounding shrill or negative, Christian ministers must speak into that mix. Beyond the din and with exceptional clarity, we need to convey what Christianity offers. More than ever, the faith needs to demonstrate how the way of Jesus Christ offers a response to suffering and death as well as offering true beatitude, the complete joy, described in the Lord's Last Supper discourse (John 15:11). Ministers should offer Christian insights for a moral life (being good), an ethical life (living well),[5] and for human flourishing.

I am not as pessimistic as my historian friend who thinks the church has completely lost touch with the culture. My experience as a pastor tells me something quite different. Every day, pastors and pastoral ministers rub shoulders with believers who are building their lives in this culture. Parishioners create homes, raise children, make livings, shop for food and clothing, prepare meals, enjoy some recreation and play, and interact with neighbors, family, and friends. They enjoy the advantages of science and technology, cherish their mobility, and value their freedom. They hear or read the news, form opinions on the day's issues, and probably vote. In short, they are contributing to the maintenance of the culture. What is more, they believe and act on their belief! They cooperate with their pastoral leaders in building the church, and they participate in the community's ministries. Pastoral theology needs to nurture such living faith.

To lay the foundation, the reader may need to reexamine some aspects of the ministry:

- Our faith must be expansive. Pastors need to understand the small part of life secular society leaves for religion. Pastoral ministry cannot permit the way of Jesus Christ to be reduced to that space. Ministers need to expand religion into all aspects of contemporary

---

4. Contemporary pluralism was a major concern of Australian-born American sociologist Peter L. Berger (1929–2017). See *The Heretical Imperative* and *The Many Altars of Modernity*.

5. I am using the distinction between morality and ethics given in Dworkin, *Justice for Hedgehogs*, 1. Morality is about good versus evil; ethics is about living well. Dworkin believes, as I do, that one cannot live well without seeking the good.

society. It must communicate the faith to make possible the formation of a Christian life.

- Authenticity remains the aspiration: the means used by the church to influence individuals and society must correspond to the gospel.

- To create an expansive religiosity, the nature of religion needs to be explored. Pastors need to become aware of how religion communicates.

Chapter 2 explores what religion offers toward the formation of the self, the community, and society. What does religion do *to us*, *in us*, and *for us*? I will call these the *functions of the faith*.

After exploring these fundamental concepts, I offer essays on the propositions of the faith from the perspective of performative truth. Part 2, chapters 3 through 14 examine creedal propositions for their potential to create a Christian life. I will explore the Nicene Creed from a pastoral dimension. All branches of theology emerge from revelation. Scripture is referenced throughout these essays to ground my reflections. Even if one is addressing contemporary situations, pastoral ministry must reflect the most basic faith propositions: Jesus Christ is Lord! (1 Cor 12:3); God is becoming all in all! (1 Cor 15:28).

The French word *essai* means *to try*. These explorations are attempts to speak the truth of our faith so that contemporary believers might shape self, community, and society. Please keep in mind that this book explores one dimension of Christian truth. It is a dimension, however, that cannot be left unexplored any longer. If pastoral ministers persist in reading what follows, I pray that ministers will acquire additional insights for communicating the way of Jesus Christ.

Part 1.

A Method for a Pastoral Theology

1

A Pastoral Dimension to Truth

FRESH APPROACHES TO PASTORAL ministry became urgent because of the expansion of lifestyle choices in our times. The claim that we live in a valueless society is mistaken. For too long, Christian churches have relied on that countercultural argument to confront the times. A simple fact belies the claim: believers construct their lives in this culture even as they believe and act on their beliefs. What confuses me are the people who make the countercultural argument. They are also participating in the social interactions that define the culture. They too are making homes, using the banks, speaking to politicians, talking on cellphones, driving cars, enjoying restaurants and their vacations, and hopping on jets to attend their professional meetings. I am concerned with two themes I hear underscoring the negative assessments: (1) religion has lost power and prestige as other forms of social interaction have risen in status; and (2) many believers long for a return of a lost golden age of religion. The loss of power is positive, at least for a faith that celebrates *kenosis* (Phil 2:5–11). It is high time to correct the church's attachment to power, domination, and control. And if there was a golden age, the expression of faith would have fit that culture. No one can reproduce the past. Trying to live the faith life that fit past cultures is like holding on to a heliocentric universe to do contemporary astrophysics. I am certain that nostalgic longings will not revitalize the faith for our times. We need fresh wineskins for new wine (Matt 9:17).

Navigating our culture is difficult. Here's why. Modern society is a fusion of four types of interaction. Each type makes up a substructure of society: (1) the distribution of goods and services, called economics; (2) the acceptable uses of power, called politics; (3) the exploration for and application of knowledge, called cognitive interaction; (4) intimate and affective relations, marriage, family life, friendships, and associations, sometimes called the private life. Each substructure has distinct forms of activities. Each has its norms and values. The values of any one subsection can become the organizing principles of one's life—for example, a scientist, a businessperson, a homemaker. Most people draw values through engagement in multiple types of interaction, selecting and prioritizing them according to needs and desires.

The combined value sets of all four subsections do not form a coherent whole. Values can even conflict. The business community's norms for competition, for instance, if applied to the family, would destroy our homes. Taken as a whole, our culture presents each person with an array of values. During the average day, people adjust to multiple settings requiring different values.

People seek a coherent self, however. Each person seeks one guiding set of values for their life choices. Subsequently, values and norms are wont to migrate across substructures. Examples are in order: Democratic power structures require a theory of human rights, equality, freedom, and self-assertion. The Catholic Church, though, is hierarchical. An American pastor can suffer tense moments when democratic values pop up at a parish council meeting. Likewise, many husbands and fathers suffer embarrassing shocks when the notion of equal rights takes root in the home in a spouse or teenager. Another example: Science has developed an open-ended definition of truth. Truth unfolds before those seeking it methodologically. That mindset conflicts with truth revealed in the distant past with its *closed* canon of writings. Preaching Scripture implies that the fullness of truth came down from above thousands of years ago.

The process that has brought our world to this moment has a name: *secularization*. When I was in the seminary and for the first years of my ministry, the *secular* was a neutral term. It was the backdrop against which a person lived life. It was a synonym for *these times* or *this age*. *Secularization* was the adaptation to the times. The progress of science, the advance of democracy and human rights, new movements in the arts: change was considered positive. It was known that secularization challenged the practice of the faith—science against revelation, democracy against hierarchy, social change against tradition. Even so, faith leaders bid us to heed the signs of the times. During the papacies of John Paul

II and Benedict XVI, the connotation of the *secular* and *secularization* changed. The terms became negative, perhaps even derogatory. A negative valuation of the contemporary world was understandable from Pope Benedict who was brought up in Nazi Germany and Pope John Paul who lived in Communist Poland. Secularization became an existential threat to the faith.

For the sake of this study, I will use these definitions of the following terms. I know these are debatable in faith circles. To glean the most from these pages, I ask the reader to indulge me:[1]

- The *secular* means these times, our age. It is the material, social, and cultural backdrop for the construction of our lives.
- *Secularization* is a process through which ever greater segments of society are freed from religious authorities. Social interaction even becomes resistant to religious influence.
- *Atheism* is the denial of the existence of God. Secularization is about diminished religious control of social interaction. Diminished religious control leads some to sense the absence of God. Secularization increases but does not necessitate the probability that people will exclude God from whole segments of their lives. The process creates the space for some to deny God altogether.
- As God's presence seems to recede, society's institutions can no longer claim divine legitimation. I will call this process *desacralization*. The seeming withdrawal of God and the desacralization of social interaction reveals a long-hidden truth: political and economic structures, our quest for knowledge about the universe, and even family structures are human constructs. As such, they are malleable. Secularization advances because choice proliferates, and human freedom expands.
- A *secularist* is a person who pushes the agenda of *secularization*, hoping to expand personal freedom by moving religious authorities further to the periphery of society where they are even less able to control or even influence individuals or social organizations.

Secularization is quite complex. It involves the differentiation of the forms of social interaction, the disenchantment of society, and the privatization and commodification of religion. This much must be said:

1. I have discussed this more fully in Schmitz, *Thoughts on Secularization*.

our times require each person to construct a coherent self out of the array of values offered from the various forms of largely secularized social interaction. The construction of a coherent self demands freedom. Secularization has contributed to a social order counting among its highest values human rights, autonomy, and personal choice in the construction of one's life, human potential and possibility—in short, freedom. Church leaders need to understand the depth of freedom's roots in our culture.

Our political structures may take up the lion's share of our public concern about freedom. But something much more profound has taken root. All forms of social interaction are being purified of past forms of domination and traditional authoritarian pressures, including those based in religion.[2] The most recent developments have brought that freedom into our homes and most intimate relationships—spaces where religion recently held sway. Choice, self-construction, autonomy, and possibility are corollaries of the value of freedom now influencing the whole of our lives.

Because of this process, a renewal of pastoral theology requires raising three soul-searching questions. The first confronts a perceptive staff each weekend: What brings people to the pews? Why do they attend? Why do they give their time and money to the church? The opposite question seems more pressing: Why are they leaving? Christian churches in first world countries are doing poorly. But let's start with the more positive question: Why do they participate?

I believe the contemporary person realizes that our society is malleable. We are even more aware that the self is changeable. We also know that the self and the social world influence each other. The search for a good life is perplexing. The promises of Christ, however, continue to be a good wager on which to stake one's life construction. Pastoral ministers need to support that choice by communicating a faith that moves believers to choose Christian values from among this culture's array of value choices. Pastoral ministers have an inescapable mission to proclaim faith that stirs contemporary Christians to freely form and reform their lives.

This certainly does not mean the leaders of the church should withhold criticisms of society and culture. Disciples of a crucified God are perpetually discontented with any status quo. Proclaiming the cross raises tension with all societies. Even so, the theology that informs pastoral ministry should be sensitive to those making their lives now.

---

2. Taylor, *Secular Age*, 149.

By rubbing shoulders with believers who value freedom, pastoral ministers should also understand that most of their congregation will not accede to a religion that uses compulsion to keep them in their place and in the pews. Fear is counterproductive. Exclusion repels most contemporaries. Commands, regulations, and decisions made without consultation are not likely to gain respect for church leaders. Using power and aligning with political parties will not end well for those preaching the truth of one killed by the religious and political powers of his day. The temptation to misuse authority is all too real for those who are dedicated to do God's will. The temptation must be resisted. In a society that values freedom, the proclamation of the faith should correspond to the aspirations of those who have taken steps on the Lord's way.

The pastoral minister comes at such questions from the viewpoint of the believer. In our times, a believer has a right to ask, What's in it for me? The second of our three questions is not necessarily narcissistic. With the array of values in contemporary society, the believer is asking the minister to compete and, more, to demonstrate the efficacy of the faith for the construction of a moral and ethical life. So, what does faith do to us, in, and for us? My shorthand answer is this: our faith provides a safe space for building a spiritual home.[3] In a spiritual home, believers should enjoy a feeling that they are part of God's creation and are connected to the universe. They should know that their lives are significant, that they are free participants in God's creating. This means that believers are morally and ethically responsible for the construction of self, one another, family, society, and their physical and human environment. Because the way of Jesus Christ prioritizes self-giving love, such love becomes the standard for all life decisions. Charity should expand outward and be expressed as peace and justice in the larger world. In this way, believers know they are directed to the good and to the true. As a result, believers should experience an inner peace. They should be assured that their failures are forgiven, that they are loved without conditions, and, at or near the end of life, they should be confident of salvation.

A pastoral minister would be right to consider the facilitation of the construction of a spiritual home to be formidable. My historian friend may be pessimistic, but the gap between the contemporary world and the church is wide indeed. For example, at least since the composition of the two accounts of creation in Genesis, the wonder of creation has

---

3. I have discussed a *spiritual home* more fully in Schmitz, *Methodology*, 12–15.

led people to believe. But consider how many preachers can glorify the Creator by expounding on the origins of the universe or the evolution of life in today's scientific terms.

Here's the rub. The secularist pushes religion to the periphery of society where it loses influence over much of the social order. Our age moves religion to some part of the private life. As a result, even for our active members, time for God in our personal and collective lives is brief. I estimate that over 80 percent of believers think an hour or two per week for worship and prayer satisfies the desire for God. Active members gather in church once a week. They probably have a routine of daily prayer. They return to church to mark annual feast days. And they come to church to sanctify important events in their family's private lives. Congregations may hear occasional homilies urging them to apply Christian values to their whole lives. But many homilies retreat from such challenges. It is far easier to escape into moralistic human-interest stories. A crucial and far grander task is missed. The Lord's way connects each moment to eternity, changes the space in which we live into God's kingdom, and incorporates a believer's life into divine life. The church experienced by most parishioners, however, seems to accept a secularist's minimalistic approach to religion. The way of Jesus Christ has been reduced to *explicit religiosity*.

Explicit religiosity is the stuff that occurs on parish grounds. It is churchy. Its language and thought patterns are those of theology, scriptural scholarship, and church history—watered down, of course, for the average believer. This is important: *Explicit religiosity* is not detached from life. Baptisms, marriages, and funerals prove otherwise. A well-oiled parish generates remarkable activity. Its parking lots are seldom empty. Some activities reach beyond institutional maintenance to support daily life. The best of its activities cares for the poor, comforts the sick and dying, assists the addicted, and so forth. The very best of its activities address the desire for God placed by the Creator in human hearts.

So, what about *explicit religiosity*? All of it is good; all of it is right. It is not enough! Pastoral ministers should be about the finest worship, engaging formation programs, in-depth spirituality, and so forth. And pastoral ministry requires the best Christian theology. Here's the rub. Explicit religion absorbs much of a minister's waking life. In contrast, it is a tiny part of an active believer's life. The whole of it—except for getting to heaven—will not appear on a list of believers' most pressing concerns. Little of it affects the growing population of those who are into spiritual issues but who cannot find a home in organized religion.

Explicit religiosity does not build the community of believers in our times. It is not enough to build a spiritual home. Perhaps it never was enough. Faith, as *explicit religiosity*, pales when contrasted with the Lord's way of life. It even fails believers. After all, baptism, confirmation, and Eucharist convey the Creator's imprint and the life-giving memory of the Lord's vision: life is fulfilled in the divine; God is to be all in all (1 Cor 15:28). Explicit religiosity cannot substitute for the way; explicit religion can only nurture the way of the Lord. It may not even nurture the way unless ministers know that religion is about life-construction. We require an *expansive religiosity*. To arrive at an expansive religiosity requires that pastoral ministers and theologians plumb the depth of our faith for a dimension that informs the construction of self and society. The essays in this book (chs. 3–14) search at length for this dimension of our truth. Here are some examples:

- *I believe* implies the agency of the believer. Because there is no coercion forcing belief and very little social pressure, the contemporary path to faith is likely to encounter doubt and questioning, flights of imagination, and a creative spirit. *I believe*, therefore, asserts freedom, since doubt, questioning, imagination, and creativity are corollaries of freedom. Since the time of the first Passover, our faith has celebrated freedom. How can pastoral ministry celebrate the divine gift today?

- *In one God* reminds us that God has created all humankind in God's own image. The truth of the one is also the truth of the unity of the entire human family. How can the pastoral minister break down social boundaries separating people?

- *Father Almighty* invites us to meditate on the nature of divine power and power, in general. Searching the Scriptures to discover the meaning of these words brings us to *Abba*, *kenosis*, and *agape*. How does that reflection reshape power in our interactions?

To get to *expansive religiosity*, we need a particular dimension of truth. Expansive religion is Christian truth as performative truth. Most theology aspires to describe ultimate reality, engaging its readers in *what is*. Performative truth takes us to the third pressing question for the pastoral minister: What does faith do? How does our faith function in shaping Christian identity? Pastoral theology's missing element is what faith does to us, in, and for us as we create our lives.

All construction projects build up from a foundation. The construction of the self, community, and society are linguistic efforts. Language is necessary for the description of the universe, our world, our society, and our self. But more than description is needed. Language facilitates the self-construction process. It is necessary for imagining our participation in the universe, our world, and society. It is also necessary for imagining our best self. And language is necessary for our relationship with God. This is not a new insight. Christianity celebrates language. St. John's first Christological insight refers to the Savior as the Word: "In the beginning was the Word, and the Word was with God, and the Word was God" (John 1:1). St. Paul said, "But how can they call on him in whom they have not believed? And how can they believe in him of whom they have not heard? And how can they hear without someone to preach?" (Rom 10:14). The insight goes back to Genesis. God creates through his Word (Gen 1:3). The first cooperative effort between God and humankind was naming (Gen 2:19–20). Language is the foundation.

Religious language is of a special kind. Doctrines tell us of reality beyond human cognition. Direct, univocal language cannot express it, even though the human species never quits trying. As a result, humans have created multifaceted language forms for such communication. Divine truth is conveyed in one of those forms; sacred truth is expressed in symbols.

Canadian theologian Bernard Lonergan offers this definition of a symbol: "A symbol is an image of a real or imaginary object that evokes a feeling or is evoked by a feeling."[4] Let me break down how Lonergan explains symbolic communication. Through symbols and the feelings they evoke, basic questions of our lives are addressed. We can reflect upon who we are, imagine our place in the world, envision our relationships with one another, conceive the makeup of society, and embed ourselves in the natural environment. In short, we have the stuff to create spiritual homes. According to Lonergan, the feelings are "related to objects, to one another, and to the subject." He describes our relationship to objects and to our environment, giving these examples: "One desires food, fears pain, enjoys a meal, regrets a friend's illness." Through symbols, the imagination is triggered: "One desires the good that is absent, hopes for the good that is sought, enjoys the good that is present; one fears absent evil, become disheartened at its approach, sad at its presence."

---

4. Lonergan, *Method in Theology*, 64.

Feelings group together. They interact to form patterns. Lonergan writes, "So love, gentleness, tenderness, intimacy, union go together; similarly, alienation, hatred, harshness, violence, cruelty form a group." A coherent self becomes possible. The patterns allow for the formation of our identities and naming our personal qualities. These patterns allow for the completion of a spiritual home. The self can survey the array of available values to discover a relatable world. Persons take in what happens around them, process the intake, and respond with action consistent with who they are. Lonergan puts it more precisely: The patterns are "the mass and momentum and the power of conscious living." Furthermore, they activate "affective capacities, dispositions, habits, the effective orientation of... life."[5]

Based on his thoughts, a definition of religious language emerges: Religious language communicates through symbols an interacting pattern of feelings, offering an effective orientation for our lives. To transition from religion to faith, I would need to add God's self-revelation to the definition. But here I am considering symbolic communication at its most basic. Symbolic communication evokes feelings that migrate into all aspects of life. In short, the gospel message, cracked open as symbols, can bring us to the way of Jesus in contemporary times and in this place.

Let me offer three approaches that contribute to an understanding of how symbols work. Anthropologist Clifford Geertz enhances the sense of Lonergan's feeling.[6] Symbolic communication conveys "moods and motives," therefore establishing the tonality of our lives. A relation with the divine evokes profound emotions in us. When speaking God-language, we imply the whole of reality, the "maker of heaven and earth, of all things visible and invisible." Because feelings group together, the moods and motives can permeate our entire lives. The tone of life becomes fundamentally set (e.g., optimist/pessimist, upbeat/melancholy, traditionalist/progressive, extrovert/introvert, this-worldly/other-worldly). Tone affects our perception of reality and our reaction to it. It affects our valuation of other people and our reactions to them. Moods and motives filter the surrounding reality, so our response can be prepared. Because we relate to the Creator, we are placed within creation, within the human and physical environment. All things find their meaning. All things receive their valuation.

---

5. Lonergan, *Method in Theology*, 65.
6. Geertz, "Religion as a Cultural System," 4.

A crucial insight of performative truth and pastoral communication is the deep level to which the pastoral minister must reach. Preachers may wish to address contemporary issues from the headlines each week. Some such preaching is necessary. More important, however, is the fundamental moods and motives, the underlying valuations. Abortion, euthanasia, capital punishment are important issues. Hearers of the word of God can arrive at the correct judgment for themselves if they are aware of the Christian valuation of life. The distribution of wealth, war and peace, and racial prejudice are important issues. The deeper level on which to explain issues of the social gospel, however, is the valuation of the Other, of people who differ from me. The foundation of pastoral communication is on the deep level of moods and motives.

American philosopher Mark Taylor can help us understand how our faith positions us in this world. Religion is an emergent and adaptive network.[7] It takes in information about its environment. It surveys the physical and material world, social institutions, cultural values, the idealization of the person, the cosmos, and its Creator. It evaluates perception through religion's symbolic communication. And it creates adaptive actions. Religion offers the ability to navigate the world, to feel secure in it, and to aspire to our better selves. Taylor says that religion creates "schemata of feeling, thinking and acting."[8] Schemata is a complicated idea. It seems to be a mindset, a way to understand, relate to, and, when necessary, change views on God, the self, and the world. Taylor helps us understand: "Schemata function both theoretically and practically first to screen data in order to detect, form, and reform patterns that simultaneously describe, prefigure, and predict entities and events and second to model adaptive actions in the real world."[9] Schemata offer a person a filter for interaction with the world. Crucial information is taken in and processed. It is assessed and critiqued. Action becomes possible.

Let me offer one example: St. John teaches us that God is love. If that truth is active in a believer's consciousness, it would be difficult to perceive the Other as fearsome, or worse, as an enemy. If that truth inspired one to action, the believer would be compelled to try understanding and tolerance, perhaps acceptance and charity.

A third contribution to understand what religion does comes from Peter Sloterdijk. He is a philosopher who was born in Holland and who

---

7. Taylor, *After God*, 12.
8. Taylor, *After God*, 12.
9. Taylor, *After God*, 16.

now works in Germany. He claims that religions are only "misunderstood spiritual regimens."[10] The radical philosopher Friedrich Nietzsche disclosed what religion had actually been: "a comprehensive theory of practicing existence."[11] Practicing existence means establishing the discipline to take actions that optimize oneself in the face of life's contingencies. This leads Sloterdijk to place religion into a category he calls *anthropotechnics*—the practice of living.[12] That term helps us imagine the content of expansive religiosity.

Anthropotechnics can be simplified to mean *consciously working on oneself*. I have been using the phrase *construction of self*. My phrase, however, does not convey an end or a point on which we are focused. The philosopher has two directional insights. Humans seem hardwired to avoid danger. Humanity developed what Sloterdijk calls "socio-immunological methods."[13] Religion is a mental and physical practice by which "humans have attempted to optimize their cosmic and immunological status in the face of vague risks of living and acute certainties of death."[14]

The second inclination is to optimize the self. It comes from a "human vertical tension"[15] that has been acknowledged since ancient times. Sloterdijk quotes Socrates: "Man is a being potentially superior to himself." From conception and birth through infancy and our first years on earth, we are totally dependent, developing beings. Perhaps we never get over the experience. Vertical tension, therefore, is a force that cannot let us alone because humankind always feels incomplete, discontented, and is striving for something. Even today, this spiritual force fascinates perpetually unfinished selves to seek "the higher and highest possibilities of human beings."[16]

Sloterdijk writes that these two forces—the need for security and the vertical tension—are the conditions of possibility for religion.[17] These factors are prerequisites for the development of religion. He bounces off

---

10. Sloterdijk, *Change Your Life*, 3.
11. Sloterdijk, *Change Your Life*, 6.
12. Sloterdijk, *Change Your Life*, 3.
13. Sloterdijk, *Change Your Life*, 9.
14. Sloterdijk, *Change Your Life*, 10.

15. Sloterdijk, *Change Your Life*, 13. While I strive for more inclusive terms in my own writing, where authors and translators use any derivation of *man* to mean all humankind, I have left it in the original.

16. Sloterdijk, *Change Your Life*, 14.
17. Sloterdijk, *Change Your Life*, 15.

a poem by Rainer Maria Rilke written as the poet contemplates a Rodin sculpture of a perfect human torso. The poem ends: "You must change your life."[18]

The religious self must change—read, construct—life. This is the heart of pastoral theology. After all, the first sermon Jesus proclaims is, "Repent, for the kingdom of heaven is at hand" (Matt 4:17). Participation in the life of the church offers the matter for the construction of the self, community, and society. In the next chapter, I will be more specific on what religion does to us, in us, and for us. I will offer the *functions of the faith*. In these times, the pastoral minister needs to expand the reach of the faith. Pastoral ministry needs to embrace the entirety of life, offering the faithful the material needed to work on oneself, work on one's community, on society, on the world, and ultimately to work to shape our response to God.

---

18. Rilke, "Archaic Torso of Apollo," in Burt and Mikics, *Art of the Sonnet*, quoted in Sloterdijk, *Change Your Life*, 21.

2

What Faith Does to Us, in Us, and for Us

WE MUST CHANGE—READ, CONSTRUCT and reconstruct—our lives. This imperative is the heart of pastoral theology. Participation in the life of the church offers the material needed to work on oneself. The construction of the Christian self occurs through relationships, actions, personal prayers, communal liturgy, the teachings one takes to heart, the ministerial, charitable extensions of the church community into society and, also, self-examination, the voice of conscience, penance, and occasional dark nights of the soul. In this chapter, I explore what participation in the faith does *to us*, *in us*, and *for us*. These are *the functions of the faith*.[1] This is faith that moves mountains (Matt 17:20).

When I ask why people come to church, sit in the pews, contribute their time and money, I find answers on various levels. Most reasons are well studied by various branches of theology. What faith does to us, in us, and for us, however, is not. How faith affects a believer may be the missing element in the church's communication and in our efforts to evangelize. Because our culture offers so many options to obtain a good life, I think this element is necessary for the presentation of the faith. It is necessary for the creation of one's spiritual home. Here are the functions of the faith:

- Faith creates community.
- Faith offers valuations—of life, of the Other, of time, of this world.
- Faith gives perspective.

1. I have discussed the *functions of faith* more fully in Schmitz, *Methodology*, 33–89.

- Faith nurtures transcendence.
- Faith comforts—by offering tenderness, by restoring a sense of living after a death, by inspiring the tears of the saints.
- Faith defines an end.
- Faith grounds life decisions.

FAITH CREATES COMMUNITY

Humans thrive in relational networks. In a culture that celebrates individuality, powerful magnets are needed to draw us into a community. And a strong adhesive is necessary to maintain the connections. Divine images cloak our faith communities in a sacred aura. Images like *the people of God*, *the body of Christ*, *the true faith*, and *the elect* consecrate our interaction. The rites and sacraments, especially the Eucharist, are the adhesive that holds the church together. Our faith provides the inducement and the adhesive bond for communal interaction.

Traditionally, communities were formed with the like-minded. Some people still long for such unanimity. Religious communities have identities, shared attitudes about the faith, about the self, and about being in the world. The whole is mutually reinforcing. It becomes a source of comfort. Communities of the like-minded, however, have the unfortunate tendency to exclude.

Today, social mobility and global corporations bring together diverse peoples in the same area. The Catholic claim to universality is becoming a reality in many, if not most, of our parishes. All Christian communities must now evolve to welcome diversity. A community of diversity celebrates pluralism. Reflections on the contemporary life journey may lead to greater appreciation of pluralism. Each of us considers our own self-construction to be generated out of informed free will. If informed free choice is predicated on others, diversity appears positive. Differences become complementary. They expand one's perception of human possibility. Human differences fire up the imagination to consider options for personal growth.

Living in a pluralistic community is difficult. It takes a deep understanding of the goodness of God creating. A believer must learn understanding and tolerance for those who differ. The possible, unfortunate side effect of understanding and tolerance, however, is a weakening of a believer's own core values. Only those who deeply internalize the faith can expose themselves to differences without becoming lukewarm or defensive or angry at the Other. Preachers and teachers should use every opportunity to demonstrate the Christian basis for tolerance, understanding, and reconciliation. Teachers and preachers should also recommend a spirituality of constant growth, a lifetime of renewal.

The hierarchical nature of church governance once fostered religious passivity in its members. The Second Vatican Council, however, altered that experience. It calls for full participation of all members in the church. A parish community should acquire an active quality. Scripture scholar Gerhard Lohfink calls this attitude "the Abraham principle."[2] Since the time of Abraham and Sarah, God has acted through God's people to make God's kingdom tangible and visible. This principle may help Christian leaders form communities supportive of self-construction and communities active in transforming the culture. Active ministry requires personal conversion. An active mindset emerges from a spirit of gratitude. When we realize what God has done for us, gratitude segues into active ministry. If participation is moved by the incarnation and the cross, Christians will soon know that the construction of self reaches its pinnacle when the self is embedded in a network of people responding to God's self-giving love by giving of themselves.

FAITH OFFERS VALUATIONS

Faith Creates the Valuation of Life

One's valuation of life underscores the valuation of everything else. The term *life* lacks specificity. It is given to sloganeering and banner art. We require more precision; we need a Christian perspective. Italian atheist, philosopher, novelist, and semiologist Umberto Eco (1932–2016) discussed faith and belief with Milan's archbishop, Cardinal Martini (1927–2012).[3] Eco asked whether Christians consider life to be the highest good. Martini responded by quoting John's Gospel: "He who loves his life (*psyche*) loses it, and he who hates his own life (*psyche*) in this world will keep it for eternal life (*zoe*)."[4] Neither our physical lives (*bios*)

---

2. Lohfink, *Jesus of Nazareth*, 44.
3. Eco and Martini, *Belief or Unbelief?*, 36–50.
4. Eco and Martini, *Belief or Unbelief?*, 48.

nor our psychological lives (*psyche*) constitute the highest good. Instead, the divine life (*zoe*) guides Christian valuations. Life shared with God gives ultimate value to human life. Baptism, confirmation, and Eucharist ritualize the aspiration. St. Paul tells us of the consequences of baptism. We live "for God in Christ Jesus" (Rom 6:11). John does the same for Eucharist. Holy Communion makes it possible to remain in Christ as Christ remains in the Father (John 6:56–57). As a result, the performatory truth of this valuation involves our image of God and the means God provides for our unity with God. Philosopher Mark Taylor writes, "The way in which God is imagined determines the way in which the self and the world are conceived and vice versa."[5]

The restoration of biblical concepts in Catholic discourse, a process begun with *Providentissimus Deus* in 1893 and continued with *Divino afflante Spiritu* in 1943 and *Dei verbum* in 1965 is moving us to change our valuation of life. Our long-held traditional valuation began in thoughts about death. Our spiritual lives were centered on mortality—understood as humanity's punishment for sin. This life was thought to be an exile, a temporary trial undergone until death and the afterlife. When we escape this valley of tears, our disembodied souls may be taken into heaven.

The Hebrew Scriptures, however, seldom propose an afterlife.[6] Salvation occurs in history. Liberation and freedom, deliverance from one's enemies, a messiah bringing justice and peace, the promised land, a new creation, prosperity—salvation is this-worldly. Jesus was thoroughly immersed in Scripture. He conveys salvation as health, liberation, and well-being. His miracles and his efforts toward an inclusive in-gathering speak of a this-worldly transformation: a new creation embracing all material things; conversion for the individual; and peace, justice, and compassion for the collective and communal. Jesus's sense of an afterlife experience is the resurrection of the body, also a this-worldly transformation. The resurrection of the body and a new creation accompany the second coming. They are a continuation into eternity of a believer's attempt to live the Lord's way of life. The model for that life is the cross and resurrection: what we give in love for others ennobles and sanctifies this life and lifts it into eternity (John 5:24–29).

Scriptural imagery suggests that our contact with God should use the preposition *in*. We can live even now *in Christ* and through him *in*

---

5. Taylor, *After God*, 22.
6. Borg, *Speaking Christian*, 197.

God. St. Paul says it like this: "Indeed [God] is not far from any one of us. For 'In him we live and move and have our being'" (Acts 17:27–28). Just as the Lord's Prayer requests, this earth can be transformed into the heavenly, and time can participate in the eternal. The incarnation and the indwelling of the Spirit become guiding symbols of our spirituality. Because we live in Christ and in God, we can imagine God's perfections as the goal of human striving. Salvation becomes the realization of human possibility. We know the finite cannot grasp the infinite, but, in this life, our coming-to-perfection in God becomes for the determined believer an ever-receding horizon into which we happily journey. Hannah Arendt gives us a term to contrast with the idiom of mortality.[7] Her term is *natality*, the emergence of new life. Natality recalls St. Paul's invitation to "live in newness of life" (Rom 6:4). It also summarizes the Lord's own offer to be "born from above" (John 3:3) and of abundant life (John 10:10).

Faith Creates Valuations of the Other, of People Who Differ

We create social boundaries by necessity. Those helping us construct and maintain our identities become our network. Our social boundaries embrace those offering support and stability and those helping us find contentment and happiness. Those I look like, think like, speak like, act like, believe like—these are included. All of us are aware of factors that group people into categories. I use the word *group* advisedly. The factors that group us do not necessarily divide us. Recognizing differences is part of identity formation. Even so, differences can be valuated as complementary and enriching. Interaction with the Other can be imagined as one element in the quality of our lives. Catholic Christians had once maintained exclusionary borders and boundaries despite the universality the faith professes. The Second Vatican Council's concern with ecumenism is changing that perspective.

Biblical imagery is also pushing us toward porous, more inclusionary boundaries. Jesus Christ fostered inclusion. His ministry and his life indicate how he treats others:

- Sinners and outcasts were welcomed. Even the religious enemies of his own people (i.e., Samaritans and Canaanites) and his people's political oppressors (i.e., the Romans) felt his compassion.

---

7. Arendt, *Human Condition*, 8.

- To maintain Jewish identity, Israel maintained purity regulations called the Holiness Code (Lev 17–27). The code demanded exclusion of people for any number of reasons. Jesus violated it regularly to heal the suffering. Jesus even introduced his own holiness code, what we call the Sermon on the Mount. The Lord's code is inclusive, embracing even one's enemies and persecutors.

- Jesus wanted his followers to disavow the relationships required for exclusive identity formation—mother, father, sister, brother (Mark 3:31–35). The people he gathered in were to become a new family, multiplying by a hundred times what one gave up (Mark 10:29–31). In that new order, fathers are not included in the reward. Fathers, as they operated in the first century, are not part of the Lord's new family; patriarchal oppression is eliminated.

- A meditation on the cross demands the critique of any power that diminishes others, any that degrades, or divides. The cross compels Christians to question all judgments of anyone society rejects or disenfranchises.

In fact, Jesus teaches that the sinner, the stranger, the outcast, and the hurting, even one's enemies, have a priority over me and mine. He warns us, "the first will be last, and the last will be first" (Matt 19:30). He teaches, "whoever wishes to be great among you shall be your servant" (Matt 20:26). His word challenges anyone who excludes or anyone who ranks people best to worst. His message is crucial for our times. Inclusive, porous social boundaries are required for the future of civilization. Christian ministers should take to heart the gospel message of inclusion.

Faith Offers a Valuation of Time

The valuation of time is a crucial factor in the quality of life. Along with the valuation of the world, the valuation of time is an element in our cosmology, our sense of being in the world. The modern world experiences linear time, always moving from present to future. In people's spiritual lives, however, people can choose to live in the past, present, or future. This choice depends on our prior valuation of the passage of time. In *The Confessions*, St. Augustine gives us a vocabulary to assess time. Past and future, he said, are real because they affect the present: "There are three tenses or times: the present of past things, the present of present things and the present of future things. These are three realities in the mind, but nowhere else as far as I can see, for the present of past things is memory, the present of present things is attention, and the present of future things is expectation."[8] Memory, attention, and expectation are mental realities fundamental in shaping the self. Although we cannot escape any of the three, one can give more weight to the past, or the future, or the present.

The present of present things is when the pastoral minister leads a community of faith. The present is always challenging. All moments in history are fraught with difficulties. Everyone has times of personal suffering. Difficulty and suffering, however, are not the only reasons for remaining in the present. Many life choices require celebration. Some events reveal the divine presence. Some people model sanctity in this life. Attention, the present of present things, becomes a minister's strategy. The requirement is called *pastoral presence*. Memory and expectation assist the minister's attention. When needed, a minister can call upon the memory of God's interventions. And the minister can call upon our expectation of a future in God. Both work in and on the present.

Pastoral ministers are likely to meet people who live in memory. Valuing the past offers a sense of continuity and stability. Memory, often selective or revised, is crucial to identity. Traditions are forged from memory. They are the present of past things, shaping the present by re-presenting revered moments. Revelation is truth given in the past and commanding the present. Authenticity is a measure of how present realities compare to the ancient truth. Memory and tradition can become problematic if they regress into nostalgia for some golden age that never really existed. Although informed by memory where some prefer to live, our faith must be alive in the present where we must live.

Pastoral ministers are also likely to meet people who live in expectation, the present of future things. Imagination, hope, and dreams may be as important for the contemporary person as our memories. They can stoke creativity. And they imply we are free, active agents who can shape things for the better. Expectation has always been a force in the Christian imagination. Since Abraham, God's people have lived in expectation, the realization in time of the divine promise and the hope for salvation. The perfection of the self, of time, and of place will occur in a transformed world.

---

8. Augustine, *Confessions*, 300.

The reforms of the Second Vatican Council opened imaginations to possibility. When church reform encountered our culture's faith in inevitable progress, however, some could see no limitations on what is changeable. Still, expectation and hope are forces in our religious imagination because they move us forward in anticipation of salvation.

As important as memory and expectation are, Augustine is correct: both are about constructing a present. When faith works correctly, it forms schemata, a way to take in data about God, the world, and ourselves. Faith should be able to take in both memory and expectation. Looking to the past, ministers can guarantee authenticity in the present. And expectation allows the minister to help navigate the present toward fulfillment. If past and future are properly focused on present realities, we may avoid twin fictions—one of a golden age, the other of a utopian future. In the present, through suffering and celebration, the pastoral minister can effectively disclose God's presence.

Faith Offers Us a Valuation of This World

As with time, we have a certain experience of this world; it remains the only world we live in. The material of the earth is altogether necessary for our existence. Spiritually and psychologically, we form a valuation of this world, of the physical and material, of our bodies, of all it takes to maintain a presence in time and place. Sociologist Max Weber found that most religions offer a variety of theories on salvation.[9] To organize the theories, Weber gives us helpful terms, *world-rejecting* and *inner-worldly*. I wish to use the terms *this-worldly salvation* and *other-worldly salvation*. When salvation is to occur on earth within the creation we sense here and now, we have *this-worldly salvation*. When salvation is beyond this world, in another world beyond our senses, in a non-material existence, we have *other-worldly salvation*. Both types of salvation are offered to the Christian believer. The way a Christian leans depends on their judgment about the goodness or evil of this world and humankind.

A decidedly other-worldly perspective was held by the church of my youth. It is illustrated in two nineteenth century prayers. Pope Leo XIII (elected 1878) wrote prayers he added to the Mass. The *Salve Regina* is a prayer through the Virgin Mary and the *Prayer of St. Michael* is through the Archangel Michael. Both paint a dark picture of this world. In the

---

9. Weber, *Economy and Society*, 541.

prayer through Mary, we cry as banished children, sending up our sighs, "mourning and weeping in this valley of tears." We ask the Virgin to bring us to our heavenly existence after our exile on earth. In the prayer through the archangel, we implore the angel for protection from the wickedness of the devil. We ask Michael to do battle against evil spirits who prowl the world, "seeking the ruin of souls."

The world becomes a battlefield. That image is confirmed in scriptural passages called *apocalyptic*. Most readers of this literature cannot see past the destructive evil and the battle with diabolic wickedness to God's ultimate victory. The authors, however, present a symbolic battle leading to God's ultimate victory over all suffering. Some interpreters read the literature factually; most read it with a soft form of literalism.[10] Despite the authors' intentions, many seem overwhelmed by the evil; many Christians feel at war with the world; and many are sure the world is near a catastrophic end.

I suppose any person in any period of history could list tragedies and hardships, confirming a dark apocalyptic vision. Many think the twentieth and twenty-first centuries manifest the end-times. Through world wars and depression, terrorism, recession, pandemics, and pending ecological disaster, the worst seems to be upon us. When we factor in the twenty-four seven newscasts instantly alerting us to the entire world's bad news, we can feel as if we are in the ultimate battle. Spiritually, the direction must be out of this world, an other-worldly escape from this vale of tears.

With the reemergence of biblical imagery, this-worldly salvation was reintroduced into the church's self-perception. God is the principal actor in history; God's salvific work is in this world. Salvation becomes the restoration of the original goodness. The doctrine of incarnation proves God's love for this world (John 3:16). Jesus's first sermon asserts that God's kingdom is at hand (Mark 1:15).

A this-worldly perspective activates believers for God's salvific work. The judgment scene in Matt 25 presupposes an active humanity. John's metaphor of the vine and branches illuminates the partnership (John 15:1–10). Before his ascension, Jesus empowers the disciples to perform the work he has done. John's Gospel says, "Amen, amen, I say to you, whoever believes in me will do the works that I do, and will do greater ones than these, because I am going to the Father" (John 14:12).

---

10. Borg, *Speaking Christian*, 23.

St. Paul proclaims our partnership dramatically: "Now you are Christ's body, and individually parts of it" (1 Cor 12:27). Paragraph 460 of the *Catechism of the Catholic Church* asserts the belief in divine-human partnership.[11] It begins, "The Word became flesh to make us '*partakers of the divine nature.*'" Then, it quotes theologians Sts. Irenaeus, Athanasius, and Thomas Aquinas to confirm the biblical assertion. This transformative reading of salvation values this world as the location for salvation. And it makes disciples agents of it.

FAITH GIVES PERSPECTIVE

A valuation of oneself is a gift our faith offers. Faith offers us an assessment of self that puts oneself in a right spiritual location in relation to God, to God's universe, to the human family, and even to oneself. Two major problems hinder the development of perspective. In an age of heightened individualism and its dysfunctional extreme called narcissism, perspective is highly problematic. It is far too easy to inflate one's worth. Developing a Christian perspective runs another risk. The nineteenth-century philosopher Ludwig Feuerbach charged Christianity with diminishing people.[12] The faith can be used—more accurately, abused—when pastoral ministers, preachers, and teachers make the faith a bludgeon to use on others. In Christian circles, too many deflate their worth and the worth of others.

Heightened individualism bordering on narcissism invites *me* to picture *myself* as the center of existence. The world should bend to *my will*. Others should be *like me*. Disappointment and failure should not befall *me*. Illness, suffering, aging—these are not *on my agenda*. Unfortunately, the mindset has invaded religion. Some have made God into their personal Santa Claus or their friendly wizards Dumbledore or Gandalf. The white-bearded man on the throne should wave away *my* problems and set *my* life right. The religious narcissist puts himself at the center with a fanciful god who is at the believer's command.

Diminishing believers may result from the same narcissistic dysfunction when the dysfunction is found in the church's ministers. The problem is as old as the Christian faith; the Lord often warned his disciples

---

11. *Catechism of the Catholic Church*, para. 460 (emphasis original).

12. See Feuerbach's 1841 masterwork *The Essence of Christianity*. The diminishment of humanity is a crucial theme of the book.

of the misuse of the faith (see Matt 23). Leaders, ministers, teachers, and preachers can lose their perspective. They put themselves at the center of existence, incorrectly valuing themselves as God's right hand. They can use power to "lord it over" those they are meant to serve (Matt 20:25; 1 Pet 5:3). They can use faith to maintain social order—or their own political agenda—as if they are God's constabulary. The arrogant can attempt to explain life's mystery when reverential silence is a far better approach. The number of Christians drowning in guilt or with profound feelings of unworthiness gives evidence that the church's ministers need perspective.

As a corrective, God's confrontation with Job comes to mind. Out of the storm, God asks, "Who is this that darkens counsel with words of ignorance? (Job 38:2; see chs. 38–41). God's words to Job demonstrate that proper perspective begins in the asymmetry between the finite and the infinite. The infinite qualities rightly attributed to God prohibit any person from claiming the center, from becoming the standard. The all-powerful one makes us look frail. The all-knowing one highlights our ignorance. The all-good one mirrors back our sinfulness. The Creator, source of all life, makes us aware of our dependency. The eternal one reminds us of our inevitable collapse into illness and death. Our desire for life after death reminds us of our need for a Savior. Alain de Botton uses the expression "*egocentric axis*"[13] to explain proper perspective; any encounter with God knocks us off that axis and offers us a welcome perspective.

Our church has gentle ways of bringing our ambitions into perspective. The Mass communicates our place in relation with the divine. We come into church with a bow or genuflection. Mass begins with a penitential rite. We listen in silence to receive God's word. The Lord's Prayer asks that God's will not ours be done. Before receiving Communion, we remind ourselves of our need for personal healing. And we recall the work yet to be completed in uniting the church and establishing a peaceful world. Before receiving the Lord, our amen emphasizes our willingness to be transformed by Christ into his instrument. Putting our lives in perspective is not the primary reason for Mass. But one cannot participate in Mass without relearning one's place in God's reality. Our weekly attendance should remind us how stubborn our egocentricity is.

The practice of confessing our sins also reminds us of the human condition. The confessor requires a constant reminder that he is a frail

---

13. De Botton, *Religion for Atheists*, 37.

and sinful human being himself. He is present to announce God's mercy and forgiveness. In the reconciliation room, a priest can become defensive, feeling that God and God's ways need protecting and the penitent needs scolding. The penitent, however, is looking for mercy. Ministers need to keep in mind that God can take care of God.

The church has additional gentle ways to put our lives into perspective. Some of the church's most popular iconography reminds us of our place in God's design. Pictures of the Annunciation recall Mary's words: "Behold, I am the handmaid of the Lord. May it be done to me according to your Word" (Luke 1:38). And pictures of the agony in the garden recall Jesus's prayer: "Not my will but yours be done" (Luke 22:42). Stations of the cross surround many of our worship sites. Familiarity may immunize us, but exposure to icons of the crucified Lord should contextualize our egos.

Sin and frailty should not monopolize the minister's image of humankind. The good news is forgiveness and salvation. Sts. Paul and John invite us to live "in Christ" and through him "in God." The preposition *in* plus *divinity* carry a message of potential and possibility. We are reminded of what the angel Gabriel said to Mary: "Nothing will be impossible for God" (Luke 1:37). We may also remember the Lord's instruction on the power of faith: "Amen I say to you, if you have faith the size of a mustard seed, you will say to this mountain, 'Move from here to there,' and it will move. Nothing will be impossible for you" (Matt 17:20). With God and in Christ, the higher things are attainable. A faith life led in Christ should compel a search for knowledge and truth, the pursuit of creativity and beauty, the possibility of goodness and justice, and the quest for the depth of love. Compassion and charity should have no limits. A dedication to peace will yield fruit. Life in God is a declaration of human possibility.

The Christian minister needs to keep the whole vision of the faith for a true Christian perspective. Acknowledging our weakness and sinfulness is healing. Knowing what we have contributed to the evil in the world is realistic. Christians are also saved. Life in Christ offers us an infinite horizon. In God, the good news is brought into this world.

FAITH NURTURES TRANSCENDENCE

The omnipresence of God cannot be a mental or cognitive experience only. God's presence must be felt. In *The Varieties of Religious Experience*,

William James writes, "Were one asked to characterize the life of religion in the broadest and most general terms possible, one might say that it consists of the belief that there is an unseen order, and that our supreme good lies in harmoniously adjusting ourselves thereto."[14] Later he writes, "It is as if there were in human consciousness a *sense of reality, a feeling of objective presence, a perception of what we may call 'something there,'* more deep and more general than any of the special and particular 'senses' by which the current psychology supposes existent realities to be originally revealed."[15] Believers give a name to the unseen order, to the objective presence of something there. We speak of God's presence, God's grace, and God's Spirit. Moments of transcendence make the divine experiential.

Writing on the craft of a poet, Michael Edwards says that poetic language makes us feel that "there is an intimate link between our body and everything that constitutes it."[16] He writes, "Naturally incarnate, we are less a soul in a body . . . than a body in a soul." A meditation on *the soul in a body* leads to a realization that each one of us is a unique creation—a necessary proposition for our self-valuation. To think of ourselves as *a body in a soul*, or a person inspired by the breath of the ever-present God (Gen 2:7), allows us to understand ourselves as surrounded, embraced, and inundated by the Spirit. It unites us with the Creator and embeds us in creation for its stewardship. The experience moves us to participate in the history of salvation. The image of a *body in a soul* raises our self-valuation beyond any humanly imposed limits. The feelings described by James of an unseen order and objective presence become conceivable.

God calls us by drawing us out of ourselves into the divine itself. Christ invites us there, and the church's sacraments direct us there. For the rare, true mystic, the experience of the divine may be direct. For most of us, God calls us out of ourselves through mediations. Our experiences become moments of transcendence. The Creator draws us to the beauty of nature or the wonder of life or the vastness of the universe. One of the Creator's most brilliant creations is the knowing person situated in a knowable universe. The pursuit of knowledge, truth, and wisdom is a path to the Creator. The Savior God of the exodus calls us out of ourselves to admire the history of liberation. The long slog of humanity toward the

---

14. James, *Varieties of Religious Experience*, 55.
15. James, *Varieties of Religious Experience*, 59 (emphasis original).
16. Edwards, *Bible and Poetry*, 62.

realization of human dignity, human rights, and freedom—even though not fully achieved—can and should move us toward the Savior. God, the source of beauty, uses human creativity to call us beyond ourselves. Art, music, and literature, as well as a well-cooked meal and a well-kept home add fulfilling dimensions to our lives.

Woven within human experience is an unseen order, an objective reality that communicates the holy, that allows for the feeling of God's presence. I've heard people tell of moments on a hike or while drifting on water that seemed to fuse them to nature and nature's God. Some people discover that when they share fears and apprehensions with others, they feel connected to the human family and God, who is Father of all. Some have told me of a clear communication, a voice, that gave them the strength to overcome depression and severe anxiety. Others tell me of a similar voice that confirmed a tough, exacting choice they were making on their life journey. Many have told me of experiences that overcame the barrier between the living and the dead. Dreams or significant signs of the deceased made them feel the unseen order. A charitable or compassionate act can give a person a sense of significance.

American sociologist Robert Orsi has researched such experiences. In analyzing what has followed upon the apparition of the Blessed Virgin at Lourdes, Orsi describes the essence of transcendent experiences. He calls them *abundant events*:

> Much becomes possible that otherwise was not. Time may become fluid. Past/present/future, as they are, as they are hoped for, and as they are dreaded, may converge. Spatial boundaries, between here and there, oneself and another, may give way. Relationships also come under the power of the unlocked imagination, relationships between heaven and earth, between the living and the dead, among persons as they are and persons as they are desired to be by themselves and others. In the abundant event and all that follows it, a certain kind of intersubjective receptivity and recognition may become possible, on earth and between heaven and earth, an awareness of being seen and known, and of seeing and knowing, so focused that in certain circumstances, it may seem intrusive and threatening; in others, deeply compassionate and supportive.[17]

---

17. Orsi, *History and Presence*, 67.

Orsi borrows an idea from William James. He calls such experiences 2 + 2 = 5 experiences, a tradition of the *more*.[18] He provides a long list of scholars from multiple disciplines who have tried to articulate these experiences. I have two favorites. Theologian Jean-Luc Marion uses the term *saturated phenomena*. And scholar Eric Santner speaks of the *attunement to the surplus of the real within reality*. Along with *holy, presence,* and *abundant event*, Orsi calls the experience an *excessive event*.[19] The subject of the experience feels lifted out of themself. But Orsi notes the experiences transpire during normal human living. He writes, "Human beings meet real presences in the midst of living their lives."[20] And he says, "The routes of presence go right through the material and political circumstances of everyday life."[21]

A function of religion, what religion does, is to open our bodies and minds, and our hearts and spirits, to an objectively real, unseen order. Our rituals can be understood as routinized transcendence if all involved are dedicated to the ritual's quality. But we can also feel connected to that reality and even participate in it throughout our daily lives. Believers can experience God directly, sometimes as a voice, or through mediums of nature, history, art, or significant daily interaction.

FAITH COMFORTS

Proclaiming an all-good, all-powerful God will always run up against the problem of evil, suffering, pain, illness, and death. It is the problem of theodicy. For the pastoral minister, the problem is existential, not academic. Other than proclaiming God's word and celebrating the sacraments, the essential task of ministry is summarized by the second prophet to use the name Isaiah: "Comfort, give comfort to my people, says your God" (Isa 40:1). The church has a treasury of symbols to communicate comfort. I wish to reflect on three spaces for comfort: (1) We can offer tenderness; (2) we can restore a sense of living after a death; and (3) we can shed the tears of the saints.

---

18. Orsi, "Problem of the Holy," 99.

19. Orsi discusses Marion's and Santner's articulation of these experiences in Orsi, "Problem of the Holy," 100.

20. Orsi, *History and Presence*, 60.

21. Orsi, *History and Presence*, 68.

Our Faith Comforts by Offering Tenderness

Atheist Alain de Botton's observations on religion can remind Christians what we often take for granted. He witnessed what every perceptive minister has seen: a beaten down parishioner lighting a candle and kneeling before an icon of the Blessed Mother.[22] Sometimes tears run down the supplicant's face. An untold number of ministers know the experience firsthand when they are the supplicant, feeling overwhelmed by the ministry. A few moments of prayer remind us that the Mother of the Lord "seems to understand everything," as de Botton writes. Reassured, we can put things back together and move on. In recognizing our emotional requirement, de Botton offers pastoral ministers a necessary insight: "That there is no sympathetic mother or caring father out there who can make everything all right for us is not reason to deny how strongly we wish there could be. Religion teaches us *to be gentle on ourselves* in those times of crisis when desperate and afraid, we confusedly cry out for help from someone."[23] To be gentle on ourselves—here's a lesson many Christians and Christian ministers sorely need.

The message is conveyed in our doctrines. Comfort is woven throughout the feasts of the Virgin Mary. Just as Mary was assumed into heaven, body and soul, Mary signifies hope that our entire situation may be redeemed. Just as surely as she was spared the effects of original sin, she is the symbol that the objectified evil beating us into infantile tears can be overcome.

Christological symbols also teach us to be gentle on ourselves, the Good Shepherd, the Sacred Heart, and the crucified God. The Good Shepherd goes to the extreme to find the lost. In Christ, we can always reclaim the right path through life. The heart of the Savior beats for us. In Christ, we find comfort that love is at the core of existence and divine love embraces us. The cross teaches us that the God-man knows suffering. In Christ, we might overcome our suffering, or at least find a redemptive way to endure it.

The church also teaches us to be gentle on ourselves as sinners. Few conscientious people can deny some proclivity to evil and some willful participation in it. Because we are conscious of the social construction of reality, we know, too, that our sinfulness adds to the objectified evil in this world. The church demonstrates wisdom in acknowledging the "double

---

22. De Botton, *Religion for Atheists*, 166–7.
23. De Botton, *Religion for Atheists*, 175–6 (emphasis added).

consequence" of sin,[24] the immediate impact on our communion with God and a "temporal punishment," the lingering effect on ourselves and others. The sacrament of reconciliation is a moment to proclaim God's mercy. If the confessor acts in the person of Christ, the sinner should feel relief and renewal. The penance can become a moment to address the lingering consequences of sin. Objectified goodness may counterbalance objectified evil. If both consequences of sin are addressed, a repentant sinner can feel enormous comfort. The confessor can deliver what God requested of the prophet: "Speak to the heart . . . and proclaim . . . her guilt is expiated" (Isa 40:2).

Faith Comforts by Restoring a Sense of Living After a Death

To bury a loved one with care and dignity is essential to one's sense of worth. Few pastoral encounters, therefore, are more important than the funeral rites. The death of a loved one provokes the sensation of staring into the abyss or unleashing primordial chaos (Gen 1:2). Done well, the rituals bring comfort. The rites assist the bereaved to step back from the void and repair a sense of order. To restore equilibrium, the Christian community should be called into service. Comfort is offered on two interrelated levels: (1) The community assures the bereaved that there is life after death and that the community can assist the deceased with prayer. (2) The presence of the community holds out the promise that the bereaved can reclaim living after the beloved's death. The ministerial community needs to make practicable the prayerful assertion in the Vigil for the Deceased in the *Order of Christian Funerals*: "We believe that all the ties of friendship and affection which knit us as one throughout our lives do not unravel with death."[25]

The first ministerial task is to assure the bereaved about the afterlife. We can draw on the performative truth of the sacraments. Baptism is the beginning of eternal life. Eucharist unites us with the resurrected Christ and the living God. Ministers of bereavement need to trust the grace of baptism and Eucharist. A believer's well-lived life will exhibit signs of eternity. During encounters with the bereaved, family and friends will almost always offer insights into significant features of the deceased's life. They will speak about the eternal, higher things: faith, hope, and love. They

---

24. *Catechism of the Catholic Church*, para. 1472.
25. *Order of Christian Funerals*, 27.

may talk about the deceased's charity, compassion, search for knowledge and truth, goodness, and integrity. They may speak about their devotion to family and church, as well as sacrifices for community or country. Perhaps the deceased tended toward the creation of beauty, art, music, the care of the home, or contact with the good earth. Because eternity starts in this life, and because we are united to the living God, these activities and attachments are signs of our life in the resurrected Lord. Because eternity has saturated this life, life after death seems reasonable.

I have also heard the bereaved speak about the inadequacies and even the sinfulness of the deceased. Those funerals test the diplomacy of the presider. Every word must be chosen carefully. Connecting the truth about the deceased with the truth of God's forgiveness and Christ's saving power can bring comfort into those moments. Once the connection of the deceased's life with the life of the forgiving Christ is made, the rites carry the rest. Bereavement ministers may wish to read Hans Urs von Balthasar's *Dare We Hope "That All Men Be Saved"?*

To restore living after one suffers the death of a loved one, pastoral ministers need to recall that the people we serve are diverse and have various reactions and needs. Some people will never return to the church where the funeral Mass was offered; others want to be in that sacred space regularly. Some will never go back to the cemetery; others will visit daily. Some will wish to join a support group soon after the funeral; others will not be able to imagine sharing their most precious feelings with strangers. Some will blame God and want time with their pastor to express their rage; others will think such anger is sinful. The minister should concede whatever scenario that allows them to see God's goodness in the death and following. Some try to return to a normal schedule of work and play as soon as the rites are over; others need time before anything like normalcy is reestablished. Because our society celebrates autonomy, and because our communities are diverse, ministers should not be surprised that the needs of the bereaved vary. This situation tests the pastoral minister. Few pastoral encounters demand more careful listening than do the meetings with the bereaved. My recommendation—if I make any—is that the bereaved should do what they feel needs to be done to find comfort. I have found that people can rectify most decisions if the choices they make prove wrong over the long run. I think the right ministerial approach is to recognize the self-actualization of the believer—unless, of course, the bereaved is thinking about doing harm to themself or others.

My inclinations were confirmed when I read George Bonanno's research on bereavement. Most people are resilient, and most people seek comfort. Bonanno writes, "We are not accustomed to thinking of grief as a process of finding comfort. The idea seems a bit odd, but this is precisely what resilient people tend to do. Regardless of what the relationship was actually like, resilient people are generally able to gain a feeling of comfort from remembering the relationship during bereavement. They are also more likely to find comfort in talking about or thinking about the deceased, which, they report, makes them feel happy or at peace."[26] Comfort rather than closure seems to be the aim of the bereavement process. After all, memories are triggered by any number of factors over an indefinite duration: a smell, a favorite food, a piece of music, a photograph, and so on. If eternal life is a continuation of the best of this life, then comfort can be found in those memories.

Faith Comforts by Inspiring the Tears of the Saints

The Beatitudes are among Christ's most popular teachings. They are requested for celebratory weddings and heartrending funerals. I wonder about their popularity. In this culture, how is it that poverty in spirit, meekness, mourning, and persecution are so appealing? The second Beatitude may be the most perplexing: "Blessed are they who mourn, for they will be comforted" (Matt 5:4). I have witnessed the power of our funeral rites. But how do we make sense out of blessed mourning?

In his book, *Tears of the Saints*, Emil Cioran offers this insight into mourning: "As I search for the origin of tears, I thought of the saints. Could they be the source of tears' bitter light? Who can tell? To be sure, tears are their *trace*. Tears did not enter this world through the saints; but without them we would have never known that we cry because we long for a lost paradise."[27] Reflection on the "tears of the saints" has a long history in Christian spirituality. Their tears are shed as a sign of penitence. They can flow as one contemplates God's love. Saints cry with empathy for the crucified Jesus. Because the cross has several meanings, it can point us to the meaning of blessed mourning. The cross gathers into one icon the suffering of all humankind. The words of Jesus carry us to that conclusion: "Whatever you did for one of these least brothers of

---

26. Bonanno, *Other Side*, 72.
27. Cioran, *Tears and Saints*, 3.

mine, you did for me" (Matt 25:40). Solidarity with suffering humanity is solidarity with the crucified Christ and vice versa.

Pope Francis speaks of the gift of tears. Inés San Martin writes, "In 2013, at Mass for the Feast of the Exaltation of the Holy Cross, the pope challenged Catholics to come face to face with human misery, as a way to fully appreciate Jesus's crucifixion." She points out how his teaching helps us to get our minds around blessed mourning: "To the pope, the act that God himself cried shows that everyone can weep too. 'The tears of Jesus serve as an antidote to my indifference before the suffering of others,' Francis said."[28] Overcoming indifference is part of the experience. The experience deepens when we come to genuine empathy. An active response to lift up the suffering takes us deeper yet. At its most profound, to take up the cross means we sacrifice self out of love so others can find a better life. In the full experience, we discover an authentic Christian existence; therefore, we find the fullness of life. Perhaps that's the lost paradise of which Cioran writes, "Were heaven and earth to disappear, the saints' tears would still endure. Out of light and tears, a new world would be born, in which we could heal our memories."[29] So, the cross is exalted; mourning is blessed; the tears of saints give comfort. As long as such tears are shed, the fullness of life remains possible.

FAITH DEFINES AN END

The foundational preaching on evil is tied in with the doctrine of original sin. Karl Rahner's explanation of it offers preachers important insight.[30] We live in situations developed before us. Although we remain free, these conditions are imposed on us. Memories of previous decisions and actions become embodied in our institutions, organizations, and traditions. How power was used, how goods and services were distributed, how children were educated, how people related: these personal choices become objectified, forming our social environment. Patterns of behavior are transmitted from one generation to another and from one person to another. A child takes after a parent; a student learns from a teacher. Role models can be athletes, celebrities, civic leaders, and pastors.

---

28. San Martin, "Pope Francis Delivers."
29. Cioran, *Tears and Saints*, 59.
30. Rahner, *Foundations*, 106.

Some of those decisions—too many—were evil and sinful. An abuse of power can become objectified in an organization and, so, become a normal part of the operations of that organization. Cruelty can become institutionalized as *good* parenting or *good* pedagogy or *good* preaching. Respectable practices can camouflage evil. Economic success, for instance, can disguise avarice and greed. Rahner writes, "This co-determination of the situation of every person by the guilt of others is something universal, permanent, and therefore original. There are no islands for the individual person whose nature does not already bear the stamp of the guilt of others, directly or indirectly, from close or from afar."[31]

This reality demands we think on four levels at once. First, we remain free. Original sin does not diminish responsibility. The self remains free to construct a life. Second, the person's decisions and actions can contribute to the objective evil in the world. Third, Jesus Christ offers salvation. Cruelty, abuse, violence, and greed may be a permanent and universal part of the human condition, but no one baptized into the freedom of God's children needs to be cruel, abusive, violent, or greedy. Fourth, the Christian community must stand against the evil embedded in institutions, organizations, traditions, personal relationships, uses of power, the distribution of goods and services, and education—and correct its own abuses of the gospel.

To navigate a world awash in universal, permanent, and original guilt, a Christian can be inspired by the end—the purposeful goal of a Christian life. *Heaven* is the term describing that end. But heaven carries connotations of a passive, nonmaterial existence that is far too different from life in this world. If the end is expressed as *heaven*, the final determination of our lives is a total break with what life is now. The end, therefore, cannot function to produce the means to the end for people engaged in ordinary life. Besides, the goal of a disembodied existence can readily be used to diminish the material and biological, doing damage to our psychic and spiritual lives. If the end is to be purposeful in our lives now, St. Paul's description of the end may be more useful. When the ministry of Christ and Christ's people is complete, God will be all in all (1 Cor 15:28). The end is unity in God; the means, then, must be of God.

St. Paul's description of baptism renders the end as the presence of future things. In Romans, Paul tells us that baptism unites us in the death and resurrection of Christ, so that we live in the newness of life (Rom

---

31. Rahner, *Foundations*, 109.

6:1–11). In 2 Corinthians, he writes, "So whoever is in Christ is a new creation: the old things have passed away; behold new things have come. And all this is from God who has reconciled us to himself through Christ and given us the ministry of reconciliation" (2 Cor 5:17–18). In 2 Peter, we are told that "we share in the divine nature" because of our incorporation into Christ (2 Pet 1:4).

The end infuses our entire lives, including the passage of time and the place we inhabit. Beginning with baptism, our lives partake in eternity. The Christian believer, therefore, has a definitive valuation of self, this world, and time. Because we are tasked with the ministry of reconciliation—"as if God were appealing through us" (2 Cor 5:20)—even those who differ, share in a definitive valuation. All times, all places, all peoples can be made holy through a ministry to consecrate it all. God can be all in all.

FAITH GROUNDS LIFE DECISIONS

In the discussion between Umberto Eco and Cardinal Martini, the cardinal put questions to Eco about the grounding or the foundation for Eco's moral decisions. He phrased the question in dramatic terms: What principles are held so firmly that "one would give his life for them?" What moves a person to act "at any cost?" Why would one "sacrifice one's life?"[32] He quotes Hans Kung: "It has become clear that only the unconditional can force unconditionally and only the absolute can bind absolutely."[33]

Questions of grounding raised by pastoral ministers might take on a different tone. Principles that compel, bind, and force seem beyond ministers who are rubbing shoulders with free, autonomous believers. Pastoral theology might ask whether there are absolutes that enthuse, inspire, and evoke a Christ-like response. The pastoral minister is working through questions that move a believer to construct a Christian life.

The pastoral minister's question can be phrased like this: Can Christian ministers offer a foundation or grounding to respond to pressing life questions? Imagine a three-way dialogue. The discussants are: (1) the *world* awash in universal, permanent, and original guilt, as Rahner describes the impact of original sin; (2) the searching and seeking *believer*

---

32. Eco and Martini, *Belief or Unbelief?*, 81.

33. Kung, *Project for a World Ethics*, quoted in Eco and Martini, *Belief or Unbelief?*, 83.

trying to put a good (read, moral), and significant (read, ethical) life together; and (3) *pastoral ministers* assisting the believer to ground her search for faith in the absolute.

The world tells us it is only sensible to accept the status quo, to go along to get along, to join the worst of humanity that we see on the twenty-four seven cable news shows. Yet, the searching and seeking believer has found goodness at the core of reality and is hoping to conform her life to that goodness. The assertion of goodness requires grounding. The pastoral minister invites the believer to meditate on her freedom, which encourages questioning, searching, imagining, and creating her life. The gift of freedom implies a gift giver. Once the minister establishes the goodness of the gift and the gift giver, the minister can speak of the God of goodness and love who invites all people into union.

The world says life is pleasurable if the self is guided by immediate impulses. The believer is aware of the *gap* between who she is and who she could become. She has come to experience the *more*, a desire for *more* of life and *more* to life. The *gap* she experiences and the *more* she desires require grounding. The pastoral minister teaches her about the incarnate God who invites us to appreciate the goodness of the material and spiritual world. Stewardship of life, of the body, and the environment are grounded in God creating and God saving. Moreover, the infinite, living God invites us into an aspirational life, into natality, a life that is open to possibility. Seeking the newness of life is grounded in sharing new life with the resurrected Lord.

The advertisement industry carries the message of this world that happiness is in self-centered acquisition. The searching and seeking believer discovers that joy is found in others, in family and friends, in community, and even in Others who differ. An orientation to others rather than self requires grounding. The minister can show the believer that the God of love invites us to overcome hard boundaries that divide humankind, to seek understanding and tolerance, to construct communities of diversity. The cessation of judgment, the appreciation of differences, the establishment of peace is grounded in our participation in God's love (1 John 4:7).

The world awash in original guilt tells me that life is a war of all against all, that each person needs to be tough, ready to bulldoze others to succeed. The believer desires a world that is caring and compassionate, where she can be gentle on herself and on all those around her. She feels a compulsion to forgive and to be forgiven. The desire for genuine peace within herself and with others requires grounding. The pastoral minister can point her to the crucified Lord who forgives from the cross and demonstrates self-giving love. The minister can promise that such love promises to unite all peoples in Christ (John 12:32).

The world reminds us of our mortality. It may quote the biblical sage Qoheleth. Since death is around the corner, would it not be best to eat, drink, and to seek constant entertainment (Eccl 8:15)? The searcher and seeker hopes time flows into eternity and that this earth is transformed to be "as it is in heaven." She desires her striving and her aspirations to make a significant if not permanent difference. Her desire seeks realization. The pastoral minister can inform the believer that she is baptized into newness of life. Her hope is grounded in God, who is the beatific vision. God inspires each of us to find transcendent beauty in nature, in the long struggle of humankind toward freedom, and in human creativity. Transcendent experiences preview the beatific vision. In addition, the minister can quote St. Paul who tells us that "love never fails" (1 Cor 13:8) and that "faith, hope, love remain, these three, but the greatest of these is love" (1 Cor 13:13).

Such a dialogue depends on performative truth. As noted above, a performative truth is not another truth or a different truth. It is a dimension of the one truth. What grounds all theology grounds pastoral theology. The pastoral theologian explores the one truth that a believer needs to construct a self, a community, society, and the world. Pastoral ministers should pursue all branches of the one truth. But they need to know that the one truth has a much-needed dimension, a performative truth. This truth grounds the construction of Christian self and community and the labor for a just society and a peaceful world. Philosophers and systematic theologians may never prove the existence of God—at least not definitively. But the pastoral theologian can readily prove our need for God. Seeking "the higher and highest possibilities of human beings"[34] depends on grounding our life choices in God.

---

34. Sloterdijk, *Change Your Life*, 14.

Part 2.

A Performatory Reading of the Nicene Creed

3

I Believe

IN *THE CONFESSIONS*, ST. Augustine offers us this insight into the search for God:

> Late have I loved you, Beauty so ancient and so new,
> Late have I loved you!
> Lo, *you were within*,
> But I outside, seeking there for you,
> And upon the shapely things you have made I rushed headlong,
> I misshapen.
> You were *with me*, but I was not with you.[1]

Augustine has us look within. In his work *The Trinity*, he demonstrates more precisely where to look. He surveys the soul. He finds the image of God in a threefold aspect of the soul: "mind remembering itself, understanding itself, and loving itself."[2] He also sees the image of God in three virtues of the soul: "sagacity, courage, and moderation"—these three "produce a trinity."[3]

Augustine proposes that the tenses—past, present, and future—are about forming the present. So, the mind remembering itself helps us to "recognize the image we are looking for."[4] Because faith is also active in the memory, recognizing the image of God gives way to the actuality of

---

1. Augustine, *Confessions*, 262 (emphasis added).
2. Augustine, *Trinity*, 379.
3. Augustine, *Trinity*, 362.
4. Augustine, *Trinity*, 383.

God.⁵ Augustine writes, "The trinity of the mind is not really the image of God because the mind remembers and understands and loves itself, but because it is also able to remember and understand and love him by whom it was made. . . . Let it remember its God to whose image it was made, and understand and love him."⁶ This leap back to the fourth century reminds us how very different we have become. I seriously doubt anyone could survey the soul and find threefold elements that remind them of God's image. I am also sure that even if we find the image in memory, we could not find God's presence in actuality.

So, what happens when the contemporary person looks within? Could the contemporary person look within to find the image of God and from that image sense the Creator and Savior? The path I have found seems counterintuitive. And it is a long journey. The path takes us into the depth of the modern skepticism, on which modernity is founded. I am referring to Descartes's *Meditations*, which were composed in 1641. *Meditations* begins with absolute doubt and works its way to God. In a similar fashion, if the contemporary person allows herself doubting, questioning, searching, even skepticism, she might find her way to God. Pastoral ministers, however, may need to assist the doubting believer to discover the path from skepticism to faith. It is not a straightforward journey.

In 1902, American psychologist William James wrote a book on religion that is still admired; it is called *Varieties of Religious Experience*. He begins his search in the feeling of helplessness, a feeling of being incomplete. He constructs this definition of religion: "Religion shall mean for us the feelings, acts and experiences of the individual in his/her solitude, so far as they apprehend themselves standing in relation to whatever they may consider as divine."⁷ Scholars of James' work suggest that his definition reflects New England Protestant individualism. For me, it does that and more. It suggests contemporary society's privatization of religion.⁸ Because each of us constructs the self out of the values we encounter on our individual life journey, we have few other options but to find our faith in our solitude.

For most pastoral ministers, being immersed in our religion, in its beliefs and rituals, in its organization and interpersonal encounters,

---

5. Augustine, *Trinity*, 382.
6. Augustine, *Trinity*, 384.
7. James, *Varieties of Religious Experience*, 36.
8. I have discussed privatization and commodification more fully in Schmitz, *Thoughts on Secularization*, 21–30.

to find faith in our solitude sounds strange. Theologian Hans Urs von Balthasar may help us understand. He develops the concept of vocation or calling.[9] A calling is personal. It takes place before any involvement in the church. What he calls the *abstract*—that is, our belief system—and the *institutional*—that is, the church as organization—are secondary. The call may come to individuals through various patterns of experiences. Upon reflection on the experience, a person may come to knowledge of God. A starting point appropriate for today's situation is to consider the altogether personal calling. We begin in our solitude.

Solitude strips off our masks; false personas fall away. Soul searching raises existential questions. We do not ask these all at once, but only when occasions demand. Periods of our lives, certain experiences, various encounters insist we fall back into ourselves to question and think. Who am I? What is life for? What is my ongoing interior conversation with myself? Does it point to my soul or my spirit or what we now call consciousness? Will I accept the values of my family and friends? Or will my life journey take me elsewhere? How do I value material, physical reality, my body? What is the good? How do I relate to others? What is love? Why does fear of failure cause such inertia? What about shyness around others? How is it I perceive beauty? Is there really truth? Why do humans suffer? Why do some do evil? Why violence? Why abuse? Why do people try to control others? How should I relate to people who differ from me? Can I change myself? Others? Reality? Does the passage of time lead only to death? Or is there fulfillment? Is there happiness? Do I have a preplanned destiny? If so, who or what composes the plan? Or am I free?

We may come to the first diabolic trick played on us during this journey into faith. Not just a few of us get off this path as quickly as possible. Not just a few of us abandon the search for the best about ourselves or the best about humanity. Questioning is stressful; honesty with oneself can generate anxiety. We can hide in perpetual entertainment; contemporary society is excellent at providing diversions. We can also posit some controlling demigod, some version of fate to guide our affairs. I find too many people look for some force to shield them from the search. I hear the questioning shut down with illusory assertions: *Everything has a purpose.* Or, *Everything works out for the good.* Some hide in religiously built mental sanctuaries: *God has a plan.* I am not sure most of us can

---

9. Balthasar, "Vocation," 114.

take these shortcuts. It smacks of magical thinking. Such illusions seem to break down in times of deprivation, suffering, failure, or illness. And worst of all, these fictional shelters hide us from our humanity. Here is a place where the pastoral minister may help. The questioning needs to be commended. The illusions of magical thinking need to be stripped away. Reality must be faced. A pastoral minister can suggest that the entire process, even when painful, can lead to a renewal of the path to God who created each of us with active, searching, seeking minds and hearts.

Because the mind and heart are created by God and may lead us back to God, we possess a nearly infinite need to question and a capacity for it. The pastoral minister can suggest that the questioning and searching are constants. They may abate for a short period. But they soon return. Every stage of our ever-longer lives seems to raise new questions. The young adult needs to find a mate, make a career, commit to values and norms. Questions arise about settling down, having children, and on. Few of us hang on to one career for our lengthy work lives. So, the career questions of youth return and trigger again the questions of finding satisfaction in life. Longer lives raise new questions. Long chronic illnesses and disabilities raise the question, *Why me?* When children leave home, what about the empty nest? How does one use the time after retirement? How can one revitalize one's most significant relationships late in life? Then, one gets to old age. How does one deal with the inevitable loss of physical strength and eventual breakdown? How does one navigate through a period of dependency that comes with advanced age? What happens when death rises on the horizon? How does one put life back together after the death of a spouse or lifelong friend?

Although some can ignore them, the questions never cease. We are never complete. The self is a lifetime construction project. Some, perhaps most of us, find the questioning and searching exciting. Each question at each stage of life implies new hope and new possibilities. Each question raises options. Living with possibility within the ongoing construction of a life requires imagination and creativity. After a survey of life's potential, after the exploration of our imaginations, the achievement of the self—although temporary—is one of life's satisfactions. We may even look forward to the process beginning again when we come to the next stage in life. Behind it all is an unavoidable conclusion: we cannot avoid our intrinsic freedom and agency. We can and must shape and reshape our lives. This makes us human.

Faith is now just a few steps away. Potential, possibility, hope, options, imagination, creativity—corollaries of freedom—require a reflection on a Creator or a creative force. Somehow, someone, or something graced human life so that we can shape our lives. Somehow, someone gifted us with freedom. When the project of the self becomes a source of joy, we conclude that whoever or whatever made us free must be benevolent, must be goodness itself.

William James says that such meditations happen in solemn, reverent moments. When we sense the grace or the gift, we come to acceptance, what James calls "a complex, a tender, a submissive and a graceful state of mind."[10] We can be overwhelmed by our reality. We can be staggered at the idea of a never-ending journey. But we also sense our freedom and our agency. In gratitude, we come to accept ourselves as active agents of our own lives.

Returning to the thought of grace and gift, we follow it to the source, to a gift giver. When we get there, we see the astounding goodness at the core of reality. The Creator or some creative force tenders the grace of freedom, potential, possibility, hope, imagination, creativity. Like a bolt out of the blue, we may suddenly recall with appreciation God's reaction to the sixth day when humanity was created: He "found it very good" (Gen 1:31). The questions make us human. The contemplation on the faculty to question leads us through that questioning to the realization of our intrinsic freedom and, beyond, to a benevolent Creator or creative force. We are on the threshold of faith.

Before we go through the threshold and on to God, we need to wrestle with another diabolic play against our humanity. The first was fear of self-questioning. The second temptation that can throw us off course is the fear of chaos. When we journey through questioning to freedom, we pass close to a frontier where humans cannot bear to go. We come to the border of spiritual chaos. In terms of human interaction, we come close to anomie, to lawlessness and normlessness. To avoid a breakdown of self and social systems into free-floating anxiety and chaos, we need what British sociologist Anthony Giddens calls "ontological security." To maneuver through the simplest everyday activities "demands the bracketing of a potentially almost infinite range of possibilities open to the individual." We require trust in an "unproven and unprovable . . . framework

---

10. James, *Varieties of Religious Experience*, 42.

of reality."[11] Ontological security stems from that shared framework of reality based on generally accepted, but unprovable, answers to "existential questions."[12] Without commonly held answers to these basic questions, we are set adrift. Giddens passes on an insight from developmental psychologist Henry Stack Sullivan that such security is more important "than the impulses resulting from a feeling of hunger or thirst."[13]

One option for a pastoral leader destroys faith. My argument, however, is again counterintuitive; I ask the reader to suspend judgment until the full argument is explained. In our times, the more one aims to shore up certitude, the more one erodes the possibility of genuine faith. Doubt and questioning are deeply coded in our contemporary DNA. Attempting to silence the questioning and suppress the doubt, a pastoral minster can lead an assembly into the idolatry of a faux certitude.

Fundamentalism is one example. Biblical fundamentalism is a modern phenomenon, articulated in the late nineteenth and early twentieth centuries. Biblical fundamentalism is most often found in branches of Protestantism. Catholics are not immune to it, however. Catholics tend toward an equivalent form of faux certitude. Catholics look for security in ecclesial authority. Infallibility may have deep roots in the history of the church, but it is also modern; it was articulated as dogma in July, 1870. I am not questioning the dogma, but, today, a Catholic's search for ontological security can find respite in an overreach of the notion of unchanging truth based in infallible authority. Philosopher Charles Taylor sees these options as a temptation of Western Christianity: "This is, of course, in keeping with the long-standing obsession of Latin Christendom to nail down with ultimate, unattainable and finally self-destructive precision the bases of final, unchallengeable, inerrant authority, be it in a certain form of Papal decision, or a literal reading of the Bible."[14] These forms of Christian certitude developed in modern times to counter increasing choice and escalating pluralism. Because the faux certitudes do not address the underlying issues, contemporary believers are unlikely to sustain that certitude. Any average student of the Bible can find fundamentalism's flaws. It is easy to find contradictory accounts of events. It is even easier to get turned off by atrocities attributed to God (e.g.,

---

11. Giddens, *Modernity and Self-Identity*, 36.
12. Giddens, *Modernity and Self-Identity*, 47–55.
13. Sullivan, *Modern Psychiatry*, 14, quoted in Giddens, *Modernity and Self-Identity*, 45.
14. Taylor, *Secular Age*, 512.

the genocide in Deuteronomy). And papal infallibility is hard to hold when a student of history learns about some of the men who have sat on the Chair of Peter. Besides, certitude is hardly conceivable when we consider what we are trying to grasp. Our finite minds are asking questions about the infinite; we are raising questions about God. We are also raising questions about the mystery of the human person. And we are inquiring about the two unsolvable mysteries at once, God's relation to the human. Taylor writes, "It will be less and less common for people to be drawn into or kept within a faith by some strong political or group identity, or by the sense that they are sustaining a socially essential ethic."[15] In ultimate matters, certitude is simply out of reach.

Security cannot be found in the denial of freedom, possibility, and potential. Ontological security cannot be found in the denial of our agency to create the self. The security is found, instead, in the God who created us in freedom and who bids us into that freedom. This is the point that Karl Rahner makes in *Foundations of Christian Faith*, in a section dealing with sin and guilt.[16] The freedom to question is necessary for faith. Rahner demonstrates that a *yes* to the free self is also a *yes* to God who has created us in freedom. A *no* to the free, questioning, searching self is also a *no* to God. In his dense style, Rahner writes, "Corresponding to the essence of freedom, such a *no* to God is originally and primarily a *no* to God in the actualization of human existence in its single totality and in its single and unique freedom."[17] To say *no* to the freedom to imagine and create the best self is a decision "against the reality of the world established by God."[18] The *yes* to the free questioning self is the affirmation of God and the way to our salvation.

I know the catechism prohibits doubt. While it distinguishes voluntary and involuntary doubt, both are sins against faith. "Voluntary doubt about faith disregards or refuses to hold as true what God has revealed and the Church proposes for belief. Involuntary doubt refers to hesitation in believing, difficulty in overcoming objections connected with the faith, or also anxiety aroused by its obscurity."[19] This teaching reflects a different age, a time of a homogenous Christian culture sometimes called Christendom. In such a culture, one's family and friends—in fact, all of

15. Taylor, *Secular Age*, 514.
16. Rahner, *Foundations*, 100.
17. Rahner, *Foundations*, 101.
18. Rahner, *Foundations*, 104.
19. *Catechism of the Catholic Church*, para. 2088.

society—would call a doubter back into the fold. The last remnants of that culture are passing. Today, family and friends are likely to celebrate the questioning and to acknowledge their own doubt. It is celebrated as *a coming of age* or as *the realization of the self*. In our culture, therefore, we must find a different path to faith. If someone passes through the questioning to the realization of the gift of freedom and on to the gift giver, our Creator, that person will have made a genuine act of faith, defined as a free decision made from the depth of one's spirit.[20]

If Rahner is correct, saying yes to the questioning self is saying yes to the God who made us with inquisitive spirits. The minister can celebrate—and by celebrating, affirm—the Creator or creative force who gifts humankind with freedom. This option sets the ideal of the questioning, searching person on a firm religious foundation; it offers a form of ontological security that avoids the oppression of the spirit. A minister who guides an assembly in this direction fulfills two basic functions of religion: (1) The minister grounds the faith. The creative force who gifts humankind with freedom is divine. Therefore, the person who finds satisfaction, perhaps happiness, in questioning is embracing the sacred. (2) The minister provides a positive valuation for the free, questioning, searching human person. Rahner expresses this aspiration: "Freedom is the event of something eternal. But since we ourselves are still coming to be in freedom, we do not exist with and behold this eternity, but in our passage through the multiplicity of the temporal, we are performing this event of freedom, we are forming the eternity which we ourselves are and are becoming."[21] The minister who celebrates the questioning and searching self, who praises the freedom to construct oneself, is grounding the faith in the God of freedom. I find myself in complete agreement with Bernard Lonergan: "The transcendental field is defined not by what man knows, not by what he can know, but by what he can ask about."[22] I have never understood how a finite mind can approach the infinite without difficulty, even some anxiety. To question and doubt seems obligatory.

Pastoral ministers must saturate their teaching with revelation. Pastoral theologians must ground their insights in the revelation. Anything else is cheating the people of God. I conclude this essay, then, with the gospel. Consider the treatment of faith by Jesus. Consider the ones in whom he finds faith. He recognizes the faith of men and women who did

---

20. Rahner, *Practice of the Faith*, 29–32.
21. Rahner, *Foundations*, 96.
22. Lonergan, *Method in Theology*, 24.

not share in his beliefs, his Second Temple Judaism. He did not ask the Samaritan woman he met at Jacob's well or her friends who came to faith that day to share in Jewish practice (John 4:4–42). Neither the grateful Samaritan leper (Luke 17:11–19) nor the Samaritan whom we call *good* (Luke 10:29–37) quit worshipping on Mount Gerizim to join the Lord on the Temple Mount. He did not demand the Roman centurion (Matt 8:5–13) or the Canaanite woman (Matt 15:21–28) convert from their pagan beliefs to embrace the one God. Jesus recognized these men and women for their remarkable faith.

Jesus never said that such faith would lead to a belief system, a creed. Instead, he said faith is empowerment. The faith he championed can move mountains (Matt 17:20) and uproot trees (Luke 17:6). Most of all, faith heals. How often the Lord asserts that the source of miraculous power is the internal faith of the ones receiving his miraculous action. How often he says, "Your faith has saved you" (see, in Mark alone, 2:5; 5:25–34, 35–43; 10:46–52).

In the scene where the Roman centurion asked for the cure of his servant, Jesus rebukes fellow believers: "I say to you, many will come from the east and the west, and will recline with Abraham, Isaac, and Jacob at the banquet in the kingdom of heaven, but the children of the kingdom will be driven out into the outer darkness, where there will be wailing and grinding of teeth" (Matt 8:11–12). Apparently, one can believe and practice without faith. But without faith, believers are doomed. If the disciples had faith, they could have calmed the storm at sea (Mark 4:35–41). Peter could have walked on water (Matt 14:28–31). The lack of faith was paralyzing; Jesus suffered this when he was among his own in Nazareth (Mark 6:1–6). The Gospels teach us even one's religious and political enemies may have faith. Just as important, believers may lack faith.

Let's give this type of faith the name *generic faith*. As I wrote, most of us who practice the faith find it strange that faith is discovered in solitude. Most of us enjoy faith within a belief system. We are immersed in beliefs, rituals, an organization, and interpersonal encounters. We have invested in it. For the practitioner, the overall experience is circular: I practice because I believe, and my belief is sustained by my practice. This is faith with belief, or, better, faith within the community of the church. But there is a prior experience, one that von Balthasar calls a vocation or a calling. I prefer a less theological name. I think the experience places one at the threshold of the fullness of faith. *Generic faith* is found in our solitude. One arrives at it through questioning and doubt. It is faith that emerges from a meditation on the one who creates us with an inquisitive spirit, the one who graces our lives with freedom, which demonstrates itself as possibility, potential, hope, imagination, and creativity. I might advance a hypothesis: if a sensitive pastoral minister were to honestly examine this experience, s/he would find that most practitioners return from full, practicing faith/belief to generic faith, to the threshold, repeatedly.

The author of Hebrews offers us an evocative definition of faith: "Faith is the realization of what is hoped for and evidence of things not seen" (Heb 11:1). The rest of the eleventh chapter offers examples of men and women drawn to action through faith. This "cloud of witnesses" gives credence to the Lord's assertion that faith empowers. This faith is found within. Most importantly, it empowers us for the creation of a believing self. It empowers us to journey across the threshold to find God through Jesus Christ.

4

In One God

PREPOSITIONS ARE IMPORTANT. *In* may be the quintessential Christian prefix and preposition: *in*carnation, *in*dwelling, *in*finite, *in* one God, *in* one Lord Jesus Christ, *in* the Holy Spirit, and *in* one, holy, catholic, and apostolic church. Why not save the keystrokes and simply believe God, Jesus Christ, the Holy Spirit, and the church? For a response, we need to turn to the exodus event. The immense relief felt by the Hebrew people when they no longer had to obey the *divine* pharaoh may have influenced the law. The Ten Commandments were given shortly after God freed them from slavery. God introduces the commandments with a reminder of their enslavement: "I am the Lord your God, who brought you out of the land of Egypt, out of the house of slavery" (Exod 20:2). How liberating it must have been for the Hebrew people to hear that Yahweh alone is God (Exod 20:3), that no human is divine, that they did not have to bow down before a human figure made into an idol (Exod 20:5), and that to use God's name to dominate others was a punishable evil (Exod 20:7).

Three millennia have dulled the impact of those commands.[1] In common catechesis, for instance, the second commandment has been reduced to a prohibition on foul language. Considering the experience of slavery, however, the commandment means so much more. Believers often bring *God* into the give-and-take of ordinary human interaction. *God* is used to give authority to one's argument. *God* can be a bludgeon to manipulate another. *God* is often used in popular piety to give credence to magical thinking. The first seven verses of Exod 20 imply that

---

1. Schmidt, "Dialogue," 63.

the true God is to be thought of differently. God is not like us. God cannot be brought down to our level. God is not our puppet. God cannot be used for our purposes, especially if our purpose is to degrade human life. Isaiah's words demand our restraint: "For my thoughts are not your thoughts, nor are your ways my ways" (Isa 55:8). Because God is infinitely greater, God's message does not come to us directly; the distance requires mediation. Each word of the Scriptures is a human construct—albeit an inspired one. The distance is denoted by the preposition. We believe *in* God.

Emmanuel Levinas helps us explore the significance of *in*. Levinas reminds us that the use of the term *God* or *Lord* is a "breakup of consciousness." Normally, words try to enclose or encompass an object. A word helps us imagine something or get our minds around it. But *God* is different. *God* is "not-letting-itself-be-encompassed." He writes of the *in* of the infinite: it is "at once the non- and the within."[2] God is the non-finite. And because God signifies the whole of reality and is everywhere, our finitude is within God. God encompasses us. This is not a new thought. An early Christian theologian Irenaeus wrote, "God contains everything and is contained by nothing."[3]

Although we need to remain conscious of the non- and the within at once, let me address the non-finite first. We cannot imagine the infinite. Levinas says the infinite is "devastating" to us; it puts us in our place.[4] He is speaking of subjectivity. The infinite negates "the subjectivity of the subject."[5] Subjectivity may be defined as our overweening desire to put ourselves and our desires at the center of everything. Care is needed here. God never oppresses. God does not limit our freedom. Even so, once we posit God, we lose our subjectivity to find our true self within the infinite. As finite beings, we do not have divine power. To keep our finitude in mind will keep us from using religion to manipulate, judge, or diminish others (Matt 7:1–5). In addition, awareness of God's infinity keeps us from using God to magnify our desire (Matt 6:25–34). Our awareness of God's infinity may also keep us from magical thinking. God is not the lonely old man on a throne waiting to grant or deny our wish, the archetype of Santa Claus or the wizards Dumbledore and Gandalf. That god is a human projection. Through his temptations, Jesus teaches us that the infinite does

---

2. Levinas, *Of God*, 63.
3. Irenaeus, quoted in Borg, *Speaking Christian*, 70.
4. Levinas, *Of God*, 66.
5. Levinas, *Of God*, 65.

not bend to finite needs or wishes—not even in his case (Matt 4:1–11). Gently, a pastoral minister must urge believers "to put aside childish things" (1 Cor 13:11). A great disservice is done to the Christian faith when *God* is misused. We need to resurrect the full meaning of those first commandments. If so, God-talk might generate a liberated spirit.

Keeping in mind God's infinity and our finitude serve a crucial function of religion. The reminder gives us perspective. God is the center. God is the core of reality. God creates, and God saves. God calls us into unity. God is supreme. Humans are not the core of everything. Humans are the ones created and saved. Humans are called. Once our image of God is free from assertions of our power over others, once the image is free from childish wish fulfillment, belief in God is the best hedge against self-aggrandizement and narcissistic tendencies. Learning to bow our heads in prayer, to genuflect, to kneel in adoration, to hear the word of God in silence are all gestures demonstrating our belief in God. And more, incorporating our beliefs into gestures shows *God* is not only a cognitive proposition. The living God is an active, compelling force in our lives. We will see in the next chapter—"the Father, Almighty"—that the active force can set our priorities and design the parameters of our lives.

To consider the finite within God shows us why *in* may be the essentially Christian preposition. St. Paul preached these words to the people of Athens: "For 'in him [God] we live and move and have our being'" (Acts 17:28). In the New Testament, the preposition is used more often in relation to Christ. Of course, Christ leads us to union *in* the Father. In Romans, baptism allows us to live "for God in Christ Jesus" (Rom 6:11). In John's Gospel, Eucharist unites us to Christ and, through him, to the Father: "Whoever eats my flesh and drinks my blood remains in me and I in him. Just as the living Father sent me and I have life because of the Father, so also the one who feeds on me will have life because of me" (John 6:56–57). At the Last Supper, Jesus affirms the interaction. He starts, "I am the vine, you are the branches. Whoever remains in me and I in him will bear much fruit." Then he says, "If you remain in me and my words remain in you, ask for whatever you want and it will be done for you. By this is my Father glorified, that you bear much fruit and become my disciples. As the Father loves me, so I also love you. Remain in my love" (John 15:5–9). John's epistles also describe this interaction. This passage uses *in* nine times:

> Beloved, if God so loved us, we also must love one another. No one has ever seen God. Yet, if we love one another, God remains in us, and his love is brought to perfection in us.

> This is how we know that we remain in him and he in us, that he has given us of his Spirit. Moreover, we have seen and testify that the Father sent his Son as savior of the world. Whoever acknowledges that Jesus is the Son of God, God remains in him and he in God. We have come to know and to believe in the love God has for us.
>
> God is love, and whoever remains in love remains in God and God in him. (1 John 4:11–16)

St. Paul composed many ways to express this interaction in Christ and through him in the Father. Paul teaches that we share in the paschal mystery, in his death and resurrection (Rom 6:1–11). Furthermore, through the Spirit, we constitute Christ's body and are individually parts of it (1 Cor 12:27). Because the Spirit is within, we can have the "mind of the Lord" (1 Cor 2:16). We can also share in the attitude of Christ: "If there is any encouragement in Christ, any solace in love, any participation in the Spirit, any compassion and mercy, complete my joy by being of the same mind, with the same love, united in heart, thinking one thing. . . . Have among yourselves the same attitude that is also yours in Christ Jesus" (Phil 2:1–5).

I could go on. Certainly, other prepositions are used for our interaction in God, Christ, and the Spirit. Using the biblical image of *in*, however, could help in the construction of a believing self for our times. Awareness of the full meaning of the *in* is required; the logic of both *non* and *within* must be held together. As Levinas said, the *in* means nonfinite. The distance between the infinite and the finite remains vast. We cannot assume divine power. We cannot bend God to our desires. We are to conform to God and to Jesus Christ. But dwelling on our finitude can diminish a person to the point of abuse. So, the *in* of the infinite must remind us of the finite within the infinite and the *in*dwelling of the infinite. Both logics, *non* and *within*, are needed simultaneously.

When I consider the rationale for belief—why it compels, why it endures—I find faith offers us both connection and participation with the force at the core of our reality. Both connection and participation are conveyed with the preposition *in*. The depth of the connection and extent of participation are enhanced by the word *one*. Surely, the *in one* God reminds us of the monotheistic tradition begun with Abraham and Sarah. *One* also expresses a unity of the triune God. The Scriptures inform us, however, that a connection with God spills over into our sphere. We are connected in the Creator to all creation; we are connected in the Savior to all humankind. God's love pours forth and fills our reality.

Our connection with creation through our life within God is extraordinarily crucial for our times. Human life and creation itself are in danger. Our physical natures are made of earth, air, and water. To despoil them puts our health—the conditions for life—in jeopardy. A warming climate and melting ice will make large parts of the earth uninhabitable with ever more people fighting over the ever-diminishing resources. The issue can be approached through science. But far too many are locked in denial. Perhaps pastoral ministers can address the issue through religion, creating deep feelings about the value of creation, our connection to it, and our participation or responsibility for it. It is a function of religion to offer valuations of this world and valuations of one another by creating deeply held moods and motives.

A couple lines from Teilhard de Chardin's *Divine Milieu* have stayed with me since I first read them many years ago: "By virtue of the Creation and, still more, of the incarnation, *nothing* here below *is profane* for those who know how to see. On the contrary, everything is sacred to the men who can distinguish that portion of chosen being which is subject to Christ's drawing power in the process of consummation."[6] A few lines later, a spirit of adoration connects worship to all of life: "Right from the hands that knead the dough, to those that consecrate it, the great and universal Host should be prepared and handled in a spirit of adoration."[7]

Teilhard's words complement the words prayed in the third and fourth eucharistic prayers. In the third, we pray:

> You are indeed Holy, O Lord,
> and all you have created
> rightly gives you praise,
> for through your Son, our Lord Jesus Christ,
> by the power and working of the Holy Spirit,
> you give life to all things and make them holy.[8]

In the fourth eucharistic prayer, we pray:

> And that we might live no longer for ourselves
> but for him who died and rose again for us,
> he sent the Holy Spirit from you, Father,

---

6. Teilhard de Chardin, *Divine Milieu*, 30.
7. Teilhard de Chardin, *Divine Milieu*, 31.
8. *Roman Missal*, 502.

> as the first fruits for those who believe,
> so that, bringing to perfection his work in the world
> he might sanctify creation to the full.[9]

St. Paul makes this same point in his Epistle to the Romans. Those who live in Christ are freed from the curse of sin and death (Rom 8:1–13). We are adopted children of God, empowered to call God "Abba, Father!" (Rom 8:14–17). The connection in Christ and in the Father extends to all creation that awaits "with eager expectation the revelation of the children of God" (Rom 8:19). Creation and the children of God look to the consummation of God's plan, the final resurrection (Rom 8:22–23). We are to wait with hopeful endurance (Rom 8:25) for a new creation modeled in the resurrected Christ.

Our participation—our human responsibility—in creation can be traced back to the original creation. As St. Paul intertwines salvation with a new creation, the author of the first chapter of Genesis situates an active humanity in the original creation. If the first creation story is read as poetry—as I think it was intended—our participation, our responsibility, becomes apparent. It begins with light (Gen 1:3). The author certainly knew the sources of earthly light, the sun and the moon. But the physical sources of light are not created until v. 14. A reader of poetry needs to give pause for considering what the light is in v. 3. When one learns that the creation stories of Genesis came from the time of the prophets, we find a solution. Isaiah announces the messiah and the salvation of Israel. The chapter begins, "The people who walked in darkness have seen a great light" (Isa 9:1). If the light referenced in Isaiah is the same light of Genesis, then light symbolizes salvation. The image carries throughout the Scripture into John's Gospel: "What came to be through him was life, and this life was the light of the human race" (John 1:3–4). The light in Genesis reveals God's plan. First, God intends to save, and, only then, God creates what God will save. When the poem was composed, God's people were likely in exile in Babylon. The light is their salvific liberation.

Reading the rest of the poem with care, we discover the people of God's responsibility for the new creation. The poem begins with God creating through verbal commands. God's word is life giving from the beginning. But the author changes God's methodology. In v. 11, God calls for partnership: "Let the earth bring forth vegetation." The earth responds and does its part. In v. 20, God calls for another partner: "Let the water

---

9. *Roman Missal*, 509.

teem with an abundance of living creatures." The waters respond. In v. 24, God calls on the earth again: "Let the earth bring forth all kinds of living creatures." The earth responds. Now, the stage is readied. Humanity is created in God's own image. Humanity is charged to fill the earth and subdue it. Humankind is tasked to nurture all of creation (Gen 1:29–30). Because this poem is about salvation, the creation of humankind in God's image is a statement that humankind can and must participate in salvation by opening themselves to the whole of creation. All humankind is saved. And in this poem, salvation includes the good earth, a theme expanded by the prophets in their dream of a new creation. The poem leaves us uncertain of humanity's response. But God was very pleased: "God looked at everything he had made, and found it very good" (Gen 1:31).

Connection with creation comes through the Creator's connection within us. Our participation, our responsibility for creation, comes from the hope of a new creation when sin and death are overcome, when all creation is made holy. Very few religious tasks are as vital as the participation of God's children in the care of creation. The corruption of creation results from sin. But for centuries, God's people have not seen the despoiling of the earth as evil. Nor have we imagined salvation to include the harmonious re-creation envisioned by the prophets. For many centuries—in fact, for a couple millennia—salvation has been limited to the soul of the person, forgetting the body. The body and the earth from which it is made were more or less to be used and cast aside.

In the creed, we recite the biblical belief in the resurrection of the body. The great commission as given in Mark may reflect the biblical idiom. We are sent on mission to "proclaim the gospel *to every creature*" (Mark 16:15, emphasis added). The stuff of which the body is made, the stuff of the earth, needs our care as we look forward to the resurrection of the body and a harmonious new creation. For the sake of life, the church needs to return to biblical images. We need to reconnect with and to participate in the sanctification of all things. Because the one God is Creator, all creation needs to be handled in a spirit of adoration.

A similar argument can be made for the sanctification of humankind. Because Jesus is Savior of the world, through our life in him, we are connected to all humankind and responsible for it. Because of our belief *in one* God who saves the world through the *one* Lord, the elect are connected to *one* human family. This mission is also a crucial religious obligation for our times. Technological advances in communication and mobility are changing the way we interact and think. Technological advances are also threatening annihilation. Our ancient faith is being tested to see if believers will rise to the challenge.

Our belief *in one* God is among the many ways that the Christian message destroys particularized social boundaries. *In one* connects us to the Savior of the world and through the Savior to all humankind. In the many boundary-breaking passages of the Scriptures, the one that is most intriguing to me is John 12:32. Jesus says, "And when I am lifted up from the earth, I will draw everyone to myself." It fascinates me because the verse expresses the goal of bringing all people together. It also instructs us on the means to draw humankind together, the self-sacrificing love of the cross.

The assertion occurs right before the passion drama begins. We are prepared for it by two similar statements from the Lord. The first is early in the Lord's ministry, adding substance to John's claim that Jesus was "fully aware" of his course (John 13:3). Jesus says, "Just as Moses lifted up the serpent in the desert, so must the Son of Man be lifted up, so that everyone who believes in him may have eternal life" (John 3:14–15). Following the Lord's prediction, John explains the repercussions of the Lord's teaching: "For God so loved the world that he gave his only Son, so that everyone who believes in him might not perish but might have eternal life. For God did not send his Son into the world to condemn the world, but that the world might be saved through him" (John 3:16–17). Those who live in Christ must have the same attitude toward the world and toward humanity.

In chapter 8 of John's Gospel, Jesus proclaims that his crucifixion will demonstrate divinity: "When you lift up the Son of Man, then you will realize that I AM" (v. 28). The proclamation is part of a protracted argument with his own people. This argument is strange. Jesus addresses "those Jews who believed in him" (v. 31). Jesus tells them his word is truth and the truth will set them free (v. 32). This promise sets off the argument with those Jews who believed in him. The core of the dispute is over who constitutes Abraham's descendants. The Lord's opponents see their descent from Abraham as a boundary. They are so proud of their designation that they cannot acknowledge that they are a captive, oppressed people, and have been for most of the last six hundred years (v. 33). The prized designation denies them the chance to see themselves as one with suffering humankind. So, they accuse Jesus of being outside the boundary; they accuse him of being a Samaritan, a religious enemy of the Jews (v. 48). Jesus responds by universalizing his mission: "Whoever keeps my word will never see death" (v. 51). The boundary designation of being God's chosen people gives way to the universal reach of the Lord's salvific action.

Matthew and Luke have quite similar assertions about Abraham's descendants. Luke quotes the Lord: "And there will be wailing and grinding of teeth when you see Abraham, Isaac, and Jacob and all the prophets in the kingdom of God and you yourselves cast out. And people will come from the east and the west and from the north and the south and will recline at the table in the kingdom of God" (Luke 13:28–29). Matthew, who was writing for Jewish Christians, has a modified version of the assertion (see Matt 8:11–12). Being God's people is a mission, not a privilege.

The nature of that mission can be gleaned from the mystery at the core of Christianity, the attractiveness of the cross. At the Last Supper, Jesus speaks of how his death is his glory and the glory of the Father. We are invited to share in the glory if we can keep the Lord's commandment: "I give you a new commandment: love one another. As I have loved you, so you also should love one another" (John 13:31–35). Jesus speaks more on love later at that supper. He says, "No one has greater love than this, to lay down one's life for one's friends" (John 15:13). This friendship requires participation in the Lord's mission: "I chose you and appointed you to go and bear fruit that will remain, so that whatever you ask the Father in my name he may give you. This I command you: love one another" (John 15:16–17). We can share in the glory of the Father and Son if we can live the love of which there is no greater.

The components of our connection and participation come together: The cross is the glory of God; it reveals God; it is the basis of our friendship in Christ; it compels disciples to bear fruit. It all comes together in the word for love, in *agape*. Universal, self-giving love is the essence of the church and the church's mission. The universal reach of self-giving love may cause disciples to shrink from the task. Where can we draw the line? What boundaries are appropriate? How much of self must I give? The Sermon on the Mount offers the answer. *Agape* is used to describe the love we are commanded to have for our enemies (Matt 5:43). The words of 1 John tie it together: "Beloved, let us love one another, because love is of God; everyone who loves is begotten by God and knows God. Whoever is without love does not know God, for God is love" (1 John 4:7–8). This is why Jesus proclaims that the cross reveals divinity. The cross reveals the greatest love possible. Its reach is universal. Its depth has no limits. The Lord commands us to love with the same love. Through it, we connect in God and can participate in God's salvific mission in the world.

In one God is a bold Christian truth. The one God is the God of Abraham and Sarah. One God is belief in the unity of the Trinity. *In one God* also describes the life of the disciples. We are invited to live in one God, in one Lord Jesus Christ, in the Holy Spirit, and in one, holy, catholic, and apostolic church. As we meditate on that thought, we must remind ourselves of our finitude. The distance, the asymmetry, cannot be overcome. That distance gives us perspective. But through Jesus Christ and his gift of the Eucharist, God can be within us, and we can be within God because God is everywhere in all things. That audacious truth offers an uplifting valuation of self.

The truth becomes a challenge when we consider how it connects God and us. Once connected, the same trust demands of us participation in the divine. Our life within the Creator embeds us in creation. We are to be the earth's caretakers. We are to restore its beauty. Our life within the Savior embeds us in humanity. The love—*agape*—calls us into a community of love. And more, it demands we bear fruit, that we carry that same divine love to all humankind, reaching as far as our enemies. When we say we believe *in one God*, we are drawn into all that the Creator has made, all that the Savior has redeemed, all that comes in the fullness of time. In a spirit of adoration, we are participants in making all things holy.

5

Father Almighty

Father Almighty exposes us to the nature of divine power. A Christian recognizes that God is the source of all power. The use of power by any believer should conform to the performative truth we can glean from the source, the *Father Almighty*. Power is not only used by civic governments. Power is found in many relationships: parent/child, teacher/student, coach/athlete, employer/employee, pastor/parishioner. When religion and power mix, the results can be dangerous. This is true in relationships between a parent and child, a teacher and student, a pastor and parishioner. All who use religious power must remain conscious of its perils. Power misused can harm people, diminish them, and abuse them. Misused religious power can render people passive, even childish. Religious power can also liberate the spirit. It can empower, freeing the imagination and inspiring creativity. Power can arouse action to better this world. Jesus understood the issues:

> You know that the rulers of the Gentiles lord it over them, and the great ones make their authority over them felt. But it shall not be so among you. Rather, whoever wishes to be great among you shall be your servant; whoever wishes to be first among you shall be your slave. Just so, the Son of Man did not come to be served but to serve and to give his life as ransom for many. (Matt 20:25–29)

Our task here—translating the propositions of our faith into performatory truth—could add to the problem or lead to a solution. How, then, do we derive from *Father Almighty* power to act positively in the church, in the world, in every relationship?

Philosopher Gianni Vattimo helped me get my mind around the difficulty.[1] After considering the history of theology, he sees two modes of interpretation, a *strong* and a *weak* mode. The strong interpretation proclaims God as almighty and derives from that proposition power to dominate or coerce. He developed a weak interpretation of the same propositions. He is moved by the doctrine of the incarnation, seeing it through the prism of *kenosis*, the outpouring of divine power for our salvation. Weak power always acts in terms of charity.[2] To explain Vattimo requires a lengthy detour into contemporary philosophy and the debate over metaphysics. What we need to proceed is the awareness that the propositions *Father* and *Almighty*, as symbolic communication, can have very different, opposing meanings, strong or weak. Our translation of the propositions into performatory truth has serious real-world consequences. Care is needed.

Vattimo is working in hermeneutics. I want to keep in mind his distinction between a strong and a weak interpretation but move into related questions for performative truth, a truth that contributes to the construction of self and society. I wish to adopt sociologist Richard Fenn's use of the word *sacred*.[3] After all, a believer confesses that all power derives from God (John 19:10–11). Therefore, all uses of power involve the believer with the sacred. When the word is used in the construction of self and society, two meanings may emerge. Fenn designates the two meanings by using a capital and lowercase S. The first, *Sacred*, is the sum total of all human possibility. The second, *sacred*, is the limitations imposed on humanity by using religion to legitimate limitations.

I suggest we do the same with power. *Power* with a capital *P* empowers. It encourages, builds up, awakens potential. Power liberates the spirit to imagine, to hope, and to create. It is open to the Other, those who differ, because the Other represents possibility and potential. The Other is someone whose very existence, differing from me and mine, challenges me to expand my horizons.

Lowercase *power* diminishes, coerces, manipulates. The intentions of the power broker may be good. Lowercase power might be aiming

---

1. Vattimo, *Nihilism and Emancipation*, 21–36.

2. See Vattimo, *Belief*; Vattimo, *After Christianity*; and Rorty and Gianni Vattimo, *Future of Religion*.

3. Fenn, *Beyond Idols*, 5.

at right order, harmony, and righteousness. But the order and harmony are forced, the goodness imposed. The imposed force degrades and oppresses the human spirit. Lowercase sacred power makes me think of the unforgivable sin (Mark 3:29). It is not only the human spirit that is oppressed; God's liberating Spirit lives within and can be suppressed.

When we mix power and religion, we can have two results: Sacred Power is used to inspire believers to discover God within. Or sacred power is used to suppress and dominate, even to silence the indwelling Spirit. Ministers must realize that the best of intentions do not justify the misuse of power. In the give-and-take of human interaction, *Sacred Power* can mutate into *sacred power*. Pastoral ministers must guard against that transformation.[4]

We would do well to meditate on John's version of the passion drama when Jesus is before Pontius Pilate. I know of no more dramatic scene where Sacred Power is contrasted with sacred power (John 18:28—19:22).

The event begins when Israel's religious-political leaders bring Jesus to the praetorium. Recall that Pilate represents an emperor who claims divinity, another religious-political combination. The Jewish leadership could not enter the praetorium because they would be defiled and unable to eat the Passover. Contact with gentiles likely occasioned the defilement. There may be some poetry here. Passover recalls Sacred Power that liberates. Pilate's sacred power, though, is violent. Rome looks like ancient Egypt, the place of slavery. Cooperation with sacred power defiles.

Beginning with chapter 18, v. 33, Jesus and Pilate engage in a discussion over Jesus's kingship. Pilate is speaking about Roman power, a kingdom of predatory violence. Jesus rejects that kingdom completely. If Jesus used such power, his attendants would be fighting for him (18:36). Jesus asserts Sacred Power, a kingdom of truth. Sacred Power critiques the power of this world; truth exposes the illegitimacy of sacred power.

In what follows, John masterfully inserts reminders of the two opposing forms of power. In scene after scene, sacred power shows itself as dishonest, conniving, abusive, and violent. Jesus is mostly silent, a sublime presentation of Sacred Power:

---

4. Richard Rorty warns Vattimo that his weak interpretation picks the best of the Christian tradition—*kenosis*, charity, love. But anyone who knows the whole of the tradition has read biblical writings that have God commanding genocide, that portray God as a warlord, having three thousand killed in God's name at Mt. Sinai. History shows, too, that Christians have relied on a strong interpretation to do violence. The point is this: we have the option now. What was done in the past can be repented; what we do now and in the future is our choice. See Rorty and Vattimo, *Future of Religion*, 29.

1. In 18:39–40, Pilate goes out to the people and announces that Jesus is the "King of the Jews": Jesus is Sacred Power. In response, the leadership demands the release of a violent revolutionary, Barabbas.

2. Using sacred power, the soldiers mock and torture Jesus (19:1–3). The scene reminds the reader that Jesus is a saving figure, what Isaiah presents as a suffering servant (Isa 52:13—53:12).

3. Pilate brings Jesus out to the crowd again (19:4–7). This time, the angry crowd itself reminds us that Jesus is the Son of God, the source of Sacred Power. The chief priests and guards demand crucifixion because, they say, Jesus "made himself the Son of God."

4. Pilate speaks to Jesus again about power. Pilate reminds us that sacred power kills: "Do you not know that I have power to release you and I have power to crucify you?" (19:10). Jesus denies Pilate has genuine Power. Sacred Power comes from above.

5. Pilate tries to release Jesus, but the leadership picks its preferred type of power: "If you release him, you are not a Friend of Caesar. Everyone who makes himself a king opposes Caesar" (19:12). The leadership endorses the power that conquered and oppresses their own people. John, then, reminds us it was the preparation day for the Passover, the feast of liberation (19:14).

6. Pilate declares Jesus to be Israel's king. The leadership demands crucifixion (19:13–16).

7. When Jesus is crucified, Pilate has an inscription fixed to the cross "Jesus the Nazorean, the King of the Jews" (19:19). The inscription prepares the reader to receive empowerment from Sacred Power. Under that inscription, disciples receive the waters of baptism, the blood of the Eucharist, and the Lord's Spirit. The leadership argues with Pilate over the inscription.

This scene is very familiar. It should not only be read to recall the sad event. It is a profound meditation on power. To complete our meditation, notice John laid a trap for the reader, which teaches us how easy it is to slip into judgmental sacred power. Before Pilate, John makes the Jewish leadership look like a mob. He may expect us to judge and condemn the Jewish leadership. Back in chapter 11, however, he records a session of the Sanhedrin, which reveals their good intentions. A political revolutionary who had moved sizable crowds would force Rome to act and do so violently. So that "the whole nation may not perish," the Sanhedrin acts (11:47–53). Unfortunately, they resort to violence. Sacred Power readily mutates into sacred power. But John makes us participants in misused sacred power if we have judged and condemned those trying to save their nation. In hindsight, we know that Christians have misused power. Using the Lord's crucifixion to justify hatred, sacred power triggered persecution of Jews for millennia.

Such a meditation prepares us to draw out the performatory meaning of *Father Almighty*. The question becomes how to share in Sacred Power. The first step is to investigate fatherhood. The two genealogies of Jesus prepare the reader for something altogether new regarding fatherhood. Matthew records forty-two generations of fathers who have sons until he reaches Joseph, the husband of Mary. He writes, "*Of her* was born Jesus who is called Messiah" (Matt 1:16, emphasis added). Luke traces Jesus's linage through sonship, each generation being the son of their father. Luke adds a few words to cast the line into doubt. Jesus "was the son, *as was thought*, of Joseph, the son of Heli" (Luke 3:23, emphasis added). I realize this contributes to the mystery of the Virgin birth. It also creates space to doubt the value of fatherhood as it was practiced in the first century.

The New Testament shows that there are two types of fatherhood. One type is the patriarchal fatherhood. A patriarch was a guardian of the social order. If the law was violated, he could rouse the clan to enforce an eye-for-an-eye form of justice—a violent type of social order. His protection, however, compromised the autonomy of members of that clan. A first-century patriarch controlled his spouse, children, his extended family, servants, and slaves. Women and children were compelled to obey him. Jesus rejects that control. He said, "Call no one on earth your father; you have but one Father in heaven" (Matt 23:9). The rejection is made clear in Mark 10:28–31:

> Peter began to say to him, "We have given up everything and followed you." Jesus said, "Amen, I say to you, there is no one who has given up house, or brothers or sisters or mother or father or children or lands for my sake and for the sake of the gospel who will not receive a hundred times more now in this present age: houses and brothers and sisters and mothers and children and lands, with persecution, and eternal life in the age to come."

New, additional fathers are not rewarded for self-sacrifice even though houses, brothers, sisters, mothers, children, and lands are awarded. I don't think this is a mistaken omission; how could the evangelist omit the key figure of the family? I think the passage is a rejection of patriarchal power. In God's kingdom, coercive power is eliminated.

The second type of father is *abba*. When God is called *Father*, the Greek word *pater* is normally used. The reference is often to Jesus Christ: e.g., the Father *(pater)* of our Lord Jesus Christ. The Aramaic *abba* is seldom used in the New Testament. Paul uses *abba* twice. Both usages empower believers by incorporating them into the divine interaction. Galatians 4:5–6 reads, "But when the fullness of time had come, God sent his Son . . . that we might receive adoption. As proof that you are children, God sent the spirit of his Son into our hearts, crying out, 'Abba, Father!'" In Romans, his message is the same: "For those who are led by the Spirit of God are children of God. For you did not receive a spirit of slavery to fall back into fear, but you received a spirit of adoption, through which we cry, 'Abba, Father!'" (Rom 8:14–15). *Abba Father* is used only when the love of Father and Son is extended to us, the adopted children of the Father.

Geoffrey W. Bromiley's abridged version of Kittel's *Theological Dictionary of the New Testament* has two brief explanations of *abba*: "An infant sound is confidently applied to God as the simplest term to express his loving attitude."[5] Later, he writes, "The invocation implies the assurance of sonship and inheritance. It marks the end of legalism and servanthood."[6] Further, Bromiley is probably correct in delimiting any familiarity conveyed by *abba*; it is not a term like *daddy*. "Familiarity is avoided by the setting of the invocation within the kingdom with its demand for submission to God's holy rule."[7] He would have us consider the Fatherhood of God in reference to 1 Pet 1:14–17, which calls God's children to holiness as God is holy. *Abba* helps us understand how God uses authority and power in relation to God's children. It helps us define Sacred Power. *Abba Father* is a formal but loving form of power, free of legalism and enforced servanthood. *Abba* draws into the divine those empowered to become adopted children.

As I wrote above, Vattimo advances what we can draw out of *Father Almighty*. To compose what he calls a weak interpretation, he refers us

---

5. Bromiley, *Theological Dictionary*, 810.

6. Bromiley, *Theological Dictionary*, 813.

7. Bromiley, *Theological Dictionary*, 810.

to the Greek term *kenosis*. Vattimo's approach, however, is problematic because there is only one use of the idea in relation to divinity, in the Philippian hymn (Phil 2:5–11). *Kenosis* comes from the Greek word *kenos*, which means empty. The verb is "to make empty." It can be used figuratively to mean "foolish" or "the use of empty words."[8] How shocking this hymn may have been in the early Christian community. *Foolish* and *empty* are unusual descriptions of divinity. But then, so is the idea of God as a slave, or God humbled, or God crucified. Paul tells us that this is the attitude towards power we must adopt:

> Who, though he was in the form of God,
>   did not regard equality with God something to be grasped.
> Rather, he emptied himself
> taking the form of a slave
> coming in human likeness
> and found human in appearance,
> he humbled himself,
>   becoming obedient to death,
>   even death on a cross. (Phil 2:6–8)

This helps us get our minds around Sacred Power. The Son of God empties himself completely for our salvation. This is Sacred Power.

We need a better foundation for our exploration of *Father Almighty* than a term used just once or twice in the New Testament. One term used very often to describe God's power is the Greek word *agape*. It translates to *love*. Greek has two other terms for love. *Eran* is erotic love, the passionate love of a couple. *Philein* is a general love one might have for the gods, for one's friends, for one's nation, and for humanity. *Agape* is a universal, self-giving, binding force. Bromiley calls it "totally sacrificial."[9] *Agape* is associated with God's mercy and forgiveness. It builds up the beloved and launches a hopeful future.

Agape describes the mutual interaction of the Father and the Son. It is proclaimed by a voice from heaven at Jesus's baptism (Matt 3:17). It is also announced from the heavens at the Transfiguration (Matt 17:5). In both cases, it is translated *beloved*. In John's Gospel, it is often used to describe the shared life of the Father and Son (John 3:35; 10:17; 14:31; 17:23–24; 17:26). This love is eternal. Jesus addresses the Father: "You

---

8. Bromiley, *Theological Dictionary*, 426.
9. Bromiley, *Theological Dictionary*, 9.

loved me before the foundation of the world" (17:24). Furthermore, agape is the very essence of God: "God is love" (1 John 4:8).

This love is unlimited; the love that is God overflows, becoming God's love for God's people. It invites us into the relationship of Father and Son: "Whoever has my commandments and observes them is the one who loves me. And whoever loves me will be loved by my Father, and I will love him and reveal myself to him" (John 14:21; see also John 15:9–10). In Paul's Letter to the Romans, he asserts that God's love for God's people is eternal. It precedes Jesus's saving death: "But God proves his love for us in that while we were still sinners Christ died for us" (Rom 5:8). At the conclusion of his prayer for his disciples at the Last Supper, Jesus envisions the totality of agape's binding power:

> I pray not only for them, but also for those who will believe in me through their word.... And I have given them the glory you gave me, so that they may be one, as we are one, I in them and you in me, that they may be brought to perfection as one, that the world may know that you sent me, and that you loved them even as you loved me.... Righteous Father, the world also does not know you, but I know you, and they know that you sent me. I made known to them your name and I will make it known, that the love with which you loved me may be in them and I in them. (John 17:20, 22–23, 25–26)

Love defines power. Paul even asserts that this love, agape, is the greatest force in the cosmos: "In all these things we conquer overwhelmingly through him who loved us. For I am convinced that neither death, nor life, nor angels, nor principalities, nor present things, nor future things, nor powers, nor height, nor depth, nor any other creature will be able to separate us from the love of God in Christ Jesus our Lord" (Rom 8:38–39).

As this love overflows from the Trinity to the disciples, it becomes the binding force within the church. At the Last Supper, Jesus instructs his disciples multiple times that agape binds and prays intensely that agape would bind the church as one (John 13:31–35; 15:1–17; 17:20–26). John's epistles likewise teach us that agape should bind us and inform the use of power in our church. One example stands out: "The way we came to know love was that he laid down his life for us; so we ought to lay down our lives for our brothers" (1 John 3:16).

St. Paul writes to the church in Corinth about agape. The Ode to Love is well known (1 Cor 13); it is read at most church weddings. But

Paul intended it to describe the right order of the church. I won't quote it here. The reader is welcome to take a break to read it while considering the repercussions of Sacred Power in the church—and its often used opposite, sacred power. Chapter 12 of First Corinthians is about the misuse of the gifts given by the Spirit. Chapter 13 offers the cure for the misuse of power by defining agape, Sacred Power.

Agape does not have social boundaries. The love of the Trinity flows forth to the disciples inviting us into the love and life shared by Father, Son, and Spirit. That same unending love is to bind us together as the church. And the same love is to overflow from the church into the entire world, bringing healing, reconciliation, justice, and peace. The Sermon on the Mount teaches,

> You have heard that it was said, "You shall love your neighbor and hate your enemy." But I say to you, love your enemies, and pray for those who persecute you, that you may be children of your heavenly Father, for he makes his sun rise on the bad and the good, and causes rain to fall on the just and the unjust. For if you love those who love you, what recompense will you have? Do not tax collectors do the same? And if you greet your brothers only, what is unusual about that? Do not pagans do the same? So be perfect, just as your heavenly Father is perfect. (Matt 5:43–48)

Matthew uses a form of the same word that describes the internal love of the Trinity to move disciples to love their enemies.

The Fatherhood of God is agape. The term Almighty is circumscribed by the same, by agape. I am not trying to limit God. God can always do whatever God wills. God has revealed God's own nature to us; God is agape. The interaction between Father and Son is agape. God's love (agape) overflows into the hearts of God's disciples. Disciples are bound as the church by agape. This love (agape) has no social boundaries. Agape must reach out even to our enemies. Sacred Power is agape. All uses of power in the church are to reflect the same love.

This realization helps understand the performatory truth of *Father Almighty*. John may have given us a formula for our calculations to live within God. We affix the prefix *all* to God's attributes. What does it mean for us to live within ultimacy? Let's begin with what John wrote: "God is love and whoever remains in love remains in God and God in him" (1 John 4:16b). A formula might be invented: God is X and whoever remains in X remains in God and God in him. X can be any of the attributes of God. God is all-knowing. Anyone who seeks knowledge remains in God and God in him. In the Letter to the Ephesians, Paul makes an addition to the formula. Paul may have known power can be misused. So, love of knowledge, its pursuit, and its application, require knowledge of love. He writes, "That you, rooted and grounded in love, may have strength to comprehend with all the holy ones what is the breadth and length and height and depth, and to know the love of Christ that surpasses knowledge, so that you may be filled with the fullness of God" (Eph 3:17b–19).

The same can be said of truth. God is the source of all truth. John's formula would take us this far. God is truth and whoever aspires to live the truth remains in God and God in him. But again, Paul adds to the formula. Love of truth requires the truth of love: "Living the truth in love, we should grow in every way into him who is the head, Christ, from whom the whole body, joined and held together by every supporting ligament, with the proper functioning of each part, brings about the body's growth and builds itself up in love" (Eph 4:15–16). The body—that is, the church—needs to love truth, but it is the truth of love that builds itself up in love.

The same needs to be predicated onto any use of power by a Christian. God is all-powerful. Anyone who uses power in God's name must know and live the power of love. It is the power of love (agape) that makes power into Sacred Power. Since the revelation that God is love, everything done in God's name should empower. It should liberate the spirit, free the imagination, inspire creativity, arouse action to better oneself and better this world. A pastoral minister's use of power should aspire to be Sacred Power, to be *agape*.

I can only begin to imagine a church that aspires for all power to be Sacred Power. I can only begin to imagine what it might mean within the church, within each diocese and parish. And I can only imagine what it might do to our presence in the world, in politics and economics, in family life, in the pursuit and application of knowledge. As we draw out the performatory truth of *Father Almighty*, we might remember what Paul teaches: *agape* is the strongest force of attraction in the cosmos.

6

Maker of Heaven and Earth, of All Things Visible and Invisible

BOTH THE APOSTLES CREED and the Nicene Creed emerged from the church's efforts to understand the revelation. Both creeds point believers toward God, the mystery of the Trinity, and the marvel of God creating. The church itself is mentioned in both creeds but only with one proposition and near their conclusions. Under the pressure of the ecclesial minister's routines, the priorities implied in the creeds can mutate. The range of tasks in pastoral ministry can lead to this mistake. A pastoral team needs to be about everything from worship, the proclamation of the gospel, the care of souls, religious formation, the HVAC system, the leaky roof, and a balanced budget. Maintaining the organization can make the church its own purpose. So, the church becomes an end—the goal—not the means. The first task of every pastoral leader is to recall that the creed professes a connection with the triune God and participation in God creating and God saving.

The phrase *of all things visible and invisible* added to *maker of heaven and earth* turns our thoughts even beyond physical creation, including our sensate self. These words warn us against limiting God in any way. God is beyond our descriptions, beyond our attempts to articulate our experience of God, beyond all our social boundaries, beyond our church. The experience of God's people does not come close to embracing the totality of divinity. Perhaps this is what the phrase in the Book of Revelation is telling us: "'I am the Alpha and the Omega,' says the Lord God, 'the one who is and who was and who is to come, the almighty'" (Rev

1:8; see also Rev 21:6; 22:13). Believers may not place limitations on God, especially the ones imposed by religious people who wrongly think they can monopolize access to God. But more importantly, these words about the absolute extension of God's presence and power may be an invitation to find God in all things, in all times, and in all people, and beyond all things, beyond time, and people. These words may be an invitation to open our hearts, souls, and minds for continuous transformation and growth toward our fulfillment in God.

William James's classic work in the psychology of religion, *The Varieties of Religious Experience*, gives us a way to experience ourselves within God's all-embracing presence and all-challenging power. James's book is the collection of the 1901–2 Gifford Lectures. The third lecture begins, "Were one asked to characterize the life of religion in the broadest and most general terms possible, one might say that it consists of the belief that *there is an unseen order*, and that *our supreme good lies in harmoniously adjusting ourselves thereto*."[1] Later in that same lecture he writes, "It is as if there were in the human consciousness *a sense of reality, a feeling of objective presence, a perception* of what we may call '*something there*,' more deep and more general than any of the special and particular 'senses' by which the current psychology supposes existent realities to be originally revealed."[2]

Two notable theologians remind us of the "something there more deep and more general." The first is Karl Rahner.[3] He writes about an unthematic and anonymous knowledge of God that is prior to involvement with the church and its self-understanding. To understand Rahner's point, I think we must consider our own socialization in the faith. Cradle Catholics, especially, have some exposure to religion before they become serious about faith. Most of the college students I taught started asking earnest questions about faith in early adolescence. They were disappointed in the response of parents, teachers, youth ministers, and clergy—all of whom dismissed their questions and doubts as a character flaw or a sin.

The period of early adolescence leads directly to Rahner's point. The unthematic and anonymous knowledge of God starts in a person's questioning about the self. In her search for purpose and meaning, a person shows herself to be "a being with an *infinite* horizon."[4] The infinite hori-

---

1. James, *Varieties of Religious Experience*, 55 (emphasis added).
2. James, *Varieties of Religious Experience*, 59.
3. Rahner, *Foundations*, 47.
4. Rahner, *Foundations*, 32.

zon does not emerge from one's limited perception. We cannot imagine ourselves as beings with unlimited space or beings with infinite power. The vision comes as a gift from a source beyond the self. Our questioning shows that we are open to the ineffable; we are beings who begin to understand the genuine possibilities of the self because of grace. The argument is complex. The point is this: our openness to God is first unthematic, prior to our appropriation of the church's theological articulation. Before church is the experience of the divine. The Catholic community would do well to take seriously the questioning of youth. Rather than a mistake or failure, rather than a sin, the doubt and questioning of youth indicates an openness to God. The more serious problem is the closed minds of adults.

I mentioned earlier a second theologian, Hans Urs von Balthasar, who also weighs in.[5] He develops the concept of *calling* or *vocation*. He writes that the calling is altogether personal. It comes before involvement in church and the church's self-understanding. What he calls *the abstract*—our belief system—and *the institutional*—the church as an organization—are secondary. The call or one's vocation comes to a person through various patterns of experiences. Upon reflection, a person may come to knowledge of God. The church, then, becomes the means for the completion of one's life journey, perhaps, as the facilitator of the reflections. The goal or end is the full realization of our unity with God.

These insights compel us to consider the interaction of searching and seeking persons within the church as an organization. Canadian philosopher Charles Taylor's sense of the interaction of persons in organizations in contemporary society helps.[6] He began with political structures. Freed from former aristocratic hierarchies, political structures have come to serve the pre-political—that is, political power structures exist to protect human rights. Taylor relates the same principle to religiosity. Ecclesial structures exist to serve the pre-ecclesial—the community exists to serve the searching, seeking individual's journey to God. This insight returns the church to being a means to God; the church is not an end. Taylor writes,

> Now if we don't accept the view that human aspiration to religion will flag, and I do not, then where will the access lie to practice of and deeper engagement with religion? The answer

---

5. Balthasar, "Vocation," 114.
6. Taylor, *Secular Age*, 512.

is the various forms of spiritual practice to which each is drawn in his/her own spiritual life. These may involve meditation, or some charitable work, or a study group, or a pilgrimage, or some special form of prayer, or a host of such things.[7]

Taylor admits these have been available to active members as optional possibilities. But he thinks the new sense of self and social systems reverses the connection for most people: "First, people are drawn to a pilgrimage, or a World Youth Day, or a meditation group, or a prayer circle; and then later, if they move along in the appropriate direction, they will find themselves embedded in ordinary practice."[8]

The Catholic community has expected believers to come to it, to overlook its flaws, to accept a delimited place in its hierarchical structure, and to conform to it. To meet the new reality, the parish community must evolve. Its purpose must include assisting people across the threshold of faith by offering experiences that build upon the person's prior spiritual journey. Then, the potential believers may find in the community what strengthens their own spiritual core. Enlightened by the gospel and fortified by Eucharist, believers may become active agents in a ministering community, participating in the construction of a compassionate society, and finding life in God. The church might understand itself as the facilitator of a lifetime's growth in faith.

We must not think that crossing the threshold into the faith community is a once-in-a-lifetime experience. A person may return to the threshold repeatedly. Various life experiences can take us there. Suffering and facing a death, for instance, often raise questions and require substantial personal growth. On its own, our expanding lifespan will also return us to the threshold. Each new phase of life brings us to questions of life's purpose and meaning. Each phrase demands a rediscovery of life in God's love.

How this dynamic plays out, how the organization evolves, is unknowable at this moment. The organized church has expected passive conformity for a long time. Ministers open to our times and to a reexamination of our structures may create inviting threshold experiences. We need to look further into two categories of threshold experiences that may have the potential to connect the searchers and seekers to the community for the continuation of their journeys. The first is spirituality; the

---

7. Taylor, *Secular Age*, 515.
8. Taylor, *Secular Age*, 516.

second is transcendent experience. Both are derived from the unseen order, the omnipresence of God, the performative truth of God the maker of heaven and earth, of all things visible and invisible.

SPIRITUALITY

Spirituality has been a humanizing force for millennia. The cacophony of experiences today, however, endangers the tradition, rendering it faddish and, therefore, likely to be passed over by seriously religious people. British philosopher John Cottingham studied the concept. He acknowledges the term is "invoked by those purveying a heterogeneous range of products and services, from magic crystals, scented candles and astrology, to alternative medicine, tai chi, and meditation courses."[9] The concept may become meaningless. We should not lose the tradition, however; it represents a civilizing concept dating from ancient times. Recall Peter Sloterdijk's invocation of Socrates: "Man is a being potentially superior to himself."[10] Furthermore, the idea may prove helpful to define today's sense of *calling*. It will take some effort to pin it down.

We can begin with von Balthasar's insight that God's calling, our vocation, arises from various patterns of experience. *Spirituality* is directing the development of the self in relation to the unseen order. Philosopher Charles Taylor offers a productive insight into the experiences that constitute *spirituality*. In the first pages of *Sources of the Self*, Taylor offers us what the vague term *spiritual* means:

> In addition to our notions and reactions on such issues as justice and the respect for other people's life, well-being and dignity, I want to look at our sense of *what underlies our own dignity*, or questions about *what makes our lives meaningful or fulfilling*. These might be classed as moral questions on some broad definition, but some are too concerned with the self-regarding, or too much a matter of our ideals, to be classed as moral issues in most people's lexicon. They concern, rather, *what makes life worth living*.[11]

What underlies one's dignity, what makes life meaningful and fulfilling, what makes life worth living: these ideas can serve as the starting point

---

9. Cottingham, *Spiritual Dimension*, 3.
10. Sloterdijk, *Change Your Life*, 13.
11. Taylor, *Sources of the Self*, 4 (emphasis added).

to define the spiritual. We can draw additional insights from two other scholars. John Cottingham comes at the term this way:

> [Spiritual] is taken to cover forms of life that put a premium *on certain kinds of intensely focused moral and aesthetic response*, or *on the search for deeper reflective awareness of the meaning of our lives and our relationship to others and to the natural world.* In general, the label "spiritual" seems to be used to refer to activities which aim to fill the creative and meditative space left over when science and technology have satisfied our material needs.[12]

Certain kinds of intensely focused moral and aesthetic response, the search for deeper reflective awareness of the meaning of our lives and our relationship to others and to the natural world: we can add these ideas to our starting point. Earlier Cottingham had identified a list of ways we enrich life. These include "not just poetry, music, novels, theatre, and all the arts, but the entire domain of human emotions and human relationships as they are experienced in the inner life of each of us, and in our complex interactions with our fellows."[13]

French philosopher Pierre Hadot studied the concept beginning with the ancient Greeks and continuing through recent times. In ancient times, multiple schools of philosophy or spirituality existed in competition with one another:

> Each school, then, represents a form of life defined by *an ideal of wisdom*. The result is that each one has its corresponding *fundamental inner attitude* . . . above all every school practices *exercises designed to ensure spiritual progress* toward the ideal state of wisdom, exercises of reason that will be, for the soul, analogous to the athlete's training or to the application of a medical cure. . . . It always involves *an effort of will, thus faith in moral freedom and the possibility of self-improvement.*[14]

An ideal of wisdom, resulting in a fundamental inner attitude, with exercises designed to ensure spiritual progress toward the ideal, implying faith in moral freedom and the possibility of self-improvement: these phrases round out a sense of spirituality. Later, Hadot will distill all this

---

12. Cottingham, *Spiritual Dimension*, 3 (emphasis added).
13. Cottingham, *Spiritual Dimension*, viii.
14. Hadot, *As a Way of Life*, 59 (emphasis added).

into two crucial aspects of spirituality: "a transformation of our vision of the world," and a corresponding "metamorphosis of our personality."[15]

For some time, people have wanted to overcome the disjunction of body and soul. Contemporary spirituality includes the body, considering it in a positive light.[16] Spirituality becomes a personal quest to bring balance and harmony to the human person all the while considering one's society and the concept of the world. In our times, spirituality tries to harmonize the psychic, the moral and ethical, the intellectual and emotional, and the physical and religious dimensions of the person. Spirituality has become a quest for the optimization of body, mind, and spirit in a harmonious relationship with society and the world.

The Greeks left us terms worth maintaining. *Askesis* is the art of living. Our lives do not come with an owner's manual. The search for meaningful and significant lives, the best ways to relate to others, how to relate to the natural world, how to maintain good health, the quest for the good, the true, the beautiful, how to keep one's equilibrium through ill health, pain, suffering, and bereavement, how to prepare oneself for death, how to interact with God—the quest for an artful life is all engaging.

To discover the art of living requires *theoria* and *praxis*. Praxis may be the more important component. But theory is logically first. Spirituality requires a sense of an objective reality beyond oneself. The ideal of wisdom derived from God, nature, or the human story sets the course. Something beyond oneself establishes the standard for an optimized self. The spiritual person feels the attraction and strives to realize that self. A short-order way to imagine spirituality is to picture a *gap* between an honest assessment of one's current condition and one's idealized optimum self.[17] Spirituality includes a disciplined effort to close the *gap*, to, step-by-step, shrink that space. Theory is one's understanding of the cosmos, nature, the social world, and the divine. If one were to understand how the world works—the laws of nature, the construct of society, the divine plan—one could know one's place in it and what it may take to harmonize one's life to that reality.

Ronald Dworkin is a philosopher and atheist. He wants to be known as a "religious atheist." That term is not oxymoronic to him. He thinks the key to religion is the discovery of an objective source of value. Dworkin

---

15. Hadot, *As a Way of Life*, 83.

16. The Vatican Council seems to embrace a spirituality that includes the body. See Flannery, *Gaudium et spes*, paras. 3, 14.

17. Cottingham, *Spiritual Dimension*, 74.

claims that many people, even those who do not participate in formal religiosity, experience a deep worldview that opens them to objective value.[18] The full, independent reality of value inspires two attitudes:

> The religious attitude accepts the full, independent reality of value. It accepts the objective truth of two central judgments about value. The first holds that human life has objective meaning or importance. Each person has an innate and inescapable responsibility to try to make his life a successful one: that means living well, accepting ethical responsibilities to oneself as well as moral responsibilities to others, not just if we happen to think this important but because it is in itself important whether we think so or not. The second holds that what we call "nature"—the universe as a whole and in all its parts—is not just a matter of fact but is itself sublime: something of intrinsic value and wonder.[19]

Although the words *ethics* and *morality* are often used interchangeably, Dworkin distinguishes them. He writes, "Moral standards prescribe how we ought to treat others; ethical standards, how we ought to live ourselves."[20] Of course, morality and ethics interact; one cannot be truly ethical without being moral. The point here, however, is how the unseen order shapes all of life, engaging a complete person and permeating all experience.

A person who agrees with Dworkin is certainly on the threshold of the Christian faith. Pastoral ministers could work very productively in the space he creates. Out of our long history of reflection, meditation, and contemplation, from a spirit of adoration and a spirit of gratitude, ministers could assist people in defining those objective values: truth, goodness, beauty, charity, compassion, and, of course, the priority of self-giving love. Likewise, the pastoral minister might strengthen the sense of wonder at God's creating, the beauty of the physical universe, and the spectacle of humanity's progress toward justice and peace. And the minster might explain the ever-existing *gap* between who we are now and what we might become. If so, the seeker should be able to see her way into life in God.

---

18. I would rebrand Dworkin's religion as *spirituality*. It is my opinion that religion requires a reference to a higher power, to the ultimate, or to the supernatural. The objectivity of value does not reach that level. It is vital to spirituality, however, lest spirituality becomes a bundle of incoherent feelings. See Dworkin, *Religion without God*, 5.

19. Dworkin, *Religion without God*, 10.

20. Dworkin, *Justice for Hedgehogs*, 191.

TRANSCENDENCE

Some experiences of the unseen order take us deeper into ourselves; these fall largely into the category of spirituality. Some experiences seem to pull us out of ourselves to something greater than ourselves; these are transcendent experiences. They are many and varied: an encounter with beauty in nature or in the arts; illumination as one pursues knowledge and truth; the satisfaction of standing on principle as one seeks the good; sensing the bonds of family, community, nation, and the human family; the discovery of our commonality especially with people who differ; that which moves us to charity, forgiveness, and understanding; moments of intimacy and the embrace of love. Some experiences pull back the veil between the living and the dead. Many people have told me about experiences of their beloved deceased communicating their well-being through dreams. Others speak of hearing voices of the beloved deceased giving them direction for this life. A transcendent experience can affirm one's life direction or pull one out of destructive behaviors. One can receive a profound sense of validation for one's efforts to optimize oneself physically, mentally, or spiritually. Group experiences—concerts, plays, marches, and protests—can override one's self-absorption. We can lose ourselves in the transcendent through well-done rituals, retreats, adoration, and meditation. In fact, we may define rituals as routinized transcendence—when performed with care. If a *gap* provides a shorthand for spirituality, the *more* can be the shorthand for transcendence.[21] We seem created to desire *more*: more than the day-to-day, more than a limited lifespan, more than fixed boundaries on our experiences. Any experience that seems to lift us out of ourselves toward something objectively greater—the *more*—is a transcendent experience.

German sociologist Hans Joas reminds us that these experiences are not always euphoric, uplifting, and positive. He reminds us they can also be negative and even violent.[22] Bereavement and serious illness are such experiences. Some soldiers who return from war speak about intense, life-changing exposure to the inhumane and the chaotic. We can lose normal inhibitions and moral sensibilities when taken into a group. One can imagine the negative transcendent when viewing a filmstrip of Nazi rallies. One can also imagine someone losing a sense of right and good when taking part in something like a mob.

21. Orsi, "Problem of the Holy," 99.
22. Joas, *Do We Need Religion?*, 10.

American sociologist Robert Orsi powerfully argues against the standard academic study of religion that reduces religious experiences to "representations of social or psychological fact, symbols of something else, but nothing in themselves."[23] Orsi studied the apparition of the Blessed Virgin at Lourdes. The children directly involved in the experience were not the only ones drawn into it. All those for whom a sense of the divine presence becomes manifest through their imagined connection to that apparition are also drawn into the sense of presence. He writes, "In these exchanges, aspects of one's life previously unknown or unacknowledged may be discovered. The imagination takes hold of the world as the world takes hold of the imagination."[24] Explicating the impact of that presence, he continues,

> Much becomes possible that otherwise was not. Time may become fluid. Past / present / future, as they are, as they are hoped for, and as they are dreaded, may converge. Spatial boundaries, between here and there, oneself and another, may give way. Relationships also come under the power of the unlocked imagination, relationships between heaven and earth, between the living and the dead, among persons as they are and persons as they are desired to be by themselves and others. In the abundant event and all that follows it, a certain kind of intersubjective receptivity and recognition may become possible, on earth and between heaven and earth, an awareness of being seen and known, and of seeing and knowing, so focused that in certain circumstances it may seem intrusive and threatening; in others, deeply compassionate and supportive.[25]

Elsewhere, Orsi describes the impact of the *holy*, how the holy transforms situations. He recalls his uncle who had cerebral palsy. His uncle participated in a Catholic ministry for disabled persons. At their gatherings, Orsi records how the disabled people were subjected to sermons on the holy that "droned on and on." In these talks, suffering people were connected to the cross of Jesus Christ. The sermons allowed the disabled persons to experience themselves as holy and to be perceived by others as holy. Orsi also relates how his uncle had a connection to Blessed Margaret of Citta di Castello, a thirteenth-century saint born

---

23. Orsi, *History and Presence*, 58.
24. Orsi, *History and Presence*, 61.
25. Orsi, *History and Presence*, 67.

with multiple handicaps. Going through his uncle's possessions after he died, Orsi gained insight into the effects of the sense of holiness:

> I got a glimpse of how living in a world focused on the broken body of God understood as a sacred gift, of how being in relation to holy figures like little Margaret within the wider web of his intimacies and associations, may have opened up to my uncle deeper possibilities of love and joy—and above all, for connectedness—that otherwise might have been closed to him. Holiness—the holiness imputed to him—the holy figures he engaged, the holiness of Jesus's suffering, the holy ground beneath his wheelchair, the holiness of others experienced in his proximity—fundamentally and really transformed his world.[26]

Orsi borrows an idea from William James, "the 2 + 2 = 5 factor of religious experience." He calls it "the tradition of the more."[27] He provides a long list of scholars from multiple disciplines who have tried to articulate this experience.[28] For example, as noted earlier, theologian Jean-Luc Marion uses the term *saturated phenomena*, and Eric Santner speaks of the *attunement to the surplus of the real within reality*. Along with *holy* and *presence*, Orsi also seems to like the term *abundant event* or *excessive event*. Although "outside oneself," these experiences transpire within normal human living. He writes, "Human beings meet real presences in the midst of living their lives."[29] And he says, "The routes of presence go right through the material and political circumstance of everyday life."[30]

I think there are two types of transcendent experiences. One is highly emotional, a bolt-out-of-the-blue experience. I will source Rudolf Otto to describe these experiences. The other type seems more rational and contemplative. Through contemplation, the subject realizes her own abilities, sensing both the limits of those abilities and something objectively greater that invites one beyond those limits. I will use descriptions of such experiences from Bernard Lonergan.

---

26. Orsi, "Problem of the Holy," 91.
27. Orsi, "Problem of the Holy," 99.
28. Orsi, "Problem of the Holy," 100.
29. Orsi, *History and Presence*, 60.
30. Orsi, *History and Presence*, 13.

The Otto/Eliade Type:

Rudolf Otto was a German philosopher. He published his most famous work, *The Idea of the Holy*, in 1917. To describe these experiences, he adapts the Latinate word *numinous* derived from the Latin *numen*, meaning God. Otto asserts that these numinous experiences are *sui generis*—unique experiences whose source remains mysterious. Because they are *sui generis*, he often uses a set of modifiers to give the reader some parameters in which the reader can imagine the event. He starts with *mysterium tremendum*. The *mysterium* "denotes merely that which is hidden, esoteric, that which is beyond conception or understanding, extraordinary and unfamiliar."[31] He does the same with the word *tremendum*. He uses dread, awful, hallow, terror fraught with shuddering, the uncanny, the eerie, the weird, the overpowering, the sense of majesty, awe. The experience leaves one breathless and overwhelmed. Such experiences give us a feeling of dependence, insufficiency, impotence—what Otto calls *creature-consciousness* or *creature-feeling*.[32] Here is how he describes these feelings:

> The feeling of it may at times come sweeping like a gentle tide, pervading the mind with a tranquil mood of deepest worship. It may pass over into a more set and lasting attitude of the soul, continuing, as it were, thrillingly vibrant and resonant, until, at last, it dies away and the soul resumes its "profane," non-religious mood of everyday experience. It may burst in sudden eruption up from the depths of the soul with spasms and convulsions, or lead to the strangest excitements, to intoxicated frenzy, to transport, and to ecstasy. It has its wild and demonic forms and can sink to almost grisly horror and shuddering. It has its crude, barbaric antecedents and early manifestation, and again it may be developed into something beautiful and pure and glorious. It may become the hushed, trembling, and speechless humility of the creature in the presence of—who or what?[33]

Otto adds a dimension of fascination so these transcendent experiences would be called *mysterium tremendum et fascinans*. These experiences are alluring and entrancing, corresponding with the sense of love,

---

31. Otto, *Idea of the Holy*, 13.
32. Otto, *Idea of the Holy*, 9.
33. Otto, *Idea of the Holy*, 12.

mercy, pity, and comfort.[34] We can experience the terrifying or the alluring. Likewise, the experiences can be awful and fascinating at once.

To assist the reader in imagining these experiences, and perhaps attuning themselves to their own experiences, I will relay the following events, which were first relayed to me by undergraduate students:[35]

- A depressed young man felt very much alone in a hospital room while suffering serious anxiety. He heard a voice communicate that he was not alone and that he has family and friends. He was told that with an intense effort he could cope with his depression. His life changed. He began showing his appreciation for his family and friends; he felt empowered to attend university; and he attempted to get beyond himself by building new friendships. When he told me his major is psychology, it all held together with a remarkable logic.

- A young woman who was into very destructive behaviors with drugs experienced an evening where the universe conveyed its disappointment with her. She looked up into the heavens and said the sky and the stars were angry. The next day, when she sobered up, she began her journey out of the destructive behavior. When I met her, she was among my best students, and she was about to finish her degree in nursing. Again, it all held together with a coherent logic.

- One other student recalls his time in bereavement at the death of his grandfather with whom he had a significant relationship. He had cut himself off from family and friends until one day while alone on a basketball court, he heard his grandfather's voice reminding him of the lessons his grandfather had taught him about making something of life and assuming his role in his family. Upon relearning these life lessons from his grandfather, he began putting things together. He left eastern Europe to come to an American university, which was his grandfather's wish.

These students did not believe in God, but each had a transcendent experience that changed their lives. These are bolt-out-of-the-blue experiences. They seem to come from some place outside the subject. The subjects sense that such communications are crucial for their lives. The experiences are paradigmatic; they become a guide for their lives.

---

34. Otto, *Idea of the Holy*, 31.
35. These experiences are conveyed with permission from the students.

Early in my ministerial life, I dismissed these events and assumed they had some psychological or physiological explanations. I no longer do. I am very careful, almost reluctant, to name the source of the experience as a divine communication. Robert Orsi warned us that some people can use God-talk to manipulate others and even to reduce them to something less than human.[36] If asked, I respond with a question, Was the experience liberating and uplifting? Has it brought them a better life or given them a sense of peace? If so, I can say that our God is a Savior and let them work out whether their experience was salvific. Too many people have described these experiences to me and therefore have helped me understand the occasions in my life when I felt lifted out of myself toward the objective other. If I can associate the experiences with that which saves, that which brings peace, uplifts, empowers, and gives life, I cautiously refer to our saving God.

The Lonergan Type:

Both Karl Rahner and Bernard Lonergan explore the transcendent by analyzing the experience of *coming to know*. I will follow Lonergan here. He starts by looking at fundamental, everyday operations. They are "seeing, hearing, touching, smelling, tasting, inquiring, imagining, understanding, conceiving, formulating, reflecting, marshaling and weighing the evidence, judging, deliberating, evaluating, deciding, speaking, writing."[37] The theologian starts us off with normal everyday apprehension of the realities about us.

The normal interaction with one's environment reveals the "psychological sense," a transcendent dimension. It first reveals itself in intentionality—that is, the operator intends the object of the operations; the knowing subject intends the object known. Lonergan writes, "By seeing there becomes present what is seen, by hearing there becomes present what is heard, by imagining there becomes present what is imagined."[38] Because we choose what we perceive, the psychological sense reveals that the operator is a free, conscious subject. In any operation, "by their intentionality" objects are made present to the subject and the operating subject "becomes present to himself" as the free active agent of the intention.

36. Orsi, "Problem of the Holy," 89.
37. Lonergan, *Method in Theology*, 6.
38. Lonergan, *Method in Theology*, 7.

The realization that we are free, active agents allows for the formulation of what Lonergan calls the transcendent method. He has defined the method as "a normative pattern of recurrent and related operations yielding cumulative and progressive results."[39] In *coming to know*, there are four recurrent and related operations:

1. The Empirical: We collect data about the world and ourselves. We sense, we perceive, we imagine, and we feel.
2. The Intellectual: We come to understand, to see patterns, make connections, and to take in the context.
3. The Rational: We reflect, marshal evidence, pass judgment on truth or falsity, and the certainty or probability of what we understand.
4. The Responsible: We concern ourselves; we establish goals; we discern action; we carry out decisions; and we commit ourselves to the good.[40]

This method begins in categorical, everyday perception and takes us to the transcendent. Each step taken leads us to a more complete life. Lonergan calls it the "eros of the human spirit." The method leads to a set of imperatives that bring us to the more fully human: Be attentive. Be intelligent. Be reasonable. Be responsible. Lonergan believes that following this method leads to human progress. To shrink from it leads to decline. Lonergan writes, "To know the good, we must know the real; to know the real we must know the truth; to know the truth, we must know the intelligible; to know the intelligible, we must attend to data."[41]

One can go further and arrive at the question of God. Karl Rahner articulates this ultimate step better than Lonergan.[42] The transcendental experience of our existence, its unlimited possibility, is a gift that all but compels us to consider the gift giver. To pursue the mystery of our existence brings us to Holy Mystery or God, just as our quest for knowledge meets a knowable universe. Rahner sees the transcendent as an ever-continuing process that works asymptotically—that is, it builds upon itself exponentially.[43] The transcendent dimension would look like a curve that increases in steepness as we continue to explore the mystery of

---

39. Lonergan, *Method in Theology*, 4.
40. Lonergan, *Method in Theology*, 9.
41. Lonergan, *Method in Theology*, 13.
42. Rahner, *Foundations*, 39.
43. Rahner, *Foundations*, 35.

ourselves, as knowing agents seeking knowledge of a knowable universe. And because we are the active agents in that process, we obtain a first order sense of our freedom. In that exploration, we discover our "final and definitive validity" and the "true self-realization" that is, for Rahner, our salvation.[44] Therefore, we begin to apprehend our saving God.

Rahner's sense of salvation is not our common belief in a disembodied existence in heaven after death. Instead, he wants us to consider "the final and definitive validity of a person's true self-understanding and true self-realization in freedom before God by the fact that he accepts his own self as it is disclosed and offered to him in the choice of transcendence as interpreted in freedom."[45] This is salvation. It is contemplation and the realization of the gifts offered, received in freedom, and fulfilled in time. Rahner writes, "Man is not merely a biological and social organism who exists in time with these characteristics. Rather his subjectivity and his free, personal self-interpretation take place precisely in and through his being in the world, in time, and in history, or better, in and through world, time, and history. The question of salvation cannot be answered by bypassing man's historicity and his social nature. Transcendentality and freedom are realized in history."[46]

Both Lonergan and Rahner demonstrate the transcendent by our search for knowledge. I wonder whether there are other paths. Could we not find the transcendent in our perception of beauty, the search for it realized in nature or in humanity's creativity? Could we not find the transcendent in the pursuit of moral and ethical goodness, in finding the good in oneself, admiring it in others, and drawing goodness out of others? And what of the possibility of human relationships, the discovery that we are capable of love and of being loved in return? Could we not find the transcendent in the extension of charity outward to the entire human family expressed as peace and justice? Would it be possible to find our true self-realization and perhaps our salvation in these and other human experiences? Would they not lead to additional imperatives? Lonergan gave, "Be attentive. Be intelligent. Be reasonable. Be responsible." Could we not add, Seek beauty! Be creative! Seek goodness! Be loved and loving! Strive for peace with justice?

God is the maker of heaven and earth, of all things visible and invisible. God's presence embellishes and fulfills all things, including

44. Rahner, *Foundations*, 39.
45. Rahner, *Foundations*, 39.
46. Rahner, *Foundations*, 40.

the searching self. Spirituality, the effort to fill the *gap* between who we are and who we may become, and transcendent experiences, the movement to seek *more*, are ways of imagining our unity with God here and now. Rahner may be correct: in spirituality and transcendent experiences, we anticipate our salvation. As we do, we are engaged with the performative truth of God, maker of heaven and earth, of all things visible and invisible.

7

Lord Jesus Christ

LORD AND CHRIST ARE titles. *Lord* asserts that Jesus shares God's power and authority. He is "God from God, Light from Light." In our tradition, God interacts with God's people for their salvation. The association of *Lord* with Jesus confirms the Lord Jesus's ongoing salvific interaction with us.[1] The title *Christ* is the Greek for messiah, the anointed one. The title *Christ* reminds us of the dream of the prophets for a messianic age of harmony, peace, and plenty. *Christ* reinforces the hope for the transformation of time into the messianic age.

The person Jesus is both Lord and Christ. *Jesus* is the name of a historical person. He is situated in time and place. He lives within a network of relationships and in a flow of events. What we know about the person is from Scripture and carries all the problems of interpretation. Care is necessary in our proclamation. In the formation sessions I offer to parishioners, I remind them the evangelists were concerned about the meaning of the Christ event not necessarily the facticity—the who, what, when, or where. A crucial part of that meaning is the assertion of the humanity of Jesus.

According to the Scriptures, he was born of Mary in Bethlehem and raised in Nazareth, where his neighbors thought of him as a normal kid, the carpenter's son. John baptized him in the Jordan, and, soon after, he underwent temptations about his future. As a young adult he moved to Capernaum. He became an itinerant preacher, reportedly capable of performing compassionate miracles. He began a religious movement that

---

1. Bromiley, *Theological Dictionary*, 489.

got away from him. He was betrayed, arrested, tried, and crucified. In the telling, the divinity of Jesus never swamps his humanity.

Written decades after the Jesus event, the New Testament is a reflection on the whole, on the Lord Jesus Christ, the person with the titles. It intermingles humanity and divinity. Jesus's teaching is reported to be the Lord's word (1 Cor 7:10; 1 Thess 4:15; Heb 1:1—2:4; Acts 11:16–17). That he is the divine word is an essential premise of John's prologue (John 1:1; 1:14). *Lord* is used for the historical person often in the Gospels. Luke uses *Lord* for the historical Jesus thirteen times; John uses *Lord* for Jesus five times.[2] The humanity of Jesus is not lost, however. The flesh-and-blood person communicates his Lordship.

The resurrection narratives stretch the limits of language. The post-resurrection events demonstrate his extraordinary, perhaps divine, qualities. He seemed to be a spirit or a ghost. He appeared and disappeared at will. He passed through locked doors. Even after the resurrection, his humanity was preserved, however. He was embraced and touched. He conversed at length. He got hungry, sitting at evening table with two disciples and cooking breakfast on a beach for seven more. His humanity was never lost even in the mystery of the resurrection and the linguistic muddle it occasioned.

The efforts of the New Testament authors to maintain the humanity of Jesus all the while suggesting his divinity inform the performative truth of the creedal proposition *Lord Jesus Christ*. The human/divine combination is essential for the Christian valuation of self, society, the world, and time. The proposition is also our source of hope, the foundation for our aspirations.

The proclamation contains a remarkable valuation of humanity. By becoming one of us, he raises all of us. The *merely* in *merely human* is erased. After Adam, the *sin* in *sinful humanity* was thought to be essential to our nature. The Lord Jesus forgives our sin and offers salvation. The Lord Jesus transforms humanity. The creedal proposition informs us about our glorious end, the purpose of our lives. St. John pushes the transformation into this life: "Beloved, we are God's children now; what we shall be has not yet been revealed. We do know that when it is revealed we shall be like him, for we shall see him as he is" (1 John 3:2). The *Catechism of the Catholic Church* summarizes the transformation that occurs in us when we unite with Jesus Christ. The paragraph quotes 1 Peter,

---

2. Bromiley, *Theological Dictionary*, 493.

St. Irenaeus, St. Athanasius, and St. Thomas Aquinas (excuse, please, the male-exclusive language):

> The Word became flesh to make us *"partakers of the divine nature"*: "For this is why the Word became man, and the Son of God became the Son of man: so that man, by entering into communion with the Word and receiving divine sonship, might become a son of God." "For the Son of God became man so that we might become God." "The only begotten Son of God, wanting to make us sharers in his divinity, assumed our nature, so that he, made man, might make men gods."[3]

This transformation carries us much further than most invocations to be like Christ. The domesticated version has us being kind like Jesus was kind, compassionate, forgiving, and good like he was. The actual challenge is immeasurably beyond anything that the WWJD crowd would have: Jesus speaks, "Amen, Amen, I say to you, whoever believes in me will do the works that I do, and will do greater ones than these" (John 14:12). Belief in the Lord Jesus Christ is aspiring to do the works that he did.

Balancing the full divinity and full humanity of Jesus of Nazareth has not been easy, historically, for the church. Nor is it now. I would guess that most believers are mild docetists, over-emphasizing the divinity of Jesus at the expense of his humanity. The pastoral minister cannot allow believers to lose the humanity of Jesus. Psychologically, losing the humanity of Jesus would have us stand without mediation before the infinite. Before a divine/human mediator was imagined, humanity was thought to pay an extreme price for coming before the infinite. To see the face of God or to hear God's voice meant death (e.g., Exod 33:20; Deut 5:22–6; Deut 18:16). Our humanity becomes impossible to bear. Standing alone before the infinite, standing without mediation, magnifies every flaw in the finite—it's like looking into the mirrors of a carnival fun house, only with serious repercussions. Without mediation, the early modern critique of religion is irrefutable. By believing, humankind is diminished, degraded, and beaten down. Moreover, in the hands of Machiavellian churchmen, the asymmetry between the finite and infinite creates the pretext to demand submission and subservience not only to God but to God's spokesperson, the power-hungry churchman. In this situation, the finite believer could not escape spiritual passivity. Such

---

3. *Catechism of the Catholic Church*, para. 460.

passivity would likely migrate into other forms of social interaction—the cognitive, political, economic, and even into our private lives. A believer would be at the mercy of forces beyond the self. The church would need to abandon hope that Christians might consecrate this world.[4]

The revelation of the Lord Jesus Christ changes the valuation of the finite and the human. We can reimagine our God, allowing our image to conform to Scripture. A lone, all-powerful figure, an absolute authoritarian wielding power without mercy is not the Christian God. After Jesus, God-language incorporates desire; divinity becomes a matter of the heart. The mediation of the Lord Jesus creates a two-way attraction. The convergence of our humanity with the humanity of the Lord Jesus allows us to imagine a divinity that pours forth the divine self to raise humanity to an exalted level. The convergence of our humanity with the humanity of the Lord Jesus also allows us to imagine humans becoming active agents in union with God the Father, becoming light and salt (Matt 5:13–6). The psalmist hints at this exaltation: "What is man that you are mindful of him, and a son of man that you care for him? Yet you have made him little less than a god, crowned him with glory and honor" (Ps 8:5–6). The prologue to John's Gospel reflects the evolution of the faith after the Jesus event: "To those who did accept him he gave power to become children of God" (John 1:12).

A human/divine Savior creates the conditions for our aspirations. As discussed earlier, sociologist Richard Fenn has defined the sacred as "the sum total of human possibility."[5] Peter Sloterdijk writes of the vertical pull of religion.[6] In our Lord Jesus Christ, Fenn's definition of the sacred and Sloterdijk's category of verticality make perfect sense. The proclamation of the Lord Jesus Christ encourages believers to hope and aspire in three ways.

The first has us looking again at the Lonergan/Rahner form of transcendence. The Lord Jesus makes it possible for us to discover moments of transcendence. We can find transcendence in the explicitly religious (e.g., adoration of the Blessed Sacrament). An expansive religiosity also opens nature to its sacred dimension as God creating. Humankind's progress toward freedom, equality, and justice becomes God saving. In addition, it makes possible the fulfillment of transcendent occasions. We are empowered to climb the ladder of finitude and see beyond. The desire

---

4. Flannery, *Apostolicam actuositatem*, para. 2.
5. Fenn, *Beyond Idols*, 10.
6. Sloterdijk, *Change Your Life*, 13.

for *more* intensifies. Through his word and through the reception of his body and blood, we can step beyond into the eternal and infinite. His command to become perfect as the heavenly Father is perfect becomes vaguely practicable (Matt 5:48). Lonergan and Rahner explore the hunger for knowledge as the transcendent occasion. But we can aspire to any of the divine attributes: goodness, beauty, truth, compassion, and so forth. Even the aspiration for power becomes sacred if power becomes Sacred Power, understood as the empowerment to lift others into a better life.

A second set of benefits occurs. Too many Christians cannot perceive or process the possibilities and potential for humanity resulting from what the Lord Jesus has done for us. The promises of Christ are jettisoned into the next life, into the disembodied existence of heaven. In this life, we are left with the merely human, the essentially sinful human—a dark version of life. Exactly why the darker view of humanity came to dominate our pulpits is beyond me. I am inclined to blame the social control demanded by the hierarchical, feudal political order that the church once sanctioned. That dark view of humankind readily functions as a pretext for social control.

The New Testament offers just the opposite. It holds out a set of objectives based on our faith in the Lord Jesus Christ, an aspirational Christianity. Promises of forgiveness, healing, reconciliation, new life, the fullness of life, abundant life, and complete joy are offered to humankind. Christ is the light for the life of the human race, and the darkness has not overcome it (John 1:3–4).

Each summer, the daily lectionary takes us to the Sermon on the Mount. I made it a habit to invite the daily Mass-goers to read the three chapters in one sitting. Most years, a parishioner asks me for time to discuss the impossibility of the Lord's vision. From the perspective of a diminished humanity, the sermon is overwhelming. Yet, it does not have to be so. What if the Lord Jesus thinks it is possible for us to aspire to perfection? What if the realization of our aspirations is some part of our life in Christ?

Preachers and catechists know the sermon—or should. Jesus recites the law, the values and norms of his day. With divine authority, he intensifies the law, values, and norms, calling disciples to the ideals of God's kingdom. The law says we shall not kill; in the kingdom, we shall not get angry. The law says we shall not commit adultery; in God's kingdom, we shall not lust for another. The law says our neighbors and countrymen are the only ones who deserve our respect; in God's kingdom, there are no social boundaries; instead, we love our enemies. Some compare the sermon to the divine law articulated by Moses. In Jesus's hands, however, intensifying the law does not lead us into a new straitjacket of legalistic morality. Instead, the Lord is inviting us into a fuller humanity. In him, we see ourselves and others with intrinsic dignity, never to be excluded, used, manipulated, or degraded. We develop appreciation for the wonder others bring into our lives. In Christ Jesus, self and society become more than the status quo. With the mediation of the Lord Jesus Christ, the desires for a higher, better form of life implied in the sermon become possible.

We can find an aspirational version of Christianity also in the Book of Signs, the first eleven chapters of John's Gospel. Normal, daily realities seem to have two dimensions. The ordinary conveys the sacred. At a wedding, an overabundance of wine communicates the messianic feast (John 2:1–12). Those grown old can experience a new birth (John 3:1–21). Water can be a spring welling up to eternal life (John 4:4–26). The food brought by the disciples communicates the nourishment gained by doing the Father's will (John 4:27–38). Bread for physical nourishment becomes the Bread of Life, nourishment to journey into eternal life (John 6:22–71). The bereaved face death having discovered an additional dimension called resurrected life (John 11:1–44). Jesus does not diminish human and material existence; he consecrates it.

In one of the first testimonies of modern atheism, Ludwig Feuerbach complains that religion robs us of the ability to appreciate the beauties of life. We do not fully appreciate a good meal shared with friends because we direct our appreciation to a ritual meal held in church. We do not fully appreciate a warm, cleansing bath because we project our pleasure on the ritual of baptism. Both the Sermon on the Mount and John's Book of Signs refute this criticism. With faith in the Lord Jesus Christ, we recover our potential. With faith in the Lord Jesus Christ, everything is blessed. The rituals of the church do not rob us of our sense of appreciation but train us to see the sacred in all things. After all, water, human touch, bread, wine, and oil reflect divinity when we gather in the one who is both divine and human.

The third benefit of professing faith in the Lord Jesus Christ is the freedom of the *more* that is introduced into our loyalties. Each of us lives within a network of relationships and institutions. Each of us derives part of our identity from our placement in a culture and society—in particularities like nationality, religion, ethnicity, race, gender, social class, educational status, even geographic region. Some degree of loyalty is rightly expected of us. Priority questions, however, naturally emerge. To whom and to what and on which occasions do we owe our allegiances? The assortment of loyalties can become a confused mess. Each of these particularities can separate us from others so we value others as lesser. In fact, allegiance to our particularities can lead us to violence against those who are not like us. Our loyalties can tie us down, bind us to thought patterns and practices of our nationality, social class, race, gender, or religion. Our loyalty to our particularities can blind us to our flaws.

We require a higher power to enable us to critique our own particularities and loyalties. To rise above our personal particularities, the feelings generated by the higher values must take a potent hold on us. The force of a higher power needs to free our imaginations, open our hearts, and allow honest assessment of our condition. In Christ, "there is neither Jew nor Greek, there is neither slave nor free person, there is not male and female" (Gal 3:28). In Christ, we are free (Gal 5:1). Our belief in the Lord Jesus Christ offers us the empowerment needed to rise above our particular loyalties and begin to discover possibilities. St. Paul makes the following assertion: "For I am convinced that neither death, nor life, nor angels, nor principalities, nor present things, nor future things, nor powers, nor height, nor depth, nor any other creature will be able to separate us from the love of God in Christ Jesus our Lord" (Rom 8:38–9). Belief in the Lord Jesus liberates us to see through all appeals to violence and through any attempt to degrade others. Aspiring to divine truth helps us see through lies, propaganda, and advertisements. We can avoid entanglements that compromise our humanity—if we proclaim that Jesus is Lord. *Lord* communicates the divine, the highest of all priorities. *Christ* offers us a messianic vision, an aspirational method around which to hope. *Jesus* reminds us that change is humanly possible.

In his definition of religion, Mark Taylor uses the idea of a schema, a perceptual framework through which we take in data about humankind, our world, and our God.[7] The schema allows us to process the data and plan to act in our world or on our own self. *Lord Jesus Christ* is such a perceptual framework. Let's see how it works:

- Professing faith in the Lord Jesus Christ does not eliminate patriotism. But it helps us sort out the tendency to equate God and country. If we truly believe that Jesus is Lord, religious nationalism

---

7. Taylor, *After God*, 13.

is inconceivable. We might see beyond the norms and institutions of the nation, correcting its flaws as we seek God's kingdom. Faith in the Lord Jesus Christ redefines patriotism, making the pursuit of justice the guiding principle of our involvement in politics. In the biblical tradition, justice is not merely giving each person his/her due. As the prophets critiqued the monarchy and the distribution of wealth, biblical justice demands we examine the political and economic systems. Biblical justice insists on actual equality, raising up the lowly—the poor, the degraded, the disenfranchised.

- Professing faith in our Lord Jesus Christ does not erase social boundaries but makes those boundaries porous. Through the Son of God, we become children of God. Through this schema, we begin to perceive all others as members of one human family made in God's own image. Those who differ from me become neighbors of mine, as the good Samaritan parable instructs us (Luke 10:29–37). Our fears of a pluralistic society give way. We begin to perceive others as mutually enriching. Because those who differ from us expand our horizons, we may realize that we have a debt to others as they contribute to our knowledge of God creating.

- In our Lord Christ Jesus, the physical world is reconceived. The creed informs us that "through him all things were made." The physical world becomes creation and we become stewards of it. And more, in our Lord Jesus Christ, the first creation awaits the new creation, a time and place of harmony and peace (Rom 8:18–25). Each believer should experience the challenge found in St. Paul: "Creation awaits with eager expectation the revelation of the children of God" (Rom 8:19).

Our belief in Christ Jesus offers us a method to perfect ourselves and our society. Christ is the anointed one, the Messiah. His compassionate miracles that realize the dream of messianic harmony are to be repeated by believers who share in his anointing. However we choose to make the dream real, the blind must see, the deaf must hear, the lame must walk, the captive must be liberated, the lion and the lamb must coexist, swords must become plowshares, and no harm or ruin should be found on God's holy mountain. The *Catechism of the Catholic Church* puts our mission succinctly: "This fullness of the Spirit was not to remain uniquely the

Messiah's, but was to be communicated to the *whole messianic people*."[8] Pastoral ministry means facilitating the mission of the whole messianic people. To proclaim belief in *the Lord Jesus Christ* is to assert that the anointed ones will prioritize their loyalties and act to construct God's kingdom.

The development of an aspirational Christianity raises one caveat in my assessment. Religion is too often reduced to morality. This reduction can leach into the religious imagination of practicing Christians, shrinking everything about the faith into an ongoing struggle between right and wrong. This may be a reason behind the culture wars. The impact of this reduction places a heavy burden on believers. Without a genuine aspirational Christianity, the valuation of the person may become conditioned by a theological anthropology that only sees human flaws, sins, and participation in evil. A theological anthropology without the saving intervention of Jesus Christ—and the vertical pull that intervention occasions—allows manipulative ministers to weigh down decent, good believers with guilt even when believers simply fall short of their aspirations. Our faith needs morality, no doubt. But it cannot be reduced to morality. The *more* is a gift that keeps us from accepting the status quo as unchangeable reality. The continuous challenge of the *more* keeps us from being wearied by life. The *more* is liberating, a divine invitation.

To fall short, however, is not participation in evil. We can and should explore the depth of love. That we fail to discover it, however, does not make us sinful. We can and should challenge the reach of our charity. That we cannot raise up every poor person in our neighborhood does not make us sinful. We can and should welcome the stranger and understand those with whom we differ; we can and should allow differences to enrich our lives. That we can be puzzled by the life choices of some others is not necessarily sinful.

I have heard confessions of good Catholics who find themselves in heroic situations—for example, the spouse who is trying to cope with the dementia of their beloved, the parent who is trying to get to their drug addicted teenage child. That they fall short of perfect heroism—that they lose their patience, grow frustrated, or pray for deliverance—is not sin. The heroic is aspirational. It is sad to listen to confessions of aging believers whose decreasing energy level forces them to cut back on their active service to the civic community or to the church. Beaten

---

8. *Catechism of the Catholic Church*, para. 1287 (emphasis added).

down by the message of an ever-sinful body, they assess their aging as an evil. They cannot see the blessing in relaxation—simply letting a day go by, or counting their blessings, or taking a walk in a park. The guilt inflicted upon believers is often the sin of the ministers responsible for their formation. The people of God need to be re-formed. The *more* is a gift to be cherished and appreciated. Failure to be *more* or do *more*, or to live heroic lives, or accept the inevitable changes that come with passing time: these are not falling into evil or committing a sin. Pastoral ministers should not treat it so.

Our belief in the Lord Jesus Christ should have us thinking of the newness of life, abundant life, the fullness of life, complete joy. Certainly, our faith recognizes the need for a transformation in us, for ongoing conversion. The juxtaposition of *Lord*, *Christ*, and *Jesus* holds forth the potential for that transformation. We humans can imagine the newness of life and abundant life; the sacred is the sum total of human possibility. Our proclamation of the creed reminds us of the vertical dimension tugging on us. St. Paul understood the vertical pull of our faith. He often advances details about the newness of life. In his First Letter to the Corinthians, he referees a dispute in the eucharistic assembly by showing them a "more excellent way" (1 Cor 12:31). He offers three eternal things: faith, hope, and love (1 Cor 13:13). In Galatians, he offers us a list of the "fruits of the Spirit": "love, joy, peace, patience, kindness, generosity, faithfulness, gentleness, self-control" (5:22). My favorite list is in his Letter to the Philippians: "Whatever is true, whatever is honorable, whatever is just, whatever is pure, whatever is lovely, whatever is gracious, if there is any excellence and if there is anything worthy of praise, think about these things" (Phil 4:8). To compete with the many versions of a good life that our world offers, it is imperative that pastoral ministers present the vertical dimension of our faith. To do so, ministers need to recognize *whatever* is excellent and *whatever* is worthy of praise, even when it takes ministers and believers outside the confines of the sanctuary.

The Second Vatican Council called believers to the perfection of holiness *according to their state in life*.[9] In addition, all believers are to share in the "priestly, prophetical, and kingly" office—in other words, the fullness of Christian ministry.[10] But the documents warn those in professional and ordained ministry that believers function "in the freedom of

---

9. Flannery, *Lumen gentium*, para. 11; Flannery, *Apostolicam actuositatem*, para. 4.
10. Flannery, *Apostolicam actuositatem*, para. 2.

the Holy Spirit who 'breathes where he wills'" (John 3:8).[11] The pastoral minister must inspire and facilitate the full participation of Christians in the transformation of self and society according to their state in life and in their own freedom. According to the teaching of the church, the nature of holiness can no longer be imagined in a single hierarchical order. To profess belief in the Lord Jesus Christ is to aspire to whatever is true, honorable, just, pure, lovely, gracious, excellent, and worthy of praise.

---

11. Flannery, *Apostolicam actuositatem*, para. 3.

8

Incarnate

SHORTLY AFTER CHRISTMAS a few years back, I attended a conference for pastors. I met a priest who came from Poland to minister to the Polish community in Detroit. The American way to celebrate the incarnation upset him. His was the standard criticism—the excess, the materialism. He preached the issue throughout the Advent and Christmas seasons. I conceded the point but cautioned him. Enduring traditions often meet deep social needs. I would guess that the largest percentage of the money spent at Christmas is for gift giving, an altogether necessary social ritual. Gift giving symbolizes social bonding, mutual care, and concern, if not love. In a society as mobile as ours, sharing gifts may take on more importance. For many reasons, families and friends can live miles apart. A gift can bridge the distance. My warning came to this: preach against the excess and materialism but commend the exchange of gifts. Besides, a grandmother rendered immobile by age or health should not endure a homily suggesting there is anything wrong with sending gifts to her grandchildren living across the country.

My point is this: Most traditions, all dogma and doctrines, all rituals, all Scripture passages are polyvalent. They communicate across multiple levels of meaning. The primary meaning of Christmas is the birth of Jesus. Would that all the trappings of the season conform to the meaning of God-with-us! The dogma, however, does not come close to expressing the full meaning of the celebration. The all-but-unpreachable doctrine is summarized by Karl Rahner like this: "By the hypostatic union, the eternal (and therefore pre-existent) Word (Logos), the Son of the Father as the second person of the Trinity, has united as his nature with his person in a true, substantial and definitive union, a human nature created in time with a body and a spiritual soul from the Virgin Mary, his true mother."[1] The biblical story is more approachable and lends itself to the range of meaning in our Christmas festivities. It celebrates the birth of a child in a stable because the inn had no vacancy. It is about a manger (a feeding trough) and swaddling clothes (a form of the diaper). It is about an ox and an ass, shepherds and sheep, magi and their camels. Certainly, it is about the Virgin Mary, her husband Joseph, and angels singing about peace.

The story has a dark side that frames the light and makes it more brilliant. Matthew tells us that King Herod governed Judea. Fear of the tyrant gave rise to a nervous dream that sent the Holy Family fleeing to Egypt. The king ordered the murder of all boys in Bethlehem under two years of age. St. Luke also suggests a dark side to the nativity story. He names the religious and political leaders of the day: Herod, Caesar Augustus, Tiberius Caesar, Pontius Pilate, Annas, and Caiaphas. The acknowledgment is more than an attempt to locate Jesus in history and more than Luke's use of the format to announce the birth of great men in that age. They suggest the tensions Jesus would soon face. The names put into sharp relief the revolutionary words of Mary in the Magnificat (Luke 1:46–55), Zechariah in his Canticle (Luke 1:68–79), Simeon's prophecy (Luke 2:34–35), and Jesus's words quoting Isaiah announcing the Lord's liberating mission (Luke 4:18–19). Luke contrasted the peaceful, liberating Savior with violent religious and political powers.

The popularized meaning has been sentimentalized; the biblical meaning itself often challenges our religiosity. The ox, the ass, and the manger are rooted in a complaint about Israel by the prophet Isaiah. The ox and the ass were smart enough to know where they are nourished, but God's people had forgotten (Isa 1:3). The shepherds indicated that the very poor and disenfranchised knew their need for God (Luke 2:8–20). Luke mentions the manger three times (Luke 2:7; 2:12; 2:16). Christmas carols make the manger a sign of the Holy Family's poverty. In Luke, the manger serves as a bookend to symbolize our hunger for divine nourishment. At the other end of Luke's Gospel, the resurrected Jesus feeds his disciples on the road to Emmaus (Luke 24:13–35). Likewise, swaddling clothes are not a sign of poverty; they are a type of diaper that King

---

1. Rahner, "Incarnation," 693.

Solomon wore when he was an infant (Wis 7:1–6). They are a sign of our common humanity that Jesus shares. In popular lore, the innkeeper is a mean fellow who turned away a very pregnant woman. The biblical meaning is likely based on a complaint from the prophet Jeremiah. To the prophet, God seemed distant, removed from Israel. He asks God, "Why should you be a stranger in this land, like a traveler stopping only for a night?" (Jer 14:8). The innkeeper was doing God's bidding; God was answering Jeremiah's complaint. Jesus was not a traveler in need of a room for a night; he is making a home among us. The biblical story refuses to render salvation *overly* spiritualized; this world and human nature are changed. It also rejects becoming *overly* sentimental; the cross bleeds into the infant's story. The whole, the light and dark, the sentiment and the challenge, draw us in.

Christmas season seems to pass before preachers get beyond the spiritualized and sentimental to the real-world challenge. At a most profound depth, incarnation is a way of thinking. God did not come among us as the unmoved mover, the ineffable, or first efficient cause. Theologians can discover all that upon rational reflection. Instead, our faith—the way we perceive God, the world, and ourselves—is defined by God being born in the flesh, in time, in a place enriched by relationships and challenged by a flow of events. Therefore, incarnation opens our perception to the sacred in our time and place, in the flow of events and the network of people in which each of us is situated. Most importantly, it opens our hearts to the possibility of God being mixed in with the whole of our lives. The incarnation teaches us about the sanctity of the material, of our bodies, of the natural and built environment. The incarnation can open our eyes to the divinely created beauty that is all about us. The incarnation also confronts us with the darkness that we must overcome. The performative truth of God's embodiment compels us to find the truth about this world, the flesh, time, and place. Sadly, we fail the truth of the incarnation if we define salvation only as an out-of-time state of being, if we become concerned only with disembodied souls in heaven.

The schemata provided by the incarnation demands we look at the whole. God in time and place can "disrupt, dislocate, and disfigure every stabilizing structure"[2]—to borrow a phrase from Mark Taylor. The incarnation insists that we find God in the people, the places, the events of our lives, including suffering and death. As it opens our eyes to the beauty, it

---

2. Taylor, *After God*, 12–13.

opens our ears to the cries of those in need, as Mary's song would have it (Luke 1:51–53). The performatory truth behind the celebration of Christmas is the eternal truth of the Madonna and Child, of mothers caring for their babies, as well as the terrible social sin that many mothers do not have the means to do so. Even with the painful side of incarnation, however, the good news of salvation emerges. We also fail the truth of the incarnation if our valuation or assessment of this world and our times cannot discern God's disruptive presence.

Karl Rahner articulates this truth. He refers us to the Lord's self-disclosure in Matthew: "All things have been handed over to me by my Father. No one knows the Son except the Father, and no one knows the Father except the Son and anyone to whom the Son wishes to reveal him" (Matt 11:27). We come to God through Jesus of Nazareth—the person who was born in that stable. Rahner writes, "It should be pointed out that this Christ-question concerning our basic religious acts does not signify merely that one can 'also' adore the one who has become man, and this 'even' in his human nature. . . . If the religious act really wants to reach God, it *always* and in every case has and must have exactly this 'incarnational' structure."[3] This truth moves the location of our salvation: "The human being must commit himself to the finite dimension of space and time in order to render the eternal present to himself."[4] This commitment demonstrates itself "in acts of practical and 'down-to-earth' compassion performed in the context of everyday human life."[5] God embodied, therefore, can be disruptive. The incarnation is a cry against violence and the degradation of the poor. It is the foundation for our mission to consecrate this world, our struggle for social justice, and our hope for peace and a culture of compassion and charity.

The "incarnational structure" is a way of thinking. Because we come to God through Jesus of Nazareth, our time, our here and now, the contemporary state of our lives and this world, enter our formation of truth. The incarnation, therefore, influences the preacher's decision on how to present gospel truth to today's believers.

Consider the evangelist John's ambiguous usage of the term *world*. Our Christmas celebration reflects John's summary of the nighttime visit of Nicodemus with Jesus: "God so loved the world that he gave his only Son, so that everyone who believes in him might not perish but might

---

3. Rahner, *Content of the Faith*, 333 (emphasis original).
4. Rahner, *Content of the Faith*, 337.
5. Rahner, *Content of the Faith*, 337.

have eternal life" (John 3:16). At Christmas, we celebrate God's love for the world and for humanity. We celebrate because of what John says in the prologue to the Gospel. Jesus brought life "that is the light of the human race" (John 1:4). The Christmas message contains a wonderful uplifting universalism.

When the celebration has run its course and the season turns to Lent and the cross, we might check the fine print. The universalism remains, but it is modified. The blessing of the incarnation, becoming the "children of God," extends "to those who did accept him" (John 1:12). John 1:5 warns us that the darkness is trying to extinguish the light. John 1:10 tells us that "the world did not know him" although "he was in the world and the world came to be through him." The next verse offers a fact that should terrify all those who claim to be God's people: "He came to what was his own, but his own people did not accept him" (John 1:11). Even the reassuring verses of John 3 end with the author raising the tension level with this world: "The light came into the world, but people preferred darkness to light, because their works were evil" (John 3:19).

We arrive at a key question: How does a teacher or preacher present the *world* in the light of incarnation? Peter Sloterdijk's book *God's Zeal: The Battle of the Three Monotheisms* offers us some insight. He sees three types of universalism. Judaism represents a *defensive* universalism.[6] Since ancient times, Israel has suffered from the aggression of others—the Assyrians, the Babylonians, the Persians, the Greeks, the Romans, then the diaspora, the pogroms, and the lowest point, the genocidal holocaust. They maintained a universal perspective because their God remained supreme, even if they were enslaved. God's major interventions in history—the exodus and the return from exile—proved the wisdom of maintaining faith through the worst situations. The faith of Israel remembered the promise of perpetuity made to Abraham and the promise of universal peace and justice in their expectation of a messiah, even in times when the promise seemed broken. A defensive universalism results.

Both Islam and Christianity engaged in an *offensive* or *militant* universalism.[7] Both have spread their faith through aggression and violence. Adherents of both religions posit a belief system which can "demand universal subordination."[8] We are concerned with Christianity here. Christian history includes the crusades, the inquisitions, and the

---

6. Sloterdijk, *God's Zeal*, 52.
7. Sloterdijk, *God's Zeal*, 55, 132.
8. Sloterdijk, *God's Zeal*, 12.

role Christianity played in European imperialism, colonization, and the enslavement of peoples of color. *Militant* universalism remains with us. The rise of Christian nationalism and the attempts to use political power to enforce Christian morality are both expressions of it. Even today, some think the faith can and should be spread through coercion. One form of universalism is militant.

Finally, there is a *civilized* universalism. It celebrates freedom and the human rights of all peoples. Because God is merciful, faith teaches toleration and understanding. And more, it learns from and incorporates the wisdom of others. Sloterdijk reminds the reader of a force in Western culture dating from Socrates: a vertical or upward pull on humans who understand that humanity wills to be superior to itself.[9] He reminds us of a phrase: "Man infinitely transcends man." Perhaps religions can feel this pull, break free of the defensive or offensive forms of universalism, and discover the benefits of civilized universalism. Perhaps, incarnation, as a way of thinking, can become a force inviting us to embrace a truth that does not demand subordination of others but that professes an offer of salvation to all humankind through God embodied.

In our times, the course of the churches might tend toward any of the three universalisms. Some among us, sensing rejection by a secularizing world, opt for a defensive universalism. Some wish to form Christian communities that insulate themselves from the world and reenforce, if not strong-arm, a traditional Christian way of life for those who select the community. These communities intend to be a sign to the world of a Christian vocation in the world by being spiritually set against the world. Early in Christian history, monasticism may have been born from defensive universalism. Pope Benedict set the tone in 2005 by choosing his papal name to honor "the father of Western monasticism." Some Christians agree with John's sense of a world in which most people reject the light and embrace the darkness.

Militant universalism is also a possibility for those who sense more darkness than light in our world. Christian nationalists wish to use force to dominate entire countries. I am saddened by those who think *God* and *guns* belong on the same bumper sticker. But some do. Most pull up short of violence but strive to use the state's coercive power to force their morality on the nation, especially their traditional family and gender roles. Many preachers, pastors, and bishops see themselves as cultural

---

9. Sloterdijk, *God's Zeal*, 137.

warriors living through an apocalyptic battle. Some have let themselves be coopted by politicians who play on fear. Personally, I tend to agree with the Lord's insight about living and dying by the sword.

Civilized universalism is an option for those who are moved by John 3:16, God's love for this world. Even if believers assess the times to be frightening, they hold to the faith that the darkness cannot overcome the light. The world offers so many options, so many lifestyles and choices, so many value sets. In our times, the expression *the global village* has emerged. No one seems far from where I am; none are distant, removed from me. News from around the globe gets to each of us in an instant. Therefore, all peoples have an impact on me and mine. In such a setting, Christians must develop an inviting vision of a counterreality, the world envisioned in Advent's prophetic expectations of a harmonious, messianic age and made visible by an infant in a manger with angels singing on high about peace. A tolerant, understanding, reconciling Christian version of civilized universalism is waiting to emerge.

To close, I would like to cite two philosophers who have observed the power of incarnation to transform our world. They will help us meditate on the social force, the civilizing universalism, that is incarnation.

The first philosopher is Italian Gianni Vattimo (born in 1936), a thinker whose scholarship in modern and contemporary thought brought him back to the Catholic Church of his youth. In his book *Nihilism and Emancipation: Ethics, Politics, and Law*, Vattimo recognizes the social force that is incarnation. He bases his insight on Max Weber's thesis that the this-worldly asceticism promoted by the Protestantism of John Calvin provided the spiritual force for the development of modern capitalism. With similar social analysis, Vattimo sees in Enlightenment emancipation and in the idea of progress "a revelation of the most authentic truth of the divine—most authentic because [it is] profoundly related to the human (Christ is God incarnate)."[10] The unfolding of the truth of incarnation made Christianity "even contrary to the explicit positions of the churches" a force "in the modern invention of democracy, equality, and social and political rights." He goes on:

> It is neither absurd, nor perhaps blasphemous, to maintain that the truth of Christianity is not the dogma of the churches but the modern system of rights, the humanization of social relations (where it has come about), the dissolution of the divine

---

10. Vattimo, *Nihilism and Emancipation*, 31.

> right of all forms of authority, even the Freudian discovery of the unconscious, which deprives the voice of conscience . . . of its supposed ultimacy, its unquestionable sacrality.[11]

I would quibble with his dismissal of dogma. The dogma includes the performatory truth that unfolds as human rights and so forth. But the key point is this: with careful analysis, incarnation can be seen as a social force even when the churches are pointing elsewhere. It makes perfect sense to me that God becoming human raises the valuation of humanity, allowing for the development of a theory of human rights and an enhanced sense of freedom.

Another voice that sees the incarnation as a powerful social force is Hannah Arendt (1906–75). She insists that we consider genuine pluralism, the uniqueness of each person. She writes, "Plurality is the condition of human action because we are all the same, that is, human, in such a way that nobody is ever the same as anyone else who ever lived, lives, or will live."[12] This realization inspires us to think about how each person adds to the whole and increases our own possibility. She writes, "The new always happens against the overwhelming odds of statistical laws and their probability, which for all practical, everyday purposes amounts to certainty; the new therefore always appears in the guise of miracle. The fact that man is capable of action means that the unexpected can be expected from him, that he is able to perform what is infinitely improbable."[13] The miraculous new is implied in an evocative term Arendt gives us, *natality*. Our valuation of human life follows the lifespan. We are born; we grow in strength; we peak; we age; and we decline physically and mentally until death comes for us. Consequently, we are preoccupied with mortality. Religions must reflect that preoccupation by having some answer to death. Consider popular prayers of our church. The Hail Mary ends with a prayerful request that Mary might intercede for us "now and at the hour of our death." The prayer before bed for children ends with these words: "If I should die before I wake, I pray the Lord my soul to take." Recall that at every Catholic Mass, we pray a eucharistic prayer that contains a petition for those who have died. Mortality seems to hang over us.

Hannah Arendt's term *natality* invites us to consider another orientation. She believes that natality sets humankind apart from all other

---

11. Vattimo, *Nihilism and Emancipation*, 31–32.
12. Arendt, *Human Condition*, 8.
13. Arendt, *Human Condition*, 178.

living things. The miraculous new—that we can expect the unexpected from each person, who is never the same as anyone else who has ever lived, lives, or will live—means that we continuously recreate our social world. What redeems and saves humanity, she believes, is the human capacity to assert our unique selves into human affairs so that our social world begins anew.

We renew humankind by welcoming unique individuals and newcomers. Each human birth is the beginning of a unique being for which families make space and give time. Then, neighborhoods and communities open themselves for interaction with the new person. Later, the larger civic and political community does the same—at least, ideally. Creating a place for the fresh voice keeps social interaction from becoming deadly routine or, worse, dispiriting. Genuine pluralism is the acceptance of the uniqueness of each person and openness to their contribution. Would that we could learn to extend such openness to every migrant, refugee, each stranger, and every person who differs!

Christianity could readily turn from mortality to natality. Creation requires it. The theological complement to the unique person is the infinite God creating. To expect sameness of the infinite God is to limit the infinite. God, the creative Father of all, is likely to create each person distinctly. To discover the foundation of natality, Arendt takes us to incarnation:

> The miracle that saves the world, the realm of human affairs, from its normal, "natural" ruin is ultimately the fact of natality, in which the faculty of action is ontologically rooted. . . . Only the full experience of this capacity can bestow upon human affairs faith and hope. . . . It is faith in and hope for the world that found perhaps its most glorious and most succinct expression in the few words with which the Gospels announced their "glad tidings": "A child has been born to us."[14]

The incarnation is a spiritual force from which a believer can experience awe in this world. God embodied, God in the flesh, in time and place, teaches us about the dignity of the person, the freedom of the individual, the value of our physical and spiritual self. The incarnation can open our eyes to the wonders of the human journey. It moved humankind to the discovery of our belief in human rights. And that belief has become realized in the social construction of institutions that celebrate

---

14. Arendt, *Human Condition*, 247.

freedom with justice. In addition, incarnation becomes a way of thinking, a schema, allowing us to take in and apply the whole truth, including that contemporaneously discovered. The past does not monopolize the truth; tradition does not need to close minds. The miraculous new also informs truth. Finally, incarnation makes us aware of God's family, the entire human race, spread over the face of an ever-shrinking earth. This is what Christmas celebrates: Jesus born of the Virgin Mary inspires human possibility.

9

Crucified

THE CROSS OF CHRIST is central to the faith. After Paul was laughed out of Athens (Acts 17:16–33), he discerned Christianity's uniqueness: "We proclaim Christ crucified" (1 Cor 1:23). Two thousand years of reflection on the cross has produced many levels of significance. For instance, one could consider death itself, exploring the performative truth of the God-man treading the same frightening path through death that each human takes. One could consider the suffering and the sick, people bearing a cross. These topics could be their own essays. I intend to reflect on crucifixion, a brutal form of capital punishment. The question is this: What does a crucified God mean for a believer?

The most likely starting point is the thesis of substitutionary atonement articulated in 1097 by St. Anselm—Jesus Christ died for our sins. To repair sin's damage to the relationship between God and humankind, a sacrifice of divine proportions was required. The idea is well-rooted in Scripture (Rom 5:6–8; 1 Cor 15:3; 2 Cor. 5:14–15; Heb. 9:15–22). Even that one line communicates multiple meanings. I am a cradle Catholic. I went to Catholic schools through my sophomore year of high school. Then I went to the seminary. Perhaps I first heard the line from a teacher who was trying to inspire my class with the transformational possibilities of God's love. More likely, I heard it from a teacher trying to control her classroom. The guilt inflicted by the words *for our sins* could quiet children, as they began to worry their classroom antics caused the nails to be pounded into Jesus's hands and feet. Later in life, I found guilt-inflicting techniques work on adults too. Religion is often used to put a spiritual veneer over social control—a cynical and sinful act by the powerful.

In the scriptural context, however, the cross does not lend itself to guilt or any other beat down. The emphasis in Scripture is on our transformation. In Romans, the cross leads to our justification, our reconciliation with God, to the reign of grace (Rom 5:15–21). Paul does not seem too concerned about the seriousness or frequency of our sins: "Where sin increased, grace overflowed all the more" (Rom 5:20). Paul, then, explains how baptism unites us with the crucified Christ so that "just as Christ was raised from the dead by the glory of the Father, we too might live in newness of life" (Rom 6:4). In 1 Corinthians, Jesus's death is followed by his resurrection, which guarantees our resurrection from the dead (1 Cor 15:12–28). In 2 Corinthians, the death of Jesus reconciles us with God and leads to a new creation (2 Cor 5:17). The resurrection of the dead and the new creation are symbols of hope for this-worldly change.

In Hebrews, the author reflects on the meaning of the sprinkling of blood on the people gathered at some temple sacrifices. Blood was thought to contain the life force. The sprinkling of blood offered to God is a symbol of the communion of believers in the divine life. The sacrifice of Jesus leads to our communion in God (Heb 9:11—10:25). This same image is found in John's passion narrative. The nascent community gathered at the foot of the cross is sprinkled with water and blood and given the Spirit. The community is incorporated into the divine life (John 19:31–37). Using Scripture to beat down believers with guilt is conceivable only if one extracts the aforementioned words from their context. In context, the cross leads not to guilt but to our transformation, to divine life and our salvation.

The correct starting point to dig into the meaning of the cross is the Gospels. The logic of philosophical theology or systematic theology cannot get close to the meaning. Logic will not convey the meaning of the cross; a crucified God is more than our minds can handle. To get our hearts and minds around the meaning of the cross takes both cognition and emotion. Scripture comes closer because it employs story. Because thoughts and feelings are readily woven together in a story, a cognitive and emotive meaning can emerge. Take the poignant moment when John reports that the crucified Jesus saw "his mother and the disciple there whom he loved" (John 19:26–27). John was likely writing about the founding moment of the church when it would receive the Lord's spirit, the waters of baptism and the blood of Eucharist. The emotional overload of that scene, however, has inspired icons, paintings, statues, and music. We are drawn into the scene—and perhaps into discipleship—because it appeals to our hearts, souls, and minds.

When the Scriptures are used for the authoritative foundation for these observations, our systematic, logical side may object. How can we prove our assertions? Intuition, alone, is not terribly convincing. I think we can be satisfied by drawing connections and seeing the affinities. When the various insights of the Lord's story begin to connect—when we see the affinities between various scriptural passages—one may be satisfied that we are approaching the truth of our faith. I will try to take the levels of meaning step by step, hoping to approach a complete picture when the pieces begin to form a whole. To draw out the performative truth of the cross, I will articulate the parts of the whole truth as they occur in the story:

- The predictions of his passion contain a redefinition of power. Coercive power is critiqued. Because the powers of the day used violence against the God of creation and salvation, coercive power is desacralized for all times. Power in God's kingdom becomes self-giving love.
- Because of the timing of the Last Supper and the passion during the Passover festival, the cross becomes a sign of our liberation. The epitome of freedom may be found in the Lord's own ability to avoid hate, anger, and revenge even as he faces hate, anger, and violence from others. Each Mass we celebrate is a reminder that our share in divine life promises us our freedom.
- The centurion's proclamation upon his death and the water and blood that flow from Jesus's pierced side make the cross a revelation of our union in divinity. The connective bond is the outpouring of *agape*. The infinite and eternal horizon of our freedom is revealed.
- We are invited to take up the cross. Self-giving love for the benefit of others is our sharing in the divine life. Self-giving love is our salvation.

Mark, Matthew, and Luke record three predictions of Jesus's death. The predictions begin to teach us about the meaning of the cross. Jesus does not mention expiation for sin in any of the nine versions of the predictions.

1. The first prediction is found in Mark 8:31, Matt 16:21, and Luke 9:22.
2. The second prediction is found in Mark 9:30, Matt 17:22, and Luke 9:43b.
3. The third prediction is found in Mark 10:32, Matt 20:17, and Luke 18:31.

The first set occurs after Jesus questions his disciples about his identity. Peter answers that Jesus is the Messiah. His answer is partially correct. The anointed one of God could be imagined as a kingly figure, a powerful personage who could liberate Israel from Roman oppression using violence, if necessary. Jesus responds by rejecting that notion of the messiah. He recalls the suffering servant songs of Isaiah (Isa 42:1–4; 49:1–7; 50:4–11; 52:13—53:12). Peter's desire for the powerful, kingly figure receives Jesus's rebuke: "Get behind me, Satan. You are thinking not as God does, but as human beings do" (Mark 8:33).

Learning to think as God thinks requires much effort from the disciples. In the second prediction, Jesus again speaks of a gruesome death at the hands of the powerful. Mark and Luke follow the prediction with another rebuke from Jesus. On a journey to Capernaum, the disciples discuss who among the Twelve is the greatest. Jesus corrects their idea of greatness: "If anyone wishes to be first, he shall be the last of all and the servant of all" (Mark 9:35–37). Then he uses a child as an example of Christ-like and God-like life.

Matthew inserts a visit by a collector of the temple tax into Mark's narrative. With some razzle dazzle—fetching a coin from the mouth of a fish—Jesus pays that tax. During the event, Jesus turns to Simon and asks him, "From whom do the kings of the earth take tolls or census tax?" (Matt 17:24–27). A contrast is drawn between the powerful of this world and the way of Jesus Christ. Then, Matthew returns to Mark's narrative, picking it up with the disciples' conversation on greatness, Jesus's rebuke, and the presentation of a child.

In the first century, the reference to a child made the contrast quite dramatic. In their commentary on Mark's Gospel, Scripture scholars John Donahue and Daniel Harrington show the difference between our concept of childhood and that of the first century:

> In first-century Palestinian society a child would symbolize not so much innocence or unspoiledness as lack of social status and

legal rights. A child was a "non-person" totally dependent on others for nurture and protection, and of course one could not expect to gain anything either socially or materially from kindness to a child. . . . By embracing the child Jesus displays his acceptance of the child (who is a social nonentity) as worthy of respect and care.[1]

Promoting a child to first-class status was a critique of the patriarchal power structure in Jesus's day. Being servant-like or childlike—becoming powerless—seems to be how God thinks.

Being powerless should not be equated with passivity. The context of the third prediction helps characterize power as it is in God's kingdom. Before the prediction, Mark tells us of an encounter with a rich man who desires to inherit eternal life. Jesus tells him to keep the law. The rich man says he does. Then, Jesus tells him to give everything to the poor. The rich man leaves sad. Jesus turns to his disciples to give a lesson on giving up everything to enter God's kingdom. This amazes the disciples, who think wealth and power are signs of God's approval. Jesus continues his lesson on how God thinks: "For human beings it is impossible, but not for God. All things are possible for God" (Mark 10:27). Power in God's thinking is the act of self-giving.

After this lesson, Jesus continues teaching about the horrible death he would receive at the hands of the powerful. Immediately after, Mark demonstrates how obtuse the disciples were. James and John, the sons of Zebedee, ask to sit at the right and left of the Lord's throne when he "comes into his glory." Jesus invites them to the cross. The other disciples are upset with the brothers. Jesus may have felt some exhaustion with the lot. He teaches them about power, again: "You know that those who are recognized as ruler over the Gentiles lord it over them, their great ones make their authority over them felt. But it shall not be so among you. Rather, whoever wishes to be great among you will be your servant; whoever wishes to be first among you will be the slave of all. For the Son of Man did not come to be served but to serve and to give his life as a ransom for many" (Mark 10:42–45). The term *ransom* helps us to transition toward a fuller understanding of the Lord's cross. The first insight into the passion story is the rejection of coercive power. The second insight defines power in God's kingdom, which is self-giving love. With the word *ransom*, we begin to see power's purpose in God's mind. Donahue

---

1. Donahue and Harrington, *Gospel of Mark*, 285.

and Harrington write, "The term *lytron* ('ransom') refers to the price for releasing a captive or for a slave to buy his or her freedom."[2] Power is for the ransom of the many.

All three predictions of his death are lessons on power—better expressed, they are critiques of coercive power. The lessons offer the conditions for true discipleship. The predictions contrast the powerful of his day—King Herod and Pontius Pilate, the Sanhedrin and the high priests—to the way power is used in God's kingdom. These lessons, however, are not directed at the powerful as social critique. The lessons are directed to the church, to us. To find the performatory lesson of the crucified one, we need to keep this contrast in mind. The critique of power implied in the cross of Jesus Christ constitutes a historically unique organization called *church* that makes self-giving love rather than coercive power the basis of social interaction.

John takes us in the same direction but does so in an original setting. The extensive trial before Pilate in the Gospel of John (John 18:28—19:16) dramatically asserts a power that "does not belong to this world," a power from above. Jesus stands before the representative of the greatest earthly power, the divine emperor. The scene is subversive. Jesus does not claim innocence. He does not flee into spiritually motivated indifference regarding worldly affairs. Jesus does not reject earthly power. Nor does he advocate a political revolution that would replace one religious-political system with another. Instead, he claims a higher power, one above the sacralized power falsely claimed by the emperor and high priest. From that vantage point, he critiques coercive power for all time. Jesus rejects coercive power wielded in the name of God. Therefore, the scene offers *space* for followers of Jesus to engage all earthly power, critiquing it from above. When Jesus raises the question of truth, Pilate scoffs at the idea. Pilate does not and cannot know about power in God's kingdom. The Lord's truth is the truth of love, *agape*. Only those who believe, only those who have heard his word can know this truth and apply it to their interaction. Marcel Gauchet offers us an insight worthy of our reflection. What Jesus offers is a release from social bonds, especially those which demand violence and retaliation in the name of God. Gauchet writes, "He instaurated a wholly different understanding of obligation, based on the autonomy of the heart."[3]

---

2. Donahue and Harrington, *Gospel of Mark*, 313.
3. Gauchet, *Disenchantment of the World*, 121.

Scripture has it that Jesus is killed at the hands of those with religious and political power. Marcus Borg makes this point: "Historically, Jesus didn't just die—he was killed. And killed not by a criminal or assassin but executed by established authority—a combination of imperial and collaborationist religious authorities. Moreover, he was not just executed, but crucified—a form of Roman execution used for a specific class of offenders, those who systematically defied Roman authority."[4] Borg could have used a stronger word than *killed*. Jesus suffered a judicial murder; his death was state sponsored. It was intended and planned (Matt 26:3–5; John 11:47–53). He did not just die nor was he just killed. The religious and political powers of the day needed to rid themselves of this itinerant preacher. He was murdered. If we don't attend to this history, we may end up spiritualizing Jesus's death, losing the social dynamic revealed in Scripture. Or the Christian message may be domesticated—the critique of coercive power lost to us.

By the cross, power changes its nature and humankind is transformed. For followers of the crucified one, power cannot be over others; it cannot be about social control; it can never be violent. Power becomes service. Moreover, the power of the cross ransoms captives and purchases freedom. Power must be wielded only as liberating love.

Jesus was not a violent revolutionary, one who would use force to overthrow the powerful. Luke tells us that Jesus called one zealot, Simon, to be an apostle (Luke 6:15). But Jesus did not follow a zealot's blueprint. His self-proclaimed purpose, however, certainly upset the powerful. At the beginning of his ministry, Luke summarizes the Lord's ministry in words from Isaiah:

> The Spirit of the Lord is upon me,
>   because he has anointed me
>   to bring glad tidings to the poor.
> He has sent me to proclaim liberty to captives
>   and recovery of sight to the blind,
>   to let the oppressed go free,
> and to proclaim a year acceptable to the Lord. (Luke 4:18–19)

The redefinition of power is apparent. A listing of the Lord's actions helps us understand what an irritant Jesus was as he lived and proclaimed a new sense of power:

- Jesus claims to fulfill the law. He violates its letter in favor of its spirit.

---

4. Borg, *Speaking Christian*, 99.

- Jesus defies the purity and cleanliness regulations that can be used to separate and exclude peoples.
- Jesus holds no teaching credentials, but he teaches with authority.
- Jesus breaks social boundaries, engaging with gentiles, pagans, women and children, his people's oppressors and enemies, even public sinners.
- Jesus taught a counterreality, or a countervision, called the kingdom of God, which implied a critique of the Roman empire's violence and oppression and Israel's religious leaders who collaborated with it.
- Jesus cleansed the temple implying a transformation of religion.
- Jesus has a charismatic bond with the people that frightened the defenders of the status quo, both religious and political.

In all his actions and in all his teachings, Jesus demonstrates a remarkable sense of freedom. His claim to a special knowledge of the Father was the basis of his freedom (John 8:31–47). His freedom was too much for the religious and political authorities; he threatened the social order they had designed. Specifically, Jesus decoupled God's name from the use of power to legitimate the powerful and their use of power. His ministry desacralized the power structures of his day—and power structures of all times. To understand what his crucifixion means for our lives, we must get our hearts around the desacralization of all coercive power.

The desacralization of power does not eliminate power but defines its proper use. The word *ransom* guides us to the point. The timing of the Lord's passion helps us excavate the meaning more deeply. In Mark, the Last Supper was held "on the first day of the feast of Unleavened Bread, when they sacrificed the Passover lamb" (Mark 14:12). Matthew concurs (Matt 26:17). Luke also agrees on the day and includes the reminder that the Passover lamb was sacrificed that day (Luke 22:7). John changes the timing but maintains the context of the Passover. At the conclusion of chapter 11, John tells us that Passover was near when the Lord's arrest was ordered. John begins the Last Supper by telling us it was right before Passover (John 13:1). The trial before Pilate and the crucifixion itself were held on the preparation day. John wants Jesus's death to coincide with the ritual sacrifice of the Passover lambs. Three times, John reminds his readers of the day of preparation (John 19:14; 19:31; 19:42). John uses references to the Passover lamb as literary bookends. In the second chapter of his Gospel, he records John the Baptist proclaiming, "Behold the Lamb of

God who takes away the sin of the world" (John 2:29). At that point in the narration, the exclamation is bizarre. Only when the reader gets to the other bookend, John's timing of the passion, does it make sense. As the passion begins, John has the death of Jesus occur at the time of the ritual sacrifice of the Passover lamb. The bookends make the entirety of John's Gospel unfold in the context of Passover liberation.

We learn more on the redefinition of power in God's kingdom. The Passover is the feast of liberation; the Passover lamb is nourishment for the journey into freedom. From the time of the Lord's crucifixion, all the power of all pharaohs becomes desacralized. One cannot claim God's approval for the use of power to manipulate, degrade, disenfranchise, or violate another. Control of others becomes sin. Based on a special relationship with God the Father, our Savior, imbued with freedom, invites us into the same freedom. As a result, power becomes the ransom of others. Power in the kingdom of God is employed to liberate.

The freedom enjoyed by Jesus of Nazareth seems like no other; it is a full, total freedom. It has a political dimension. The trial before Pontius Pilate makes the representative of the greatest political power the world had ever known look foolish and cowardly. Jesus's sense of freedom had a religious dimension: Jesus lived by the spirit not the letter of the law. He broke purity and cleanliness norms. He taught without religious credentials. Jesus forgave sin. He claimed a special relationship with God the Father. Jesus cleansed the temple. His teaching estranged him from the religion of his day; he was condemned by the Sanhedrin and the chief priests. In addition, Jesus removed himself from the patriarchal household and began a new, inclusive family of God's children. And he violated social boundaries, showing compassion even to his people's religious and political enemies. His full, total freedom was not anomie, lawlessness, or nihilism. His freedom had a transcendent quality to it. Social boundaries were broken to show God's love for all the suffering with no distinctions. He forgave sinners, even tax collectors and prostitutes, to emphasize his mission of inclusion, the in-gathering of all God's people. Religiously based social control is also abandoned for the sake of human freedom. His evocative teaching on the Sabbath reveals the Lord's intent: "The sabbath is made for man, not man for the sabbath" (Mark 2:27). His freedom to confront coercive power offers us the fullness of life and our own freedom, components of our salvation.

His executioners could not begin to understand his freedom. They may have feared the liberation of the people; they may have foreseen their loss of status. Whatever moved them, it became easy to accuse. In their dark hearts, his freedom looked like fanatical religiosity, political treason, or diabolical behavior (Mark 3:22). They interpreted his transcendent freedom as madness (Mark 3:21–22; John 10:20). Because of their reaction, we are shown the perfection of his freedom. He did not allow himself to be imprisoned by anger, hate, or the desire for revenge for his executioners' anger and hate. St. Luke makes this point most effectively. Jesus forgave his executioners from the cross (Luke 23:34).

The powerful of his day murdered Jesus. But the cross does not become a symbol of victimization; it should not drag us into victimization. The cross remains an act of self-giving. Jesus shows us how to stay above hate and anger even as detractors pull us into the ugliness. He teaches us how to avoid compromising our spirits even when faced with violent power (Matt 26:52). As he remains totally free, he inaugurates the freedom of the children of God (Gal 5:1).

This excavation of the meaning of the crucified God can go even deeper. The four evangelists agree that the cross reveals divinity and invites us to share in divinity. Crucifixion and Eucharist are intrinsically tied together. At the Last Supper, Mark, Matthew, and Luke record the words for the institution of the Eucharist. The cross, of course, is included. Here is Mark's record: "While they were eating, he took bread, said the blessing, broke it, and gave it to them, and said, 'Take it; this is my body.' Then he took a cup, gave thanks, and gave it to them, and they all drank from it. He said to them, 'This is my blood of the covenant, which will be shed for many'" (Mark 14:22–24). Luke writes about a cup before the consecrated bread and consecrated cup. To the offering of the bread, Luke adds, "This is my body, *which will be given for you; do this in memory of me.*" And when the cup is given to the disciples, he changes the word *many* to *you*. The blood is shed for you (Luke 22:14–20, emphasis added). Matthew follows Mark mostly but makes a significant addition after *many*; he adds *for the forgiveness of sins* (Matt 26:28), which is used at Mass. Matthew does not take the forgiveness of sin in the direction that Anselm took it, however. He does not imply a sacrifice to assuage a just or angry God. The words of institution communicate self-giving. Jesus gives us his body and gives us his blood for our transformation.

The self-giving of the Eucharist seems to connect with the words in the Philippian hymn, the words of *kenosis*. Recall Paul's quotation of the hymn:

> Rather, he emptied himself,
> taking the form of a slave,
> coming in human likeness;
> and found human in appearance,
> he humbled himself
> > becoming obedient to death,
> > even death on a cross. (Phil 2:7–8).

Imagine a two-tiered emptying. First, the Son of God empties himself of divinity. And then, Jesus of Nazareth empties himself of life. Both are for us. The words instituting the Eucharist seem to connect us to *kenosis* and, therefore, to the love, to *agape*, shared by God and his Son, which overflows into our hearts and souls. In John's version of the Last Supper, all these themes come together and culminate in these words. Jesus says, "I have told you this so that my joy may be in you and your joy may be complete. This is my commandment: love one another as I love you. No one has greater love than this, to lay down one's life for one's friends" (John 15:11–13).

The performatory truth of the crucified God can be discovered in these affinities: (1) The cross and the Eucharist are replete with Passover symbols. (2) The self-giving of Jesus and the emptying of divinity are connected and become expressions of God's love, of *agape*. (3) When we eat his body and drink his blood, God invites us into that love and into the freedom of God's children. The gift of liberation is beyond our imagining. Since we are united with God in that freedom, our free spirits anticipate infinity and eternity. No greater freedom can be known than the freedom that has an infinite, eternal horizon. We are set free over against all power that attempts to dominate us; we are set free to aspire toward an infinite horizon, to share divine life.

This is confirmed by one more affinity, one more connection. When Jesus dies on the cross, Mark has a centurion, a pagan soldier, exclaim, "Truly this man was the Son of God" (Mark 15:39). The question of Jesus's identity hangs over Mark's Gospel. The messianic secret in the first half keeps the reader engaged. Peter's confession revealing the truth behind that secret is about halfway through the text. Then, the Gospel moves forward from prediction to prediction to define the type of Messiah Jesus is. At his death, the Lord is finally identified as the Son of God. Earlier in the Gospel, a demon named Legion knows that Jesus is the "Son of the Most High God" (5:7). The demon is silenced when Jesus commands it to enter a herd of pigs that runs down a hill to be drowned in the sea (5:1–20).

Before the centurion, no human makes that identification. Most importantly, none of the disciples acknowledge what the centurion does. This makes the centurion's proclamation more dramatic. Even pagans can see that self-giving love for the salvation of others is divine.

In their own way, each of the evangelists communicates that the cross reveals divinity. Matthew adds elements of a theophany to Mark's account. The earth quakes, rocks are split, tombs are opened, and saints rise from the dead. Then Matthew records the centurion's proclamation (Matt 27:51–54). Luke omits the proclamation itself. He simply records that the centurion "glorified God" (Luke 23:47). Self-giving love is divine.

John had another way of taking us to the same place. In fact, John takes the sacred moment further by incorporating us into the divine life. Before his passion, Jesus declares that, when he is lifted up from the earth, he will draw everyone to himself (John 12:32). As Jesus is dying, he hands over his spirit to the disciples who are standing by the cross (John 19:30). When he dies, a soldier pierces his side (John 19:31–37). The water of baptism and the blood of the Eucharist sprinkle the first Christian assembly. From the cross, Jesus fulfills what he had said about the Eucharist in the sixth chapter: "Whoever eats my flesh and drinks my blood remains in me and I in him. Just as the living Father sent me and I have life because of the Father, so also the one who feeds on me will have life because of me" (John 6:56–57). We are united to Jesus and through him to the Father through the eucharistic remembrance of the cross. The self-giving love of Jesus lifts us into the divine life of Father and Son.

What does the cross mean for believers?

- No earthly power can claim a divine legitimation since the political and religious powers crucified the Lord. The murder of Jesus desacralizes all coercive power.

- We are offered a new definition of power for our lives in God's kingdom. Rejecting coercive power does not render us passive. The cross is active self-giving love for others. Power in the kingdom is service to others, or better, the ransom of others.

- The context of the Lord's crucifixion is the Passover feast. The Lord's giving of self is our liberation.

- The memory of saving liberation by divine intervention remains part of the Eucharist. Every Mass should bring it to consciousness.

The ultimate purpose of our self-giving should be the ransom of others.

- The cross and Eucharist are the self-giving of the life of Jesus of Nazareth. They remind us of the *kenosis* of God, the emptying of divinity, for our salvation. Both reflect divine love, *agape*. The Lord's self-giving allows us to abide in God.

- As he dies on the cross, Jesus's divinity shines through. We are invited into the divine life especially when we give of ourselves for others.

To complete the performatory truth of the crucified God, we must recall that we are called to take up the cross: disciples are to give ourselves out of love for others (Mark 8:34–38). John records an evocative image to define our ministry: "Amen, amen, I say to you, unless a grain of wheat falls to the ground and dies, it remains just a grain of wheat; but if it dies, it produces much fruit" (John 12:24). Perhaps, if each disciples lives the self-giving love of the cross and if the church uses only the Lord's definition of power, the Lord will draw all people to himself.

A undomesticated and despiritualized cross can lead us back to our starting point, to the idea that Jesus died for our sins. If we open ourselves to the full impact of the cross, our sins are put into stark relief. How many of our failures reject self-giving love, holding firm to our particularizing identities—my nation, my race, my gender identification, my religion, my class, my possessions, my power, my well-being, and my pleasure? Evil afflicts our lives when we allow those identities to make us feel superior to other people. Evil is inflicted on others when we attempt to force our likeness on others. Furthermore, so many of our sins result from grasping for more power, more wealth, more of the earth's resources. Many, perhaps most, of our sins result from serving the self. A meditation on the crucified God offers us the solution. The self-giving love of the cross is our salvation.

10

Rose Again and Ascended

WHENEVER I CONDUCT BIBLE classes, I need to disabuse believers of facticity questions: What really happened? Which evangelist is correct? I show them the differences in the biblical accounts. Where did Jesus preach his finest sermon—on the mount as in Matthew or on the plain as in Luke? Who was at the foot of the cross—a Roman centurion but no disciples according to Mark or a small assembly of disciples as in John? The questions cannot be resolved with recourse to facticity. I explain the transformation in the way people think. Modern historians ask *who, what, where,* and *when*. Only when the facts are established should moderns ask *why*. We are prisoners of our age. The gospels are premodern; they are theological texts. If they are history, they are history as purpose and meaning. The *why* question was first in the minds of the evangelists.

No event or series of events bend the factually inclined mind more than the Easter and ascension texts. No two biblical authors concur. Luke wrote both his Gospel and the Acts of the Apostles; how can a teacher explain his two different versions of the Lord's ascension? Both Mark and John have multiple endings to confuse things. And Paul records resurrection events that differ from the evangelists. I'll let the Scripture scholars sort all that out. Pastoral theology can try to discover the meaning established by the biblical authors and move on to the meaning of resurrection and ascension *for us*. What is St. Paul's newness of life? What is St. John's fullness of life and complete joy? When does eternal life begin? The stumbling block for pastoral theology is the lack of a common treatment of the resurrection and ascension by biblical authors. Pastoral theology, however, must ask what it means to live in Christ and share in resurrected life.

To get the full truth from these texts, we can examine three dimensions of the truth: (1) Each event has meaning in itself. One can contemplate the question, What does it mean that the God-man died on a cross, rose from the dead, and ascended into heaven? (2) One can expand on that question: What does the meaning in itself have to do with our salvation? (3) A third question is necessary for pastoral theology: What does the meaning in itself for our salvation have to do with the construction of self and society in our times?

For example, the pastoral meaning of the cross and resurrection may be expressed this way: To construct the Christian self, we must do what the Lord did. He died on the cross out of love that we might be saved. For us to take up the cross means that we give of ourselves out of love for others that they may enjoy a better life. The resurrection means that the life Jesus gave was returned to him miraculously. In our faith lives, resurrection means what we have given in love for others will be returned in ways beyond our wildest imaginings. Resurrected life invites us beyond the horizon of our dreams, hopes, even imaginings. Resurrected life, however, should not be pushed into some distant, unknown future—the next life or heaven, the second coming or the new creation after his return.[1] Resurrection and ascension are symbols of this-worldly transformation. They are symbols informing us that our life in self-giving love will bring us to the fullness of life and complete joy just as certainly as God raised Jesus from the dead.

Because each evangelist communicates the theological meaning he discerns, the effort to draw a generalized meaning from these events is difficult. It is not satisfying, however, to let each account stand on its own as if each author were explaining a unique event. We cannot settle for John's sense of resurrected life, for example, or Matthew's, or Mark's, or Luke's, or Paul's. Christ's resurrected life, which we share through baptism, must have common elements in which we participate. The texts have enough agreement to offer the meaning of resurrection and ascension for our faith lives. But it takes some legwork. It helps to bring the symbols in the texts together in *configurations*. Implications can be drawn from each configuration, and the whole—the performatory meaning of resurrection and ascension—comes into view.

---

1. Lohfink, *Jesus of Nazareth*, 24–34.

1. Configuration 1: Women going to the tomb, the empty tomb, and angelic instructions.
2. Configuration 2: Galilee, a hungry Lord, touching the resurrected body, locked doors, and instant disappearances.
3. Configuration 3: Ascension and omnipresence.

CONFIGURATION 1

All attempts to draw meaning from the resurrection texts begin with the women who go to the tomb and find it empty. The narratives have women in the leading roles. In the resurrection texts, Jesus was risen before the women arrive, and the tomb is empty. In most accounts, angelic figures offer instructions about the resurrection. Then, the tomb is left behind. In Matthew and Mark, the women flee from the tomb. In Luke, the women inform the disciples about the resurrection; the men are dismissive. Peter goes to the tomb, sees that it is empty, and returns home. In John, Mary of Magdala sees that the stone has been removed. She runs to tell Peter and the beloved disciple, who run to the tomb. They enter; they begin to believe; and they return home. Mary stays at the tomb. She encounters the risen Lord. She then goes to the disciples to proclaim the good news. The tomb itself is forgotten. Let's look at each Gospel.

Mark has Mary Magdalene, Mary, the mother of James, and Salome bring spices to the tomb to anoint the corpse (Mark 16:1–8). When they arrive, the stone has been rolled back. They enter the tomb and see a young man dressed in a white robe. The young man tells them of the resurrection. He instructs the women to tell the Lord's disciples. The women fail; instead, they flee. Mark writes *his* ending: "They said nothing to anyone, for they were afraid" (Mark 16:8).

This ending completes Mark's unique theology. Part of his purpose for composing the Gospel is to offer a basis for reconciling disciples who had failed. Every known disciple in Mark's Gospel fails. When Jesus is arrested, Mark writes, "And they all left him and fled" (Mark 14:50). He drives the point home by recording the tribulation of one young disciple. The crowd who arrested Jesus tried to seize the young man. He ran with such intensity that his clothing was torn off and he ran away naked (Mark 14:51). This scene is made even more dramatic because of Peter's protest that the disciples had given up everything to follow Jesus (Mark 10:28). There is poetry, then, when the scene with the naked young man is followed by the Lord's trial before the Sanhedrin, during which Peter denies the Lord three times. Only the women were left to follow Jesus to the cross. They stood off at a distance, however (Mark 15:40).

Mark's ending requires the reader's engagement with the text. An active reader asks something like this: If the only witnesses to the resurrection say nothing to anyone, how do we know about it? Since all disciples fail, including the women, the reader must conclude that the resurrected Lord somehow reconciled the disciples and empowered them to reconstitute the believing community. The disciples who fled when he was arrested, the young man running away naked, Peter's denial, the women leaving the tomb in fear: Mark drives home the point that disciples require reconciliation. Because all humans fail, the reader is left with the conclusion that reconciliation is a divine act. Mark's unique theology is vitally important: the Christian community requires the divine grace of ongoing reconciliation. The risen Lord is present to unite the community by forgiving and reconciling failed members.

Matthew records two women going to the tomb at dawn after the Sabbath, Mary Magdalene and the "other Mary." Repeating what happened when Jesus died, Matthew writes that "there was a great earthquake" as an angel of the Lord descends from heaven and rolls back the stone (Matt 28:2). The guards go numb with fear. The angel instructs the women about the resurrection. He asks them to speak to the disciples about a meeting in Galilee. The women are fearful but overjoyed (Matt 28:8). They leave the tomb and do as the angel requested. On their way to the disciples, the women are the first disciples to meet the risen Lord (Matt 28:9). They worship him. He repeats the request for a meeting of the disciples in Galilee. Before recounting the Galilee appearance, Matthew tells what became of the guards, how they were bribed to lie about what had happened to Jesus's body (Matt 28:11–15).

In Luke, a larger group of women goes to the tomb: Mary Magdalene, Joanna, Mary the mother of James, and unnamed others. They are from Galilee and are followers of Jesus. When they arrive at the tomb, the stone has been rolled back. They enter the tomb. Two men in dazzling garments appear. They remind the women of what Jesus taught while he was still in Galilee. The women leave the tomb to tell the disciples. The eleven dismiss the women for speaking nonsense (Luke 24:11). Only Peter gives them the benefit of the doubt. He goes off to the tomb.

Luke uses geography to convey his unique theology. Jesus took the good news from Galilee to Jerusalem. After the good news arrives at the center of Judaism, Galilee is recalled but recedes into the past. After the resurrection, the disciples stay in Jerusalem until they receive the Spirit. Then they take the good news from Jerusalem to Rome, the power center of the known world. Luke's point? The progress of the gospel is continuous.

In John, only Mary of Magdala goes to the tomb. The stone had been removed. She does not enter, but she goes to Peter and the beloved disciple. Those two run to the tomb. Peter enters the tomb first; the beloved disciple follows. After they see the empty tomb, they return home (John 20:10). Mary stays near the tomb. The risen Lord appears to her, but she does not recognize him. She inquires what he may have done with Jesus's body. All at once, Jesus makes himself known to her (John 20:14). She attempts to embrace the Lord. Jesus says, "Stop holding on to me" (John 20:17). He is ascending to the Father. In John's theology, resurrection and ascension are one movement. The appearances of the resurrected Lord to all the disciples except to Mary are post-ascension. This allows John to establish an ongoing, never interrupted, and never-ending presence of the resurrected Lord. The tomb is forgotten after Mary announces to the disciples that she has seen the Lord.

In this first configuration, I think there are two areas for our contemplation. All four Gospels tell of the importance of women in conveying the good news of the resurrection. Especially because males dominate discipleship in the Gospels, one cannot miss the women of the resurrection. Could this be a symbol of the inclusiveness of the earliest church? Recall what St. Paul wrote in his Letter to the Galatians around 53–54 CE: "For all of you who were baptized into Christ have clothed yourselves with Christ. There is neither Jew nor Greek, there is neither slave nor free person, there is not male and female; for you are all one in Christ Jesus" (Gal 3:27–28). The resurrection signals the beginning of a new creation first predicted by the prophets. They foretold a harmonious existence in God's new creation. Equality may be part of that harmony—Jew and gentile, slave and free person, male and female. If the early church was, in fact, inclusive, the power of patriarchy soon blotted out the memory. The realization of the dream of harmony, however, demands we deal honestly with this memory in our times.

The other matter emerging from this configuration is the empty tomb. The angelic figures direct the disciples away from the tomb. They are to meet the risen Lord elsewhere. They are not to assemble in that shrine to violence and torture, that place of death. Disciples are not to waste energy over this world's temporary victory. Matthew helps make the point when he tells us of the soldiers who were supposed to guard the tomb. They fell as if dead when the angel rolled back the stone. The Jewish leadership bribed the soldiers to lie about what had happened. The powers of this world may be cunning. They may enjoy temporary success. But the gospel of resurrected life triumphs. Not until the fourth century—about when the church began to accumulate imperial power—was a shrine built over the tomb.

The church is not to become a cult of victimization—not then, not now! The death of Jesus and the subsequent martyrdom of the saints can embarrass living Christians. With some notable exceptions, the church is secure in this world. Discipleship is not so costly. Still, the cross upends our comfort. Instead of understanding the command to take up the cross as a way of life—giving of self out of love for the benefit of others—some see the cross factually. Some Christian leaders relish playing the victim. Some even imagine becoming martyrs. Many in leadership assume a counter) role. Here's the problem: victimization is dispiriting; it darkens our mood and clouds our vision. Others, those who differ, are imagined as persecutors and enemies. Therefore, victimization keeps us from seeing the good in others and from noting the developments toward the good in this world. We cannot participate in resurrected life if we are stuck at the tomb.

At dawn on the day of the resurrection, the tomb was empty; supernatural forces appearing as angels sent disciples away from it. The church has an option other than victimization and countercultural pushing and shoving. St. Paul offers us words from which we can take courage: "It is Christ [Jesus] who died, rather, was raised, who also is at the right hand of God, who indeed intercedes for us. What will separate us from the love of Christ? Will anguish, or distress, or persecution, or famine, or nakedness, or peril, or the sword? . . . No, in all these things we conquer overwhelmingly through him who loved us" (Rom 8:34b–37). Secure in his love, we can leave behind the empty tomb and develop a persuasive vision of resurrected life.

CONFIGURATION 2

The second configuration displays the obvious strain on language to convey these events. Some commentators try to explain the Easter appearances.[2] The texts, as they are, hand on to us saturated events, *sui generis* revelations. Out of an excess of meaning, a believing reader can take lessons to deepen a relationship with the risen Christ. The events in themselves should not be rationalized. The texts are revelation; we should hear them speak.

The texts of the resurrection and ascension communicate two dimensions simultaneously: a spiritual dimension and a physical, material dimension. By spiritual, I mean a supernatural happening, something beyond the laws of nature. The risen Lord could pass through locked barriers. He could be seen and not recognized but then suddenly known. He could disappear at will. Something beyond the normal took place in the risen Lord's appearances. Resurrected life seems to burst human limitations so those who share resurrection—read, the baptized—can enjoy a life of possibility.

Just as interesting—and vital for us—is the physical, material, and familiar dimensions that are also part of these appearances. The revealed possibilities are in this world. Let's look at the material dimension of the resurrection appearances.

The return to Galilee must be noted. St. Luke has multiple references to Galilee in his text but does not have disciples return there. His unique theology pushes the Gospel always forward. It will not allow for a return to the past in Galilee. The other evangelists insist on returning to the Lord's home. Mark tells us that the women who had come to the tomb were told to arrange a meeting in Galilee. They fail. Other authors added endings to Mark's Gospel to affirm the Galilee meeting. Matthew tells us the overjoyed women did arrange the reunion in Galilee. The eleven went to the stipulated mountain. They encounter the risen Lord there.

John has two endings. The first is in chapter 20. The appearances of the resurrected Lord are in Jerusalem. After Mary Magdalene meets the risen Lord just outside the tomb (John 20:11–18), she goes to the disciples to proclaim her encounter. Jesus meets the disciples on the evening of that same day. He reveals himself a week later, dispelling all doubts. The second ending in chapter 21 takes place on the shores of the Lake of Tiberias, also known as the Sea of Galilee. The second ending all but ignores the resurrection appearances in the first. It implies that

---

2. Lohfink offers an interesting explanation of the resurrection appearances. I do not think such efforts are necessary to uncover life lessons for Christian living. In fact, all of them I have read take us too far into the realm of conjecture. Lohfink, *Jesus of Nazareth*, 294.

the disciples went back to their occupations after the crucifixion. Galilee was familiar. It was home. Family and friends were left there when the disciples journeyed with Jesus.

The location had theological meaning as well. Matthew (4:12–16) records what is found in Isaiah (Isa 8:23–9:1). In the time of the prophet, Galilee became the first region of Israel conquered by the Assyrians. Isaiah predicts a restoration. When Jesus begins his ministry, Matthew quotes the prophet: "Galilee of the Gentiles, the people who have walked in darkness have seen a great light, on those dwelling in a land overshadowed by death light has arisen" (Matt 4:15–16). After he has risen, Galilee meets its Savior.

This much is certain: Galilee is a place on a map. To the disciples, Galilee is home and a place to make a livelihood. In the first century, it was a place of diversity, Galilee of the gentiles. It had a painful history. After the Assyrians came the Babylonians, then the Persians, then the Greeks, and then the Romans. In Jesus's time, Galilee was oppressed by the Romans and governed by the Herodians. The beginning of the Lord's ministry was there. At the end, the resurrected Lord brings his light to that place.

The simple reality of place opens our eyes to other common, everyday matters that are caught up in the resurrection. The resurrected Lord invites touch. In John 20:17, Mary of Magdala seems to embrace the Lord. The risen Christ prevents the embrace because he was completing his upward journey to the Father. Later that same day, when Jesus appears to his fearful disciples, he shows them his hands and his feet (John 20:20). A week later, Jesus invites doubting Thomas to put his finger in the wounds of his hands and his hand in the gash in his side (John 20:27). In Luke, during his final meeting with the disciples, the risen Lord also invites touch: "Touch me and see, because a ghost does not have flesh and bone as you see I have" (Luke 24:39). In Matthew, the two women meet the risen Lord on their way to inform the disciples of the resurrection. "They [the women] approached, embraced his feet, and did him homage" (Matt 28:9).

The risen Christ demonstrates another everyday feature: he gets hungry. On the road to Emmaus, Jesus accepts an invitation to dine with two fleeing disciples (Luke 24:13–35). At table, Jesus transforms the supper into Eucharist, perhaps the original format of Christian Eucharist (1 Cor 11:17–22). Later that same day, when Jesus meets with the eleven, he asks for food: "'Have you anything here to eat?' They gave him a piece of baked fish; he took it and ate it in front of them" (Luke 24:41–43). In the second ending of John (chapter 21), Jesus appears at dawn on the banks of the Lake of Tiberias. The disciples had returned to their former occupation. Jesus notices that they had failed to catch anything. He arranges a miraculous catch. The risen Lord had already started a charcoal fire and was cooking fish and toasting bread. Jesus asks the disciples to contribute newly caught fish for the breakfast. Jesus serves the meal with gestures recalling the Eucharist (John 21:1–14).

Place, touch, and food, then, show continuity. The Risen Lord is Jesus of Nazareth. They also communicate a this-worldly reality to resurrected life. Resurrection affects this world, the flow of history, our material well-being. Combined, the material and spiritual say that the resurrection is transformational. The new creation is unfolding in place and time. Resurrected life lifts us into a new mode of being human in this world.

The incarnation insists the divine is present to us: Emmanuel, God in the flesh, God in time and place, in history, in us. Resurrection and ascension make the arrangement eternal. The wonder of resurrected life informs us that life is more than a valley of tears, more than an exile, much more than a test, a trial, or a battle. We are not to return to the tomb. The kingdom of God is at hand; we can be baptized into the newness of life and live for God in Christ Jesus (Rom 6:1–11). Constructed in the resurrected Christ, constructed in self-giving love, the everyday can be holy. In it, we can find goodness, beauty, truth, and sanctity. Resurrected life informs us that what we have given of ourselves out of love carries us to God.

CONFIGURATION 3

If the resurrection texts bend the mind, the endings of the Gospels must send fundamentalists and the factually inclined into orbit. The endings, however, contain necessary truths for us.

Mark's own ending (Mark 16:8) excludes resurrection appearances and the ascension. Some Christians must have been upset; someone added a more acceptable ending. Most of the material is borrowed. The author yanked some materials out of their original contexts (Luke 10:18–19). They placed it in the resurrection texts, stressing the post-resurrection empowerment of disciples. The resurrected Jesus says, "These signs will accompany those who believe: in my name they will drive out demons, they will speak new languages. They will pick up serpents [with their hands], and if they drink any deadly thing, it will not harm them. They will lay hands on the sick, and they will recover" (Mark 16:17–18). The resurrected Lord, then, ascends into heaven to take his seat "at the right hand of God" (Mark 16:19). The image of Jesus sitting on God's right is shorthand for the assertion that the resurrected Lord is everywhere as God is everywhere. The last verse of the new ending underscores his omnipresence: "They went forth and preached everywhere, while *the Lord worked with them and confirmed the word through accompanying signs*" (Mark 16:20, emphasis added). The ascension does not create a spiritual void. The Lord is not absent. He remains to empower disciples for the mission.

Matthew's ending is similar. Jesus meets with the eleven on a mountaintop. The risen Lord empowers the eleven: "All power in heaven and on earth has been given to me. Go, therefore, and make disciples of all nations" (Matt 28:19). The mission to "all nations" is significant. Earlier, Jesus had sent his disciples only to the lost sheep of the house of Israel (Matt 10:6). And he said to a Canaanite woman, "I was sent only to the lost sheep of the house of Israel" (Matt 15:24). The magi from the East and Jesus's outreach to gentiles, the unclean, and sinners hinted that the mission was to expand. After the resurrection, the empowered disciples are to take the mission to everyone. There is no ascension in Matthew. Instead, we find the promise of ongoing presence: "And behold, I am with you always until the end of the age" (Matt 28:20).

In neither of John's two endings do we find an ascension. Unique to John's theology, the resurrection and ascension appear as one movement to the Father. Except for the appearance to Mary of Magdala, the risen Lord's appearances happen after the ascension. Both endings are from a narrator. Both affirm that he had written enough that we will enjoy "life in his name" (John 20:31). This implies that the resurrected Christ remains present; he remains "the way and the truth and the life" (John 14:6).

Luke gives us two accounts of the ascension. The ending of the Gospel takes place on the same day as the resurrection. The risen Lord meets with his disciples. He tells them of the mission to all nations beginning in Jerusalem. He also tells them of their empowerment: "And behold I am sending the promise of my Father upon you" (Luke 24:49). They go out to Bethany where the risen Lord is taken up to heaven. At the beginning of the Acts of the Apostles, Luke offers us another version of the ascension. Forty days pass between the resurrection and the ascension in this account. The disciples meet with the risen Lord on Mt. Olivet, which is near Jerusalem. The disciples ask the risen Lord when the liberation and restoration of Israel would happen. At the beginning of his mission, Jesus had defined his ministry as a mission of liberation (Luke 4:18–19). In his final moments on earth, he affirms that liberation remains in his saving plan. Then, the risen Lord promises empowerment: "You will receive power when the Holy Spirit comes upon you" (Acts 1:8). Jesus is lifted up and a cloud takes him out of sight. Angels chide the eleven: "Men of Galilee, why are you standing there looking at the sky?" (Acts 1:11). The angels promise a second coming of Jesus. Luke has logic on his side—perhaps this is the reason the church adopted his version for its feast days. The risen Lord's physical appearances stopped. The ascension explains why. The coming of the Spirit, however, reassures all disciples of the divine presence. A promise of a second coming offers disciples hope for the completion of God's kingdom and the realization of the dream of freedom.

The endings of the Gospels assure believers of ongoing divine support for a mission to all nations. The ministry of Jesus of Nazareth that began in Galilee now continues by the empowered disciples. The endings of the Gospels tell us of this truth: the saving God is present to us in this world for the mission to this world.

The performative truth of the resurrection and ascension assists us to understand newness of life, fullness of life, complete joy, and eternal life. These images are transformational. They offer believers a dynamic future. In the resurrected Lord, this world is preparing for the world that is coming. In him, each disciple is changing in preparation for total unity with God.

It is crucial we locate resurrected life in this world. We must still anticipate total fulfillment at the end—our personal end and the end of the age. The resurrected Lord, however, is now present to us. Scripture scholar Daniel Harrington wrote these words in his commentary on Matthew: "An event reserved for the end of human history has happened in the midst of human history. In the special case of Jesus, God has shown his eschatological power by raising Jesus. To this extent at least the Kingdom of God is among us."[3] Resurrection and ascension transport us into the end time. They situate the end time, however, in our times. The end

---

3. Harrington, *Gospel of Matthew*, 413.

of history is in history. Becoming literal about the word *end* is a mistake. The end is not the annihilation or destruction of world or the universe. The end is the goal, the fulfillment, the purpose that continues to unfold, that continues to draw us forward into Christ. The spiritualized physicality of the resurrected Jesus invites us to imagine and strive for our fulfillment in this world.

Theologian Karl Rahner points us in the same direction. The resurrection compels us to consider the essential unity of the physical and spiritual. Rahner writes, "For basically speaking, it is inconceivable either in terms of modern anthropology or biblical anthropology that there should be any absolute division between a fate which we attribute to the physical side of the human being and the fate which he undergoes at the spiritual level and in his personhood."[4] Elsewhere, he writes of the impact of the resurrection itself on our spiritual-physical reality: "For he rose again in his body. That means he has already begun to transform this world into himself. He has accepted the world forever. He has been born as a child of the earth, but of the transfigured, liberated earth, the earth which in him is eternally confirmed and eternally redeemed from death and futility."[5] In the same article, he invites us to remain at home in this world and to unite with God in this world. The resurrection of Jesus makes this-worldly salvation conceivable: "We, therefore, do not need to leave it [this world]. For God's life dwells in it. If we seek the God of infinity (and how could we fail to?) *and* the familiar earth as it is and as it is to become, in order to be our eternal home in freedom, then one way leads to both. For in the Lord's resurrection God has shown that he has taken the earth to himself forever."[6]

When Matthew breaks the narrative about the resurrected Lord with the bribery of the guards of the tomb, he is not simply tying up loose ends (Matt 28:11–15). When Luke tells us that the disciples asked Jesus about the liberation of Israel right before the ascension, he is not showing us how obtuse the disciples are (Acts 1:6–7). And the angelic warning not to stare up at the sky is not a bit of humor breaking the solemnity of the Lord's leaving (Acts 1:11). All three suggest that end-time salvation is now, in history. All three help to define the mission resulting from the Lord's resurrection. God is taking the earth to himself forever. Liberation *from* the old order of violence, oppression, sin, and death is possible;

---

4. Rahner, *Content of the Faith*, 311.
5. Rahner, *Content of the Faith*, 320–21.
6. Rahner, *Content of the Faith*, 322.

liberation *to* aspire to God's goodness is open to us. Sadly, liberation from the old order does not immunize us from those who would abuse, manipulate, oppress, and use violence against us. After all, we are uniting with Christ who was crucified. A meditation on the cross and resurrection of Jesus, however, keeps us from a greater sadness. It liberates us from any proclivity we might have to abuse, manipulate, oppress, and do violence to another. The meditation will unlock for us the possibility of living in God's goodness.

Resurrection and ascension have an upward motion. We might write off this movement as a reference to the cosmos before Galileo, to an earth sandwiched between heaven and hell. Instead, the upward movement might be an invitation to experience the vertical dimension of life, a transcendent tug toward a mystical bond with the divine in this world. For the individual Christian, the vertical tug means being lifted out of the tomb of the self to connect with and participate in the consecration of this world. As Rahner insists, it is the path to liberation and ultimate freedom. Ultimate freedom is imaginable because unity with God is our end. In Christ, our horizon continually recedes into infinity. Life becomes eternal. The resurrected Lord is always with us; he is raising us to the newness of life.

A pastoral minister needs to learn the language of the higher things, of the vertical dimension. By preaching and teaching the resurrected Lord, we might facilitate the creation of the mystical bond with the earth and with humankind. The bond may be the foundation for the re-creation of all that is. From the times of the prophets, a harmonious new creation has been foretold. The resurrection of Jesus is the beginning. Rahner wrote that we are eternally redeemed from death and futility. What we give of ourselves in love is never lost. Our love renews the earth and carries us to God.

11

Come Again in Glory

SIX HUNDRED YEARS OF foreign occupation taught Israel how to preserve the faith and engender hope through terrible times. Assyrians, Babylonians, Persians, Greeks, and Romans left their mark. Israel kept the faith. Through the centuries, authors who opposed the oppressors or predicted victory over them likely came to a quick and painful end (Dan 3). To communicate hope, Israel invented apocalyptic literature. Over-the-top imaginative, symbolic language allowed Israel to hide a hopeful message from the occupiers while invigorating the faith of believers. Victory over the oppressors would come in God's time.

I don't know what percentage of Jewish believers were in on the game. Christians restructured the genre by identifying the coming Son of Man with the second coming of the Lord. End-time prophecy had an intense immediacy; the second coming was to occur during the lives of the first two generations of Christians. Paul had to deal with the Lord's delay by the middle of the first century. The prediction that not all the original disciples would die before the second coming is found in Mark 13:30 and its parallels, Matt 24:34 and Luke 21:32. References are also found in Matt 10:23 and John 21:20–23. Not all Christians understood the imaginative nature of the literature, however. The second coming seems to be a divine promise stuck in a dystopian fantasia. The literature can be taught in a manner that raises anxiety and fear. This world becomes a place of immorality and strife, a battleground with overpowering evil. Jesus needs to return to set things right.

Literalism can turn the imaginative into the real. Literalism affects the doctrine even now. I don't think my formation was unusual. In my youth, the apocalyptic literature was taught as fact; the terror and destruction, the second coming, and the last judgment frightened us. Only in seminary courses did I learn of the symbolic quality of the literature. Only then could I read it as a literature of hope. Most believers and far too many preachers do not enjoy such training. These days, I wonder about the motives of teachers and preachers who insist on a literal meaning of apocalyptic texts. I am sometimes amused and sometimes repulsed by those identifying current events with specific verses of the texts. I know they can generate fear, and fear can be used for social control. Fear might keep a few people in the pews.

A factual or fundamentalist interpretation of the literature needs to account for one obvious fact: a delay of two millennia is more than a delay. Except for a few Sundays a year, only fundamentalist Christians are likely to concentrate on the end-times. To Catholics, a homily on the second coming as a future event immediately gives way to the Liturgy of the Eucharist that celebrates the presence of the Lord that very day. Can Jesus be more present than in the Real Presence?

The purpose of apocalyptic literature is to engender hope. It is not a prophecy, however. It does not forecast the future. The authors targeted their present. They knew the members of their faith communities were enduring hardship in the moment. The literature offers assurance that God remains present even as believers face contemporary catastrophes. It is the assertion, against all contrary evidence, that the God of Israel has been, is, and will be the God of salvation. Cardinal Martini writes, "It is not a frustration with the present, but rather the prolongation of an experience of fullness—in other words, 'salvation,' as it was construed by the early church. There isn't now, nor will there be, a power human or satanic that can challenge the hope of believers."[1] A pastoral perspective that is honest with the text needs to restore reassuring hope in the present tense. If the literature means anything to us, the immediacy of hope needs to be restored. Violence, chaos, and evil are present. But evil cannot overwhelm good. The devil, the symbol of all evil, is not God's equal. God's saving presence is working. As a result, judgment and the end-time must become present tense. We are judged by the world we are currently constructing. The end is our fulfillment; knowing it allows us to strive in the present to

---

1. Eco and Martini, *Belief or Unbelief?*, 20.

reach it. The combination should do what this literature did: inspire an active hope, a hope that true Christian engagement with the world leads to a new heaven and new earth. Cardinal Martini makes three points necessary for the contemporary church's reading of these texts:

1. History has a meaning, a direction, and is not a heap of absurd, vain facts.
2. This meaning is not purely immanent but extends beyond itself and thus is not a matter for calculation but for hope.
3. This vision does not extenuate but solidifies the meaning of contingent events into an ethical locus in which the meta-historical future of the human adventure is determined.[2]

Throughout the twentieth and twenty-first centuries, the world has suffered apocalyptic-level catastrophes. Perhaps we have lost hope in meaningful history and an ethical locus guiding the human adventure. In 1997, Umberto Eco listed contemporary calamities:

> Uncontrolled and uncontrollable proliferation of nuclear waste, acid rain, the disappearing Amazon, the hole in the ozone, the migrating disinherited masses knocking, often with violence, at the doors of prosperity, the hunger of entire continents, new, incurable pestilence, the selfish destruction of the soil, global warming, melting glaciers, the construction of our own clones through genetic engineering, and, according to mystical principles of ecology, the necessary suicide of humanity itself.[3]

Years later, the list remains frightening. Had he written today, little would be subtracted, and he could have added economic depressions and recessions, unimaginable destructions in countless wars, the reemergence of communist and fascist dictators, genocide, terrorism, AIDS, and COVID, the growing gap between the rich and the poor, and those with wealth paralyzing democratic governments from responding to crisis after crisis. Many of our social institutions have failed or are thought to have failed. On top of it all, modern culture has created mind-numbing entertainment that is always on our devices to help us avoid genuine problems—the new opiate of the people.

I am not sure whether a similar list could be composed in other periods in history. It must be acknowledged that a catalogue of the worst

---

2. Eco and Martini, *Belief or Unbelief?*, 31.
3. Eco and Martini, *Belief or Unbelief?*, 21.

without a comparable one on human progress is misleading. Disingenuous political and religious demagoguery occur without balance. A question remains: Are there lessons in the apocalyptic texts and the promise of the second coming to give Christians hope for our times? Can they provide a Christian ethic on which to construct a future? To answer these questions, a pastoral response needs to search the texts for three insights:

- What is a Christian response to apocalyptic-level destruction and chaos?
- What does *judgment* mean?
- Is there an *end*?

A CHRISTIAN RESPONSE TO CHAOS AND DESTRUCTION

Matthew's Gospel offers disciples guidance for trying times. When Jesus sends his disciples on their first mission, the Lord anticipates the world's negative response. He directs them to endure to the end (Matt 10:22). He warns his disciples to fear only those who can kill the soul (Matt 10:28). Later, when Matthew records Jesus's apocalyptic teaching, he warns disciples that the pressure of the times can cause disciples to hate one another (Matt 24:10). And he warns that evil may cause the love of many to grow cold (Matt 24:12). The contemporary church still needs these lessons.

The Revelation of John presents the Son of Man's critique of seven churches (chs. 2–3). The Son of Man notes the strengths and weakness of each church. Wilfrid Harrington writes, "John is not addressing an abstract 'Church'; he speaks directly to communities of men and women, communities good, bad, and indifferent. The messages peg Revelation firmly to our world. It is a word of hope addressed to people who need hope, people who may falter. The messages, like so much of the New Testament, bring us encouragement."[4]

The Son of Man critiques seven churches. The churches in Smyrna and Philadelphia received praise. The negative critiques of the other five hint at a framework for a Christian response to troubled times.

The church in Ephesus performed its good works, had endurance, did not tolerate wickedness in its midst, and tested the authenticity of

---

4. Harrington, *Revelation*, 56.

leaders. But the original love (*agape*) of the community had been lost and its works deteriorated over the years.

The church in Pergamum sustained the faith even though they lived where Satan's throne is. Some of its members, however, were tempted into idolatry and heresy. The city was a center of emperor worship. Christians who abstained from emperor worship were considered disloyal to the empire and subversive. Under threat, some Christians participated in the cult.

Thyatira was praised for its works, love, faith, service, and endurance. In fact, their last works were better than their first. The problem in the community was assimilation. An influential prophetess pushed them in that direction. Harrington says the question was "conformity to the prevailing culture for the sake of economic survival or social acceptance."[5]

The church in Sardis had a good reputation, but the Son of Man thought they were a dead community. The good works in which they once engaged were dying. They needed to awaken.

Laodicea was a wealthy town. The church relied on wealth for its self-image. The Son of Man critiqued the church for being lukewarm. Relying on the sources of the town's wealth—garment making, a medicine for eyes, and banking—became the problem. To the Son of Man, such faith was naked, blind, and poor.

Chaos, violence, and destruction can move individual believers and the church community to abandon the good news. In addition, individual believers and the church can be pulled into the times. The church can try to fight fire with fire, using the methods of those causing the chaos, violence, and destruction. It can use coercive power as politicians do. It can use the techniques of the wealthy to shape society at the expense of the poor. The marks of success of the wealthy and powerful can be imagined by inauthentic church leaders as the marks of success of the church. Scripture names the symptoms of failure: if we use the ways of the world, the love of many will grow cold, divisions will cause disciples to hate one another, and individuals may experience the death of their souls.

We can learn from Matthew and John how to create an ethic for our apocalyptic times. These lessons are implied in the evaluations of the churches:

---

5. Harrington, *Revelation*, 66.

- The Christians must never be robbed of a sense of agency to construct self and society. The Christian self must always be imagined as free to act. The believer, then, must be steadfast in good works, in self-giving love.
- The goodness of love is the Christian response to evil. Inclusion, understanding, and tolerance are required to offset division and prejudice. Peaceful nonviolence is the Christian answer to aggression.
- The love of truth is the antidote for deceit and propaganda. The witness given by charity and compassion makes a lie of consumerism. Self-giving love is how a Christian faces off against hate.
- When evil intensifies, Christians need to deepen their commitment. In tough economic times, for instance, more charity is required. When political leaders deceive, the search for truth must increase.
- Apocalyptic literature warns us repeatedly to persevere. In troubled times, it is necessary to hold fast to the cross, to *agape*.

The active Christian self is constructed by affirming Christ's presence. In the first chapter of Revelation, the author repeatedly commends reflections on the presence of the risen Christ. In v. 4, we receive a greeting "from him who is and who was and who is to come." In v. 8, the Son of Man makes himself known: "'I am the Alpha and the Omega,' says the Lord God, 'the one who is and who was and who is to come, the almighty.'" And in vv. 17 and 18, the Son of Man says: "Do not be afraid. I am the first and the last, the one who lives." The presence of Christ makes possible our endurance and inspires our good works. Christ's love is the response to any threat to the community. Because Christ is present, love intensifies, and our souls enjoy salvation.

I believe this is the performatory reading of the Lord's predictions of a second coming. Matthew introduces the coming of the Son of Man with these words: "*Immediately* after the tribulation of those days . . ." (Matt 24:29, emphasis added). He follows the prediction with the lesson of the fig tree: "In the same way, when you see all these things, know that *he is near, at the gates*" (Matt 24:33, emphasis added). Then, he gives us assurance of Christ's presence: "Heaven and earth will pass away, but my words will not pass away" (Matt 24:35). Matthew purposely confuses the time frame: "But of that day and hour no one knows, neither the angels in heaven, nor the Son, but the Father alone" (Matt 24:36). After Matthew presents the tribulations, the assurance of the Lord's presence, and then confuses the time frame, he records three parables that warn Christians to stay awake and be prepared and affirms the need to act. The parables present a stark contrast between those Christians who persevere and those who do not. Christians are warned in the parables of the faithful and unfaithful servant (Matt 24:45–51); the ten virgins, five wise and five foolish (Matt 25:1–13); the talents, the two servants who invest their master's funds wisely and the one who buries the funds (Matt 25:14–30). Christians are required to engage with the world using the example of Jesus of Nazareth. The works of self-giving love must give witness to the God of love. If believers persevere, we become participants in the new creation.

Judgment

When the final judgment is presented to Catholic audiences, the most likely text is the judgment of the nations in Matt 25:31–46. On judgment, however, Matthew's Gospel is complicated. It contains these judgment scenes:

1. Matthew 19:28–30 records the judgment of Israel. The apostles participate as judges. Jesus demands that they become qualified (20:24–28). Because the Son of Man came to serve, a judge is made worthy through service.
2. Matthew 24:1–2 contains a judgment on the temple. Before the prediction of its destruction, Jesus describes false and dangerous forms of religion. He also foretells the destruction of the city of Jerusalem, whose leaders resisted the all-inclusive in-gathering of God's people.
3. Matthew 24:29–31 records the coming of the Son of Man to gather in the elect, the church.
4. Matthew 25:31–46 communicates the coming of the Son of Man to judge the nations.

The judgment of the twelve tribes of Israel presupposes that Israel has heard the gospel of self-giving love. Such love is the criterion for judgment: "When the Son of Man is seated on his throne of glory, [you apostles] will yourselves sit on twelve thrones judging the twelve tribes of Israel. And everyone who has given up houses or brothers or sisters or father or mother or children or lands for the sake of my name will receive a hundred times more, and will inherit eternal life. But many who are first will be last, and the last will be first" (Matt 19:28–30). The judging apostles must qualify: "whoever wishes to be first among you shall be your slave. Just so the Son of Man did not come to be served but to serve and to give his life for the ransom for many" (Matt 20:26–28).

The apostles' qualifications take on heightened importance in the judgment on the temple. Jesus attacks false forms of religion before the prediction about the temple. The antagonism between Jesus and the religious leadership of his time may be historically factual. It explains why the religious leadership joined the Roman oppressors to destroy Jesus. But Matthew may have had other reasons for recording the tension. After the destruction of the temple (CE 70), Christians were expelled from synagogues and may have held deep resentment. Writing about a decade after the temple's destruction, Matthew may not have had in mind the Jewish leadership but may have been warning Christian leaders of dangerous forms of religiosity. By then, some Christians leaders may have needed such lessons. Daniel Harrington affirms the factuality of the denunciations but adds, "The prophetic warnings of Jesus in Matt 23:13–31 can serve as a checklist for all who exercise leadership in church or synagogue. Excessive casuistry, misplaced priorities, overemphasis on externals, etc., are found in every religious denomination."[6] This also remains a lesson for contemporary church leadership. As problems increase for the church in the world, Christian service must remain the norm for the leaders.

The gathering of the elect—the gathering of Christians—occurs in Matt 24:29–30. The preceding chapters serve as the criteria for the ingathering. And the event is followed by parables that separate the elect from nominal Christians, the parables of the faithful or unfaithful servants, the wise and foolish virgins, and the talents. The whole reinforces an earlier teaching from the Sermon on the Mount: "Not everyone who says to me, 'Lord, Lord' will enter the kingdom of heaven, but only the one who does the will of my Father in heaven. Many will say to me on that day, 'Lord, Lord, did we not prophesy in your name? Did we not drive out demons in your name? Did we not do mighty deeds in your name?' Then I will declare to them solemnly, 'I never knew you. Depart from me, you evildoers'" (Matt 7:21–23). Christians who retreat from the mission to consecrate this world are judged harshly, even if they prophesy, perform miracles, or drive out demons. Active Christian engagement is required.

---

6. Harrington, *Gospel of Matthew*, 327.

This brings us to the final judgment scene, the judgment of the nations (Matt 25: 31–46). Two questions are required for interpreting this passage: Who are *the nations*? And who are *the least brothers of mine*? Preachers often make *the nations* to be all people, living and dead. And the *least of the brothers* are the world's poor, hungry, thirsty, naked, and so forth. But that may not be the meaning intended by Matthew. Since Israel and the elect are already judged, the *nations* may be those who have not heard the gospel, who are not convinced by its preachers, or who drop away because of flaws in the church. The *least brothers* may be Christian believers undergoing hard times, having been ostracized from family and friends, or having been persecuted by religious and political leaders. The text identifies Christ with the brethren in need. The identification of the church with Christ is well attested to in Scripture. This passage may reward nonbelievers who care for Christ in the persons of needy Christians.

If this is a correct interpretation, a couple deductions are possible. Many Christians ask whether those who leave the church or who never become Christian can be saved. The answer is yes. Their salvation is based on lessons from the first three chapters of Genesis. All people are created in the image of God (Gen 1:26), and all people carry the breath of God within them (Gen 2:7). All people are drawn to goodness, therefore. Those who live that goodness—those who are decent, caring, and humane—are saved. Those who are kind to Christ's body, the church, will enjoy eternal life. Of course, this requires the church to seek real interaction with all people of goodwill, even those who do not practice our religion.

The identification of *the least brothers* with the church carries an implied judgment on the church. The elect and the people of God have heard God's word and are witnesses to the cross. In the closing of Matthew's Gospel, disciples are sent to the nations being judged in chapter 25. If the disciples are unfaithful servants, or foolish virgins, or ones who bury their talent, the nations will not be drawn to Christ's body. In John's Gospel, Jesus says the cross will draw all people to himself. But if Christians don't take up their cross, outsiders cannot be drawn to it. Matthew has warned disciples from the beginning of the Lord's ministry of such failure. In the Sermon on the Mount, the Lord asks about salt losing its taste and light hidden under a bushel basket (Matt 5:13–16). In Matt 25, the nations—all those who do not believe—are judged. The church and each disciple has a mission to the nations (Matt 28:16–20). Ultimately, any failure of the nations is ours. Matthew may be offering a profound lesson on how to think about and live with those who differ—the Other. He is tasking members of the church to acknowledge people of goodwill. It is the church's role to draw the goodness out of the Other.

Matthew is concerned with judgment; John is concerned with condemnation. Here are passages by John on condemnation:

1. John 3:16–21 is the narrator's conclusion after the encounter of Jesus and Nicodemus.

2. John 5:19–30 is the Lord's teaching on the resurrection of the dead.

3. John 12:23–36 is the separation of those who live in darkness and those who live in the light.

After the encounter between Jesus and Nicodemus, the narrator offers an explanation. He asserts that God loves the world and adds that the Son of God came to save the world. God did not send the Son to condemn. The narrator says, "Whoever believes in him will not be condemned, but whoever does not believe has *already* been condemned because he has not believed in the name of the only Son of God" (John 3:18, emphasis added). The *already* implies that the judgment is concurrent with the choice of light or darkness. The one choosing is judging themself by their choice. Those who prefer darkness will live with their own wickedness. Those who believe will live their lives in light, their works "clearly seen as done in God" (John 3:21).

In John 5:19–30, Jesus himself teaches. He assures us that the Father does not judge anyone but gives life. The Son is given the power of judgment, but he, too, wishes to give life. Eternal life is already offered to those who "hear his word" and believe in the Father. That person "*has eternal life*" (John 5:24, emphasis added). The Son will also call the dead out of their tombs. Those who have done good deeds are called to the resurrection of life. Those who have done wicked deeds are summoned to the resurrection of condemnation. Neither the Father nor the Son condemn; both call us to life. Our works judge us.

In chapter 12, Jesus says that the hour of judgment is the hour of his passion: "*Now is the time of judgment on this world*; now the ruler of this world will be driven out. And when I am lifted up from the earth, I will draw everyone to myself" (John 12:30–31, emphasis added). Jesus separates those who walk in darkness and those who walk in light, becoming children of light. The reader knows the source of light. Jesus's act of self-giving love on the cross is the light to the world. Those who live it—that is, live according to the self-giving love of the cross—have passed through the judgment—already, now.

Scripture is not systematic theology. It follows a storyline not a rational, logical development. I think it offers the following guidance through apocalyptic times:

- Those who succeed through the judgment are those who are persistent. They live the gospel despite the times. The church must have an honest, realistic valuation of the world. In bad or evil times, Christians cannot take up the ways of the world, the ways of power or wealth. Violence, deceit, chaos, manipulation, and evil can never be the methods of believers.
- The judgment is based on our works, our deeds. The question is whether we live the self-giving love of the cross in the face of present evil. Agency is crucial to the valuation of the Christian self.
- Neither God the Father nor God the Son condemn. The judgment is a self-judgment. Our choice of light or darkness puts us in light or in darkness now and for eternity.
- The nations, nonbelievers, are judged according to the Creator's gift of goodness. Common decency and the humane treatment of others seem to be the criteria. The church must seek alliances with all people of goodwill.
- Implied in the judgment of the nations, however, is a judgment on the church because we have a mission to the nations. If nonbelievers are not saved, the church has failed to give witness to the cross.

The best illustration of concurrent judgment I know is in Thomas Merton's *The Seven Story Mountain*. About the cause of World War II, Merton writes,

> They did not realize that the world had now become a picture of what the majority of its individuals had made of their own souls. We had given our minds and wills up to be raped and defiled by sin, by hell itself: and now, for our inexorable instruction and reward, the whole thing was to take place all over again before our eyes, physically and morally, in the social order so that some of us at least might have some conception of what we had done. . . . There is something else in my own mind—the recognition: "I myself am responsible for this. My

sins have done this. Hitler is not the only one who has started this war: I have my share in it too."[7]

Thomas Merton's brother, John Paul, was called up to military service. Before he left for the war, he visited Merton in Kentucky. John Paul was quickly prepared for baptism. He left for the war, and he served as a pilot. He wrote his brother but does not mention the bombing raids he undertook. Thomas Merton senses what was happening in John Paul's soul. He writes, "John Paul had at last come face to face with the world that he and I had helped to make."[8]

I think this is the message of the Scripture on judgment. The world is our construct. Our works, our deeds make it what it is. The judgment is not pushed off to some indefinite future. Believers do not experience judgment only after death. The general judgment does not wait until the end of the world. Because we construct our world, the contemporary world is a verdict on us. It is a reflection on our souls. If we have bought into the ways of the world—its greed, violence, deceit, and abuse of persons—we will live and relive apocalyptic destruction. If we persist with the self-giving love of the cross, we already know the joy of eternal life.

Religion is a desire deep in our souls to connect with and participate in the power at the core of all that there is. Merton's insight into the war renders that desire practicable. The mystic in us can sense the connections. Our involvement is a two-sided coin. The individual is influenced by the direction of humanity, the social order, and the entire creation. The individual is also a participant. Each person contributes to the make-up of the social order, the well-being of society, and even to the state of the ecosphere. Through the indwelling of the Spirit of Christ, the believer in his/her freedom can participate in a new heaven and new earth, in the new creation.

This is not a novel insight. The Gospel of John makes the point that each of us adds to the light or to the darkness (John 1:10–14; John 3:16–21). Connection and participation might be summarized in an idea that the church still needs, the idea of *communion*. The idea is mostly associated with Eucharist. We are in communion with Jesus Christ and through him with the Father. The eucharistic communion makes us the church, and as church, we are the body of Christ. The catechism quotes St. Thomas Aquinas: "Since all the faithful form one body, the good of

---

7. Merton, *Seven Story Mountain*, 248.
8. Merton, *Seven Story Mountain*, 402.

each is communicated to all the others."⁹ The idea is also reflected in the doctrine of the communion of saints. A mystic union exists among all who have ever served the Lord and who serve him now. The catechism says, "Between them there is . . . an abundant exchange of all good things."¹⁰ The catechism implies that the sins and evil of the living detract from the common store of goodness, but the good overwhelms the evil that may be done. *Communion* is a traditional word. Some of the church's directors of religious education think the word carries too much baggage. I think the word should be restored. In the meantime, connection and participation may remind us that we are constructing selves, society, the world—and the world that is coming.

This realization, however, should never be used by preachers to burden believers with guilt. The definition of sin includes full knowledge of the evil and one's full intent to participate in it. The Merton brothers were not the efficient cause of World War II, not as Hitler was. The pastor must remain aware of causation when alleging guilt. When a person throws away food because it is beyond the expiration date, she is not guilty of starving others. The existence of hungry and starving people, however, is a judgment on a wasteful culture. Being aware of the connection of all humanity and all creation and being attentive to our participation in humanity's direction should transform everyone's dietary habits.

Apocalyptic literature is consciously symbolic. As such, it draws us in. The literature works to create moods and motives, schema for the construction of our lives. *Heightened awareness* is some part of the purpose of apocalyptic literature. A spiritual genius may achieve perfect awareness. For the rest of us, awareness is an element of a lifetime of spiritual growth.

THE END

Because apocalyptic-level destruction is constant, because our judgment is living in the world that we are constructing, and because the literature itself engenders hope, a pastoral minister should explain the end-times in a present time frame. Cardinal Martini wrote that the literature "solidifies the meaning of contingent events into an ethical locus in which the meta-historical future of the human adventure is determined."¹¹ The end must

---

9. Aquinas, quoted in *Catechism of the Catholic Church*, para. 947.
10. *Catechism of the Catholic Church*, para. 1475.
11. Eco and Martini, *Belief or Unbelief?*, 31.

be that ethical focus that launches the Christian church into the future of the human adventure.

The current fad of books and movies based on apocalyptic-level destruction paint a bleak picture of humanity's future. The end is the near total annihilation of civilization and the human species. The most upbeat of this entertainment has a person or a couple finding an oasis in which to begin again. This does not represent the intention of the biblical texts! The scriptural images of the end are, without exception, positive. It all ends in a new heaven and a new earth, a harmonious new creation, a new Jerusalem. The end is triumph and victory. Christ is the Alpha and the Omega, the beginning and the end. God is the one who was at the beginning, is now, and will be forever. St. Paul offers us the most evocative image. Christ will put all his enemies under his feet, the last being death. Christ then presents his kingdom to God the Father "so that God may be all in all" (1 Cor 15:28). The end is a hopeful, enlivening vision.

St. Paul also offers us insight into the interconnection of all reality and the vital role Christians play in bringing about the glorious end. In his Epistle to the Romans, chapter 8, he reminds us that there is "no condemnation for those who are in Christ Jesus" (v. 1). The identification of Christ with the members of the church is vital to Paul: "The Spirit of God dwells in you" (Rom 8:9); "Christ is in you" (Rom 8:10); we are "children of God" (Rom 8:14). We prove our adoption because the Spirit allows us to recognize God as "Abba, Father" (Rom 8:15). This leads to Paul's great insight that connects us in Christ with God the Father, and through God with all creation. Connection (read, communion) makes us participants: "I consider that the sufferings of this present time are as nothing compared with the glory to be revealed for us. For creation awaits with eager expectation the revelation of the children of God" (Rom 8:18–19). The end becomes our inspiration. The Christian is in the Spirit and in Christ. We are, therefore, connected with God who is becoming all in all. As we are united in Christ with God, we are being swept up in the eagerly expected cosmic re-creation. These thoughts are essential to the dynamism of Christianity. To know the end is also to know the means. The goal is God being "all in all" (1 Cor 15:28); the means is Christ being "all in all" (Col 3:11). Christ is in us. Anticipation becomes aspiration becomes action. The end-as-fulfillment creates a crucial implication of our faith: the social order and each person are transformable. Paul said it: "All creation is groaning in labor pains" (Rom 8:22). And "we ourselves, who have the firstfruits of the Spirit, we also groan within ourselves as we wait for adoption" (Rom 8:23).

The pastor must know the times we are moving through. The secular world is the stage on which this dynamic plays out. Secularization is a process through which all personalities and all parts of all societies become malleable.[12] Although secularization is currently lamented within the church, the development may be positive for Christianity. We cannot live in actionable hope if the person and society are cloaked in a fabricated divine aura, a legitimation based on a contrived affirmation from God. Human constructs—political or economic structures, for example—are human and cannot carry the aura of unchangeability that comes from claiming divine endorsement. Responsible agency should never be removed from the self and from selves acting communally. Preachers should never deny God's greatest gift other than life itself, the gift of freedom. The world is malleable; it is our construct. Each person is malleable; each person can convert. Likewise, social systems can change. Our politics and economics are human constructs. Those who give them divine legitimation are engaged in propaganda. Great care is needed with God language, especially when we speak of God's plans for a person or God's involvement in history. To invigorate the dynamism of Christianity, we must do what Jesus of Nazareth did. Temples need to be cleansed. The human spirit needs to be open to the malleability of self and society. Life in Christ means desacralizing all current structures to discover anew human possibility.

Faith in Jesus is also faith in the free person and his/her changeability. This faith is supported by history and therefore can launch our future. Leszek Kolakowski (1927–2009) was a scholar who took a second look at religion because the predictions of its demise proved false. To my knowledge, he did not become a believer. But he could see the positive developments in history resulting from Christianity. He writes,

> But Jesus remains alive in our culture not only for those who believe in his divinity or even just in his supra-natural mission. He is present in our culture not only through the dogmas of this or that religious community but through the value of certain precepts which were genuinely new and which—crucially—remain vital not as abstract norms but living principles, enduringly bound up with his name and his life as handed down by

---

12. I have discussed disenchantment and differentiation more fully in Schmitz, *Thoughts on Secularization*, 630.

tradition and quite independently of that tradition's historical accuracy.[13]

He offered us five points. I doubt any Christian minister requires much explanation. I will offer Kolakowski's statement of these precepts and my brief elaboration.

1. "Abolishing law in favour of love."[14] Love is the highest of high things. All other goods—for example, truth, justice, righteousness—must be informed by love.

2. "The hope of eliminating violence from human relations."[15] The abuse of others, denial of their freedom, or the use of force or coercion are never of Christ.

3. "Man shall not live by bread alone."[16] Beatitude comes from appreciating beauty; seeking knowledge, truth, and wisdom; in contributing to the common good in peace and in justice; and in discovering the depth of love.

4. "The abolition of the idea of a chosen people."[17] Social boundaries are necessary for identity formation. But they must be porous. An encounter with the Other—with those who differ—is mutually enriching. No people, nation, or individual ranks above another. Being Christian is not a privilege; being Christian is a mission.

5. "The essential wretchedness of the temporal world."[18] The perfection of this world is beyond us. Each of us is frail; each of us fails. Everything alive dies. Everything will be destroyed. This realization allows us to accept ourselves, forgive ourselves, and to go easy on others. The insight stretches us to care for others in need and to care for the earth, which is in need of restoration.

Kolakowski's last point requires our consideration. After the incarnation and resurrection, suffering might seem even more absurd. If God is with us and within us, why is there still pain and suffering, why does sin and death still have a hold on us, why do apocalyptic tragedies mount

13. Kolakowski, "Jesus Christ," 153.
14. Kolakowski, "Jesus Christ," 153.
15. Kolakowski, "Jesus Christ," 154.
16. Kolakowski, "Jesus Christ," 156.
17. Kolakowski, "Jesus Christ," 157.
18. Kolakowski, "Jesus Christ," 157.

up? Philosopher and theologian Emmanuel Falque makes such questions an important part of his work. Our salvation in Christ overcomes neither the finitude of this earth nor our own finitude. Instead, our salvation in Christ offers us another way through time and this world. When we become open to God-with-us, new possibilities for life open before us. I like what he says about the effects of the resurrection: "There are not *two worlds* but *two different ways of living the same world.*"[19] He quotes a French Jesuit theologian Francois Varillon: "We confuse *another world* and *the world becoming other.*"[20] We remain finite, frail, subject to sickness and death, and we remain in a world given to sin and evil. In Christ, however, we find the way through it. We discover possibilities for forgiveness, compassion, and self-giving love; in Christ, we find the grace to seek that which is above.

Finally, anyone can name occasions of the church's failures to live the Lord's principles. Anyone can find hypocrisy in Christianity's long[21] history—indeed, in Christianity's pretenses today. Kolakowski quotes La Rochefoucauld's axiom: Hypocrisy is the homage vice pays to virtue. There will always be more the church and each believer can do. And because judgment is current, Christians will always feel its weight. Kolakowski's reading of the Lord's precepts remain at work, playing on the Christian community and each Christian individual to participate in the construction of society. The point is this: the ongoing unfolding of history demonstrates that Christ is changing our culture and our world and, most importantly, each of us. The world is becoming *other*. Pastoral ministers need to demonstrate that the church is Christ's body, and that in him, the end-as-fulfillment is open to us.

---

19. Falque, *Metamorphosis of Finitude*, 102.

20. Francois Varillon, quoted in Falque, *Metamorphosis of Finitude*, 102. See also Falque, *Guide to Gethsemane*.

21. La Rochefoucauld, quoted in Kolakowski, "Jesus Christ," 155.

12

In the Holy Spirit, the Lord, the Giver of Life

IN THE BIBLICAL TEXTS, the amazing message about the Holy Spirit is how the Spirit symbolizes our multidimensional union with God. At the very beginning, a mighty wind swept over the abyss (Gen 1:2). The breath of God was blown into the dust, forming humankind (Gen 2:7). Wisdom was God's artisan during creation (Prov 8:30). The same Spirit who was present at creation was with Jesus of Nazareth from his conception through his ascension. The Spirit was given to disciples on Pentecost. The Spirit led the church through its first phases; the same Spirit guides the church even now. And the Spirit is given to believers upon their initiation.[1] The Spirit empowers us to act in Christ; the Spirit unites us to God's people, the church; and the Spirit dwells within us.

Three assertions by St. Paul assist us in getting our heads and hearts around the function of the Holy Spirit in creating a Christian self. In his Letter to the Romans, Paul writes, "For those who are led by the Spirit of God are children of God. For you did not receive a spirit of slavery to fall back into fear, but you received a spirit of adoption, through which we cry, 'Abba, Father!' The Spirit itself bears witness with our spirit that we are children of God" (Rom 8:14–16). A few verses later, Paul writes, "In the same way, the Spirit too comes to the aid of our weakness; for we do not know how to pray as we ought, but the Spirit itself intercedes with inexpressible groanings. And the one who searches hearts knows what

---

1. Schmaus, "Holy Spirit," 649.

is the intention of the Spirit, because it intercedes for the holy ones according to God's will" (Rom 8:26–27). And in 1 Corinthians, Paul writes, "No one can say, 'Jesus is Lord,' except by the holy Spirit" (1 Cor 12:3). The finite perceives the infinite through an invitation from the infinite. The Holy Spirit allows us to know God as *Abba*, as Father, and to know Jesus as Lord. It is the Spirit who moves us to prayer. Referencing the gifts of the Spirit, Michael Schmaus writes, "Hence the gifts are special salutary modifications of the openness to God which is intrinsic to human nature."[2] The Spirit opens us to the infinite possibility that is life in God. Given that some metaphors see God as above, we can say that the Spirit turns us to a vertical dimension. Others tell us that God is everywhere; the Spirit turns us outwards to creation and to the human family.

The turning outward is a necessary work of the Spirit, necessary because it turns us away from sin and allows us to discover a way through finitude. Emmanuel Falque offers us a definition of sin. It is an "attitude of self-enclosure in our own finitude."[3] I cannot imagine a single evil act that does not begin in a person's preoccupation with the self, one's needs, desires, one's own perceived suffering and pain, one's own requirement for temporary relief and pleasure. It is the "self-enclosure in finitude" that separates us from God. The Spirit is the "divine power active in the world or rather God himself insofar as he is acting in man and in the universe, in history, and in nature."[4] The Spirit is a power or force vigorous enough to turn us away from self to God, to one another, and to this world. The Spirit can open our hearts to experience God's presence in our lives.

Through the sacraments of baptism and confirmation, our access to the Spirit is from within. As Paul says, "The Spirit bears witness with our spirit" (Rom 8:16). The infinite is within the finite in a way that leaves the finite free. The Spirit bursts the chains that imprison the self in self-absorption. The Spirit works from within, convincing us that the self is incomplete until we open our heart, mind, and spirit to God. In fact, the freedom of the finite is enhanced because the Spirit offers us an infinite horizon. Gifted to us at baptism and confirmation, the Spirit is our openness to God.

I need to acknowledge a danger. In an age of individualism sometimes sinking into narcissism, the statement that the Spirit works within—the Spirit speaks to one's own spirit—can lead to the misappropriation of the

2. Schmaus, "Holy Spirit," 648.
3. Falque, *Guide to Gethsemane*, 24.
4. Schmaus, "Holy Spirit," 642.

Spirit. The Spirit can be claimed for one's private, self-absorbed agenda. Pastoral ministers may encounter this assertion; it is difficult to refute. This danger bears some relation to what St. Paul found in the church at Corinth; the gifts given by the Spirit were not being used for the greater good. Ministers may counter such claims by reminding members that the Spirit works from within to unlock the heart, mind, and spirit to God. The upward/outward movement to God turns the self beyond self-interest, first toward mediators of God, especially the church-community, and then toward the divine itself.

I rarely argue with the catechism. In listing the gifts of the Holy Spirit, however, the catechism says that the gifts of the Holy Spirit are "permanent dispositions which make man *docile* in following the promptings of the Holy Spirit."[5] The dynamism that occurs in us by the indwelling Spirit is lost by the word *docile*. Isaiah was the first to list the Spirit's gifts. They are wisdom, understanding, counsel, strength, knowledge, and fear of the Lord (Isa 11:2). The church added a seventh, piety.[6] *Docile* is unfortunate; the gifts empower. Isaiah names these gifts in reference to the messiah, the anointed one of God. His ascendency brings a time of justice to Israel. His governance raises the poor and strikes down the ruthless and the wicked. Then a time of harmony affecting all creation begins: "The wolf shall be the guest of the lamb and the leopard shall lie down with the young goat; the calf and the young lion shall browse together, with a little child to guide them. . . . They shall not harm or destroy on all my holy mountain; for the earth shall be filled with knowledge of the Lord as water covers the sea" (Isa 11:6–9). The catechism notes earlier, "The fullness of the Spirit was not to remain uniquely the Messiah's but was to be communicated to the *whole messianic people*."[7] If the Messiah and the messianic people are about justice and harmony, the correct word for describing the Spirit's promptings is *empowerment*.

The same may be said of the listing of the gifts of the Spirit in St. Paul's First Letter to the Corinthians. Paul's list includes wisdom, the expression of knowledge, faith, the gift of healing, mighty deeds, prophecy, discernment of spirits, varieties of tongues, and the interpretation of tongues. Paul's concern was the abuse of the gifts by the members of the church in Corinth. Paul counters the abuse with a stern reminder that the gifts are given for service and good works. Paul asserts that "God

---

5. *Catechism of the Catholic Church*, para. 1830 (emphasis added).
6. *Catechism of the Catholic Church*, para. 1831.
7. *Catechism of the Catholic Church*, para. 1287 (emphasis original).

produces all of them in everyone." Individuals receive the gifts "for some benefit" to the church (1 Cor 12:7). The ultimate benefit is our incorporation into the body of Christ. Paul's exposition on the right use of the gifts leads him to his oft-quoted Ode to Love in chapter 13, the finest expression of ecclesiology in the church's history. Following the same logic, St. Thomas Aquinas asserts that love is the "proper name of the Holy Spirit."[8] To love as Paul describes and to be formed into the body of Christ requires the terminology of desire, endeavor, and action. To become the body of Christ for a service through love defines the upward/outward movement prompted by the Spirit. Love, after all, is the highest of high things (1 Cor 13:13).

In his Letter to the Galatians, Paul lists the fruits of the Spirit as "love, joy, peace, patience, kindness, generosity, faithfulness, gentleness, and self-control" (Gal 5:22–23). The church adds goodness and chastity.[9] The context for Paul's list is a meditation on freedom. Paul asserts that those living in the Spirit enjoy liberation from the law. In fact, "there is no law" (Gal 5:23) that checks the aspirations of life in the Spirit. The chapter begins with the powerful words, "for freedom, Christ has set you free" (Gal 5:1). Openness to God is the liberation of our minds, hearts, and spirits. In the Spirit, we are set free to enjoy freedom. We become open to the infinite horizon of possibility and can contemplate our potential. Once again, this is not the language of passivity or docility. Nor is it the language of individualism or narcissism. The gifts and fruits of the Spirit form the vocabulary for active engagement in our world, in our community, especially for participation in our church, and for the construction of self free of self-absorption. Paul commissions the believer: "Serve one another through love" (Gal 5:13).

The Spirit turns us upward/outward to God. But the infinite God must be mediated to finite humans. This is not a new insight. St. Thomas Aquinas writes, "Whatever is received into something is received according to the condition of the recipient."[10] Any analysis of the "condition of the recipient" includes life in this world here and now, one's culture, one's society, one's relationships, and one's self. The Spirit reveals the space, time, and the people through which the divine may be encountered. Furthermore, the Spirit reveals the ministry of service through love to which each of us is called.

8. Aquinas, *Summa Theologica* 1.37.1.
9. *Catechism of the Catholic Church*, para. 1832.
10. Aquinas, *Summa Theologica* 1.75.5.

Genuine care is needed here. At a minimum, we know that nothing can limit God; nothing may constrain the Spirit of God. But that's a minimal claim. To grow closer to a correct assertion, our God-talk must encompass the dynamism of life in the Spirit. Early in John's Gospel, the evangelist conveys the Lord's meeting with Nicodemus. Jesus speaks of "being born from above." Nicodemus expresses puzzlement. Jesus responds, "The wind blows where it wills, and you can hear the sound it makes, but you do not know where it comes from or where it goes; so it is with everyone who is born of the Spirit" (John 3:8).

The movement of the Spirit is suggested in the wind heralding creation (Gen 1:2): "and a mighty wind sweeping over the waters." Everett Fox translates the beginning as the "rushing spirit of God hovering over the face of the waters."[11] Robert Alter prefers "God's breath hovering over the waters."[12] The psalmist took up the theme: "Send forth your spirit, they [all creatures] are created, and you renew the face of the earth" (Ps 104:30). The primal wind is also the breath the resurrected Lord breathed on his disciples to inspirit them (John 20:22). This same wind is revealed on Pentecost: "And suddenly there came from the sky a noise like a strong driving wind" (Acts 2:2). What an image for the indwelling of the Spirit—a strong wind blowing where it will! The image carries connotations of power and force translating into a spirituality of action sourced with vision, imagination, creativity, hope, dreams, and desires.

The image demands we contemplate our life *in God*. The Spirit liberates us from the absorption with the self, opening us to God, turning us upward/outward. Because the Spirit works from within, it seems to implore us to come to terms with modernity's sense of self as the free, active agent in creating self, community, and society. We can base this reassessment of our valuation of the person on our creative potential in the Spirit. It is the source of our desire to recreate the face of the earth.

To get to the free, creative soul, we need to replace the objectified God, often imagined as the old man on a throne awaiting our subservient bows, waving a wand to bestow or withhold favors. The image of an objectified God creates separation and, therefore, distance between God and humanity. As a symbol, an objectified God informs the schemata through which we perceive everything around us; it creates the moods and motives for our lives. Because the image of God and our self-image

---

11. Fox, *Five Books of Moses*, 13.
12. Alter, *Five Books of Moses*, 17.

have a high degree of correspondence, the objectified image of God works to create religiosity based on separation and division: the Creator over against creation, the spiritual over against the material, the eternal against time, the heavenly over against the earthly, believers verses nonbelievers. It separates the sacred from the secular or the sacred from the profane. Religion becomes what I have called explicit religion.[13] As a result, religious life is set over against daily life.

This same separation is moving Christianity further from the best of our contemporary age. Science is teaching us of the dynamism of the physical universe. That dynamism requires new thoughts on truth itself. Currently, the theology rooted in unchanging truth keeps church members from appreciating that dynamism. The old terms were *actuality* set over against *potentiality*. Our theology holds that actuality is perfect; our secular world is teaching us that, in an evolving universe, perfection is also in potentiality. Likewise, as novel forms of communication and avenues to mobility are developed, the contemporary world is beginning to celebrate pluralism. But symbols of distance, separation, division shape thoughts of *us* against *them*, the people of God over against the Other, who is judged to be lesser for no other reason than their failure to acknowledge our God. If God remains the old, bearded man, the objectification of God produces tension between male and female. Organizationally, the image of the objectified God produces rank over against rank depending on a supposed closeness to the divine: the monastic or religious clergy over against the secular clergy, the clergy as a class over against the laity, the celibate over against the sexual.

It all evaporates if God is reimagined around the preposition *in*. The categories of *objective* and *subjective* melt away. The Spirit, who is divine breath blowing where it will, dwells with-in, in-spiriting, in-spiring. Division gives way to harmony; the body is in-spirited, the sacred is found in the secular, time participates in eternity. The Lord's Prayer is not a pipe dream; God's will can be done on earth as it is in heaven. Scientific truth and theological truth can find common expression. God did not create once in order to be done with it. God is creating; the universe is dynamic, evolving, expanding. The Christ is saving; the church is reforming; the Christian self is converting. In the Spirit, all is journeying forward on the Lord's way.

---

13. I discuss *explicit* and *expansive religiosity* more fully in Schmitz, *Methodology*, 26–31.

I find this reimagined divine offers a foundation for Paul's assertion that "for freedom Christ set us free." All that counts, he says, comes through the Spirit, by faith. The result in us is "faith working through love" (Gal 5:6). St. Paul writes that once we experience our liberation in the Spirit, we cannot "submit again to the yoke of slavery." Once the Spirit liberates us from self-absorption, we cannot return to the *status quo ante*. The upward/outward movement prompted by the Spirit becomes the definitive directionality of our lives. We become open to God. A critical awareness of our flaws and our possibilities develops, allowing for continuous conversion and permanent state of transformation. An encounter with the Other, with those who differ, enriches life. Nature becomes Creation; believers become its stewards; those who pursue knowledge and wisdom about it are its sacred personages. Humankind becomes God's family; believers are one with that family; God is our Father. Those who create understanding, tolerance, and reconciliation are its prophets. The desire for the *more* will not be satiated. The *gap* between who I am now and who I might become is never overcome. The *more* and the *gap* are permanent fixtures of a spiritual home, a cause for the celebration of freedom for freedom's sake.

The same Spirit given to each initiated Christian is guiding our church. The Second Vatican Council affirms that the same upward/outward movement is meant for the direction of the church. In *Lumen gentium*, the dogmatic constitution on the church, the authors write, "Many elements of sanctification and of truth are found outside its [the church's] visible confines." And the council declares the church to be "always in need of purification," needing to follow "constantly the path of penance and renewal."[14] Anyone who has lived through the period after the Council realizes how difficult it is to overcome religiously entrenched ideas and power structures. Only with confident awareness of the divine-blowing wind can we reach beyond ourselves to find comfort in change.

One challenge for the church is a reassessment of the balance between the collective and the individual. A turn away from the image of the objectified God triggering division and separation and a turn toward the preposition *in* will change the relation between the church as a community and the believing individual. Charles Taylor has written about the premodern conceptualization that emphasized the collective to the point where the individual could not identify the self without reference to the

---

14. Flannery, *Lumen gentium*, para. 8.

collective. The *I* was folded into the *we*. The self found its purpose and meaning in family, tribe, nation, and religion. Modernity changed that arrangement. Theories of individual human rights and the active agency in the construction of self and society transformed the collective into a supportive mechanism to protect the rights of the individual and to facilitate individual actions to obtain the individual's legitimate aspirations. This is true of religious organizations as well. The collective organization, the church, must see itself as the facilitator of a believer's progress toward God, in terms based on the individual believer's experience.[15]

To date, the church has only begun to adjust to modernity. Because the change is not complete, dissonance emerges between our teaching on baptism, confirmation, and Eucharist and the reality of ecclesiastical structures. The organization still demands conformity. The subservience and passivity of the self to the collective is still expected. The sacraments, however, communicate that believers are made "partakers in divinity."[16] The organization—as important as it is—is not the goal of faith. The Spirit moves believers toward fulfillment in the divine. The church facilitates and nurtures the journey. The church in the Spirit must gently but resolutely turn believers outward to God's creation, God's family, and ultimately to God.

I have written in chapter 1 about explicit and expansive religiosity. Explicit religion is the stuff of the sanctuary, the rites, the formation efforts, and the values behind the ecclesial organization. It is necessary and good; the organization—the structured church—is in the Spirit. Explicit religion nurtures the believer. The believer, however, is also in the vortex of the blowing-where-it-will Spirit. The believer requires an expansive religion, a religion that finds the sacred in all of life, that empowers the believer to create a spiritual home in this world.

Our openness to mediators of divinity might use St. Paul's words as a guide: "Whatever is true, whatever is honorable, whatever is just, whatever is pure, whatever is lovely, whatever is gracious, if there is any excellence and if there is anything worthy of praise, think about these things" (Phil 4:8). Paul's repetition of *whatever* is the key to an expansive religiosity. Certainly, Paul includes the *whoever*. One can imagine a long litany: those who love and allow themselves to be loved; those who bridge differences, reconcile, find peace; those with integrity and authenticity;

---

15. Taylor, *Secular Age*, 514–15.
16. *Catechism of the Catholic Church*, para. 460.

those who serve the common good; those who seek justice; those who lift up the poor; those who heal; those who create; those in music, literature, and the arts who enrich life; those who nurture; those who empower; those who teach and convey a love for learning; those who share the prosperity their work is creating; those who make us laugh; those in labs who pursue knowledge of creation; those laboring to apply the knowledge for the improvement of life; those who act to liberate humanity; those who show us how to re-embed ourselves in God's creation.

Paul's *whatever* should include the *wherever* and *whatever*. Sacred space cannot be limited to church buildings. Our homes allow the tensions of the day to dissipate and remind us that the best relationships are of love. Nature can give us solace and heal a bruised soul. A good teacher knows a classroom is a sacred space to unleash potential. Certain things can remind us of key moments in life's journey and certain people who made the journey a joy. Expansive religion is based on the Spirit revealing the sacred in the material and, most importantly, the sacred in our loves and affections.

In the process of declaring a saint, I understand that the church looks for the miraculous, for an event that defies normal causality or the laws of nature. Saints, I suppose, should be exceptional. But the viability of the Christian community depends more on St. Paul's *whatever, whenever, whoever*. If the church uncovers and proclaims the true, the honorable, the just, the pure, the lovely, the gracious, we might be convincing about the presence of the all-good God. If we could point to Paul's *whatever*, people may experience the Spirit moving them to consecrate this world. Pastoral ministry must find the goodness in the *whoever* and declare it from the pulpit and in the formation programs. By proclaiming the excellent and that which is worthy of praise, the pastoral minister is working in the Spirit to inspire the excellent and to aspire to that which is worthy of praise.

13

Who Proceeds from the Father and the Son, Adored and Glorified

IMAGING A TRIUNE GOD for formulating self, community, and society is a uniquely Christian undertaking. We must start at our beginning, with the human condition. Finite humanity's striving to reach for humanity's end in the Almighty God is nothing less than audacious. By nature, the human is marked by limitations. Humans are weak and frail, destined for death. Our weakness and our demise can turn us inward, making us withdraw into strategies for self-preservation and, perhaps, self-aggrandizement as a futile attempt to compensate. Humans have a proclivity to evil; all of us sin. Humans are dependent. We require the material, natural world for our sustenance. But we are quite shortsighted. Humans foul the air we breathe, the water that is almost sixty percent of our body weight, and the soil composed of chemicals constituting the rest. Humans also depend on other humans. But some have described human interaction as a war of all against all. Of course, humanity is capable of magnificent accomplishments. Our capacity for knowledge can improve the common good. We can build, harness nature, produce goods and services, and heal. Much of what we imagine, we can do. Our ability to formulate values and our attempts to live by those values are also praiseworthy, even if those values are applied unevenly.

Except for God's self-revelation, imagining unity in the triune God is pretentious. In the divine communication, however, we learn that wholeness is achieved only in God—wholeness defined as being at peace with our incompleteness and dependency. In addition, our deepest desires and aspirations are met only in the divine. The desire to reach our end in God may be over the top, but the desire and the striving are altogether necessary. St. Peter summarized our striving, writing, "His divine power has bestowed on us everything that makes for life and devotion, through the knowledge of him who called us by his own glory and power. Through these, he has bestowed on us the precious and very great promises, so that through them you may come to share in the divine nature, after escaping from the corruption that is in the world because of evil desire" (2 Pet 1:3–4).

When such biblical imagery moves us, the preposition *in* comes to define our interaction with God. The objectification of God—the old man on a throne, humanity subjugated before him—gives way to the God in whom "we live and move and have our being" (Acts 17:28). God who creates, God the Son who is incarnate, the Christ whom we receive to become, the Spirit who dwells with-in, who in-spirits and in-spires: these melt away the objective-subjective antithesis. To make this point, Marcus Borg quotes St. Irenaeus: "God contains everything and is contained by nothing."[1] God always remains greater; the finite cannot grasp the infinite. And the infinite has come to dwell "in the innermost center of human existence," as Karl Rahner wrote.[2] As a result, God is not set over against humanity; the spiritual is not set over against the material; eternity surrounds and includes time; God's will can be done on earth as it is in heaven. God created and is creating. Christ saved and is saving. Through the Spirit, we abide in the creating, saving God. Through the openness to God provided by the indwelling Spirit, we connect with the power at the core of existence. We are called to participate in the creating and saving. That is our mission; that is our fulfillment on earth. In the end, there can be harmony—between God and humankind, within the human family, and between the collective and the individual; and we can discover harmony in the self. The last assertion is the most amazing: reconciliation with God can be felt in oneself. The infinite, triune God can draw into the divine even an incomplete, dependent individual. The purpose of our lives is our formulation of a response to the invitation into the infinite, the divine Word. God contains everything; God is becoming all in all.

---

1. Irenaeus, quoted in Borg, *Speaking Christian*, 70.
2. Rahner, *Content of the Faith*, 373.

How does one approach the worship of such a God? How does one govern a community living in that God? What aspirations should believers rightfully entertain because they believe in that God? In this chapter, I explore a pastoral theology, the performative truth, of the triune God. This will be the dimension of the one truth that reaches into our hearts, minds, and souls, allowing us to construct a Christian self. Scripture begs us to inquire in this direction. Jesus prayed to the Father, on the night before he died, "I have given them the glory you gave me, so that they may be one, as we are one, I in them and you in me, that they may be brought to perfection as one, that the world may know that you sent me, and that you loved them even as you loved me" (John 17:22–23). St. Paul says it like this: "All of us, gazing with unveiled face on the glory of the Lord, are being transformed into the same image from glory to glory, as from the Lord who is Spirit" (2 Cor 3:18). I will briefly explore *glory* at the end of this chapter. For now, we note that this is our purpose, our end: to share in God's glory.

The scriptural *in* is transformative. Starting in the human condition, it becomes apparent that only the one true God communicated to us as three divine persons can raise the person into divine participation. To conceptualize God as three persons allows us to perceive God as the whole of our reality. The creating Father generates all things. The divine Logos, the Son, saves all things and invites us into his body through eucharistic communion. And the Spirit works from within, directing us outward and upward to the divine. The revealed conceptualization of divinity as Trinity envelops and permeates *everything* and *all of us*. The eternal God revealing the divine self from the beginning of time, through history and until now, saturates time, including each moment of every life. Karl Rahner makes this point: "Sustained by God's grace itself, [the believer] has absolute confidence that the absolute God as such has come absolutely close to him."[3] Furthermore, that which mediates God to us is considered "divine in the strict sense of the term." Rahner stresses the point that God's self-communication enables us to speak about the actual, infinite God because God's self-communication is the absolute God and not a created mediator, an emanation, or an avatar. God's self-communication comes to us as the persons of the triune God and the divine qualities that are of the very nature of God. The God we worship is

---

3. Rahner, *Content of the Faith*, 383.

"close to [us]" in "concrete salvation history."[4] For us, God is at once the infinite, all-powerful God and the divine Logos and the indwelling Spirit, together, inviting us beyond ourselves into divinity. We must take note of the directionality of this proposition. God is coming to us, revealing the divine self to us, filling our world. The inquisitive spirit in us pursues God. But the success of our union is guaranteed because God comes to us. This realization is crucial for our valuation of this world, of others, and our valuation of the self. It is also important for a proper perspective.

The reader who has made it this far may be comfortable with my methodological propositions: performatory truth looks to the symbolic dimension of the truth of our faith. Symbols create feelings in us, the moods and motives undergirding our lives. They are schemata, modes of perception, allowing us to take in and process data about the world, ourselves, and God. And then symbols move us to take informed action in our world and upon ourselves. To advance my reflections, I would like to recall two trinitarian images that somehow stayed with me over the years since theology school. Although St. Thomas Aquinas meant the expressions to describe the really real, I wish to explore the symbolic dimension. The first term to be considered is *procession* and the second is *relations*. In both these concepts, God is imagined as moving toward us. St. Thomas allows us to envision God coming at us, filling our universe, our world, ourselves. What's more, according to Thomas this movement toward us is essential to God's nature. If so, we should not conceive of God without a procession toward us for the sake of a relation with us. The idea radically transforms our valuation of self, of humanity, and of this world. The movement of God toward us defines our end and grounds our aspirations.

Unfortunately, we will need to root ourselves in terminology that is foreign to the modern mind. Here is how St. Thomas maintains the infinite that is beyond the finite while allowing the same infinite to come absolutely close to the finite. This is crucial to Thomas's argument; there is no *potentiality* in God; all is *actuality*. In Greek thought, potentiality and change are imperfect. God cannot be imperfect. God cannot change. God has no potentiality. *Actuality*, the complete, the unchanging, is perfection. Actuality is the real. It is the nature or essence of a being. It is necessary. The opposite of *actuality* is *accident*. Accident is not meant in the sense of spilled milk. Accident implies contingency, movement,

---

4. Rahner, *Content of the Faith*, 383.

potential, change, or extension. An accident is not essential, not part of the essential nature of a being.

For humans, procession and relation take us outside the self. Both terms signify an outward extension or outward movement. Intellect and will comprise a person's essential being; both are within. Neither procession nor relations are essential, necessary aspects of human nature. They are accidental. Contemporary psychology works in different categories and comes to different conclusions. But we are moving around in the ancient mind where much of our doctrine is explained—for better or for worse.

In God, there are no accidents and no extension. All is actuality. Here's the rub. The creed says the Spirit proceeds from the Father and the Son. Thomas must come to terms, therefore, with *proceeds* or *procession*. Because all in God is actuality, Thomas simply asserts that procession in God is an aspect of the divine actuality. Procession becomes some part of the essence of God; procession is of God's nature. There are two such processions. From eternity, the divine intellect generates the Logos, the Word. In our finite perception, the Logos, the Word is directed to us in time as Jesus Christ. St. John says it like this: "For God so loved the world, that he gave his only Son. . . . For God did not send his Son into the world to condemn the world, but that the world might be saved through him" (John 3:16–17).

The second procession is from the divine will expressed as Love, the Holy Spirit. According to our finite perception, the Spirit moves outward from God toward us. John quotes Jesus saying, "For if I do not go, the Advocate will not come to you. But if I go, I will send him to you" (John 16:7). The Son of God comes down from heaven into this world to us; the Spirit of God descends upon us and remains in us. Thomas insists that both processions, the Logos and the Spirit, are of God's essential nature. If we perceive our interaction with God with the scriptural *in*, we may perceive the processions of Logos and the Spirit coming to us from God's essence, from God's very nature. How this transforms our perception—of the world and of ourselves! From God's very nature, God is filling our world with the divine presence, including our flawed, wanting hearts and souls. Because God-moving-toward-us is essential to our notion of God, incarnation, and indwelling—the processions of Christ and the Spirit— may be imagined as God coming to embrace us—and more, God filling the space between the finite and infinite with the divine self.

The same can be said of relations. Human relationships are movements outside ourselves, extensions of ourselves. Therefore, relations are not of our essence; they are accidental. Again, contemporary psychology arrives at a different conclusion. For Thomas, however, human relations are not of our very nature. In God, however, relations are real.[5] That means they are of God's essence, of God's nature. God has four relations: God to the Logos and the Logos to God; God to the Spirit and the Spirit to God. Because baptism, confirmation, and Eucharist communicate our relationship—our communion—in Christ and in the Spirit, God's outward movement to us becomes a source of our valuation.

These images, as symbols, can guide our thoughts on our interaction in the triune God. Both procession and relations can become wonderfully evocative symbols even as they challenge us to the core of our being. In the human condition, outward movement is not of our nature; relations are not necessary. Self-centeredness can seem fulfilling. Caring primarily for self can seem imperative (see the philosophy of Ayn Rand). The commercial world depends on the primacy of self-concern: *I must have*; *I want*; *I deserve*. Such desire is the basis of our consumer economy and is drummed into us. As noted above, Emmanuel Falque sees this "withdrawal or self-enclosure into one's own finitude" as the nature of sin.[6] But much of the political and economic structures of this world tempt us into such self-enclosure.

The outward movement to the world and to others may seem ancillary for humanity in the sinful, human condition. Christians, however, share in divinity. In a Christian symbolic universe, the outward movement of the divine to us becomes essential, necessary for our self-imagining. To become sharers in divine nature, the outward movements of God require an outward movement from us to our surrounding reality. Such a direction becomes imperative for believers. The procession and relations in God become the foundation of an aspirational Christianity. Necessary outward movement unites us to creation and to others. Essential outward motion helps us aspire to love as self-giving love—as *agape*. This movement is necessary because it is the source of our enrichment as humans as we reach out to God's creation and God's family, both of which, in turn, mediate the divine to us. If our imaginations are steeped in that directionality, even radically different life choices, orientations, and cultures may

---

5. Aquinas, *Summa Theologica* 1.28.1.
6. Falque, *Guide to Gethsemane*, 24.

be understood, tolerated, and may even become elevating. If our imaginations are so directed, nature, even when threatening, becomes a revelation of sacred creation. Being *in* the Creator transforms our relation to the material environment. As a schema, a mode of perception, this necessary outward vision helps us re-value time: we can embrace a future, even a future leading to death, as a blessing. We can experience that future as a guide through the present. Procession and relation are essential to God; they must transition from accident to essential in the Christian self.

The repercussions for the Christian community, the church, are interesting. To join in the procession of the Logos, we need to become more aware that all members constitute the body of Christ (1 Cor 12:27). The Second Vatican Council calls each of us into full active participation in worship, governance, and the ministry of the Church. In *Lumen gentium* (the dogmatic constitution on the church), the council says, "The faithful who by baptism are incorporated into Christ, are placed in the People of God, and in their own way share in the priestly, prophetic, and kingly office of Christ, and to the best of their ability carry on the mission of the whole Christian people in the Church and in the world."[7] The same ideas are incorporated into canon law. The full workings of the church are included. All members share in the "priestly, prophetic, and royal office."[8] This transformation of church structures is not simply an organizational principle; it is a theological imperative. The full participation of each believer in all aspects of the faith is necessary for the realization of the Christian person living in God. A Christian self, then, cannot be devalued—that is, perceived as a passive recipient of the church's benevolence. As partakers in divinity, each member is an active agent in Christ's ministry.

Canon law and the council use phrases that are suggestive even if their original meaning is not. The intended meaning of phrases like *in their own way*[9] or *according to their state in life*[10] were to secure the authority of hierarchical order—the bishop over the priest and religious, the clergy over the layperson. The phrases, however, could begin wonderful discussions about a genuinely pluralistic community enabling all members to express their unique perspectives on the ministry of Christ's body.

---

7. Flannery, *Lumen gentium*, para. 31.
8. *Code of Canon Law*, 204.
9. Flannery, *Lumen gentium*, para. 31.
10. Flannery, *Lumen gentium*, para. 42.

My question is this: What if we allow our imaginations to roam around in our different perspectives—inspired by the blow-where-it-will Spirit?

Full participation is not an add-on, not auxiliary to one's baptismal responsibility. Full participation is not for the few and not to be monopolized by the hierarchy. It is to become part of what is essential to the Christian self, part of one's Christian nature. For those who think an hour for worship is enough, the words of St. Paul offer a stark warning: "For anyone who eats and drinks without discerning the body, eats and drinks judgment on himself" (1 Cor 11:29). Paul's reference to *body* here is the assembly and the organization becoming the body of Christ. I think it is fair to ask what happens if a member of the clergy suppresses the active engagement of any other member of the body?

A believer needs not spend more time in parish meeting rooms. The consecration of the world means that the work of the church proceeds outward from the church into every form of human interaction. Full participation in the body might be engagement in politics or the economy or the search for knowledge or the enhancement of family life, albeit modeled on Christ.[11] If the whole of the community felt compelled to dialogue using the logic of God-coming-toward-us, the church may risk authentic engagement with the world. The procession of the divine Logos into our world—expansive religiosity—complements and completes worship. Fully participating members process outward, moved by the indwelling Spirit to take the divine Logos from the altar into the world.

The outward procession of the divine Logos obliges the leadership of the church. Full participation of the laity requires facilitation and celebration led by church leaders. The Second Vatican Council proposed an ideal to launch an expansive religiosity. The laity have authority and should speak to the church's involvement in the world. *Apostolicam actuositatem*, the decree on the apostolate of the laity says, "The characteristic of the lay state being a life led in the midst of the world and of secular affairs, laymen are called by God to make their apostolate, through the vigor of their Christian spirit, a leaven in the world."[12] Because the council sees the laity in all phases of the church's life—the priestly, the prophetic, and the royal or kingly ministries—and because the council defines a sphere for lay ministry—the world and secular affairs—church

---

11. Flannery *Lumen gentium*, paras. 35–36.
12. Flannery, *Apostolicam actuositatem*, para. 2.

structures are needed to give voice to their insights and celebrate their contributions for the consecration of the world.

Allow me to offer an example. My city boasts of a highly rated children's hospital. I learned of some of the research on childhood cancer from a parishioner who has labored in that research. Families have asked me to pray with them in the neonatal intensive care unit. I have visited extremely sick children in the hospital any number of times. I do not know about the religiosity of the doctors, nurses, scientists, and technicians of the hospital. But if I were to try to define *miraculous*, I would start there. Should not the church, inspired by the blow-where-it-will Spirit, celebrate their work? Could we imagine a Sunday dedicated to healing children? I do not think this is an add-on, a secondary accidental aspect of the church in the world. Without the celebrations of goodness, without celebrations of the points at which humanity touches divinity, our valuation of humankind and the times we are living through are bound to become negative—in fact, quite dark. Our valuation of persons follows. Our valuation will get stuck in the evil, the sinful, the destructive, and violent. If the divine nature in which we participate guides our vision, the church can come to terms with the contemporary world through celebration of humanity's best. Our faith will be reenergized as our eyes are opened to God's presence. The outward movement of the divine intellect directs us.

Just as we share in the procession of the divine intellect, we share in the procession of God's will expressed as Love, as the Spirit. On a symbolic level, human relationships take center stage. This is not familiar territory for the church that has lifted the monk as the ideal of perfection and has celibate male priests lead its communities. Of course, the council redefined Christian ideals when it called all believers into the perfection of holiness according to their state in life.[13] This ideal has not been realized as of now. The procession of the divine will as Love allows us to see all loving relations as an expansion of God's presence.

St. Thomas puts it bluntly, "Relations exist in God really."[14] Relations are essential to God. His is not a new thought. St. John writes, "Beloved, let us love one another, because love is of God; everyone who loves is begotten by God and knows God. Whoever is without love does not know God, for God is love" (1 John 4:7–8). In his Gospel, John records the Lord Jesus defining love. Jesus says, "No one has greater love than this, to lay

---

13. Flannery *Lumen gentium*, para. 11.
14. Aquinas, *Summa Theologica* 1.28.1.

down one's life for one's friends" (John 15:13). Self-giving love is the love to which Christians aspire. The cross is the supreme symbol of such love.

Just like Thomas defined procession in God differently than procession for humans, Thomas asserts that relations in God are substantial. In his thinking, our relations are nonessential or accidental. The really real relations in God can serve as a symbol. Even if relations are not essential for humanity in the sinful, human condition, relations must transition to the essential for the Christian self because sharing in divinity is our goal. The Christian self begins to perceive reality differently. What we do in love, we do in God. Relations transition from ancillary to primary, from accidental extensions of our self to our very nature.

The confessional sometimes reveals some flaws in the popular understanding of church teaching. For instance, I hear many confessions where a married person or a parent confesses as sin that they have not given enough time to God, even though they are giving all they can for spouse and children. Sadly, contemporary religiosity has become explicit. But John writes, "*Everyone* who loves is begotten by God and knows God" (1 John 4:7, emphasis added). When one's time and energy, one's full being, are devoted to spouse and children—providing for them and nurturing them—that time and energy are of God.

The same can be said of all relations. Our self-imagining includes the necessary relations in the triune God. Therefore, John's *everyone who loves* can change our valuation of our world. All affections and friendships become essential to our Christian image of the self and should be celebrated in our Christian communities. Christ's love, however, reaches beyond those close to us. Jesus's salvific act affects the entire world and all peoples. Out of such love, we are instructed to love even our enemies and persecutors (Matt 5:43–48). The procession of God's love comes at humankind in a variety of ways; our love extended into the world may become understanding, tolerance, justice, and peace.

Our ministry in this world shares God's glory (2 Cor 3:7–18). In Paul's writings, references to our sharing in God's glory are projected into the future when the Lord returns. For example, in Romans Paul writes, "I consider that the sufferings of this present time are as nothing compared to the glory to be revealed for us" (Rom 8:18). But one cannot read Paul's predictions without a sense that the glory to be experienced redounds into the present moment. We share in the divine glory even now. His vision of the future is certainly a case of Augustine's "present of future things."[15]

Paul offers us indications that God's glory permeates the present. Paul's feeling for his own people, "his brothers in the flesh," indicates that God's glory is evident in this world. Paul writes, "They are Israelites; theirs the adoption, the glory, and the promises" (Rom 9:4). The ministers of God in Hebrew Scriptures shared in the glory. For instance, Moses is named as sharing in God's glory (2 Cor 3:7). The purpose of Paul's references to past glory, however, is to stress the glory of the present ministry. In fact, the glory of the past has faded because ministry in the Spirit is so much more glorious (2 Cor 3:8). Just so, the glory of God is shared through all who minister in the Lord. Let me repeat what was quoted above. "All of us, gazing with unveiled face on the glory of the Lord, are being transformed into the same image from glory to glory, as from the Lord who is Spirit" (2 Cor 3:18). This is an indicator of the meaning of *glory* for us. Ministry is self-giving love expressed in the name of the church. Ministry transforms us into the image of Christ. The ministry of the new covenant lifts us from glory to glory.

I am looking for a performative truth. I believe the precepts and propositions of our faith contain an existential dimension for us. The precepts and propositions help define who we are as Christian selves. In John Fuller's novel *Flying to Nowhere*, an abbot of a monastery that welcomed pilgrims spoke about pilgrimage as "a symbolic act." It is "the outward sign of an inward direction. It is the earnest of our spiritual condition, a manifestation of the natural tendency of life to seek its fulfillment."[16] Perhaps all religious rites have such secondary meaning, a meaning manifest when the rites are thought of not in themselves but as symbols. Of course, religious rites are good in themselves. A pilgrimage to a site designated as holy does not need any other explanation. To the extent a religious rite allows one to experience the holy or the divine, its existence is justified. My question is this: Could not religious rites also manifest the inner desires that anticipate one's fulfillment in the divine?

We might think of the adoration of the Blessed Sacrament in light of the procession of the triune God. If so, our direction through this world might be partially drawn from the act of adoration. If eucharistic adoration focuses our minds and hearts on God's glory, it becomes the outward

---

15. Augustine, *Confessions*, 300.
16. Fuller, *Flying to Nowhere*, 24.

sign of our inner desire to share God's glory. The act needs no other reason; it is good in itself. The act may have another meaning as well. The act of adoration my transform our vision. It may facilitate a spirit of adoration for all that Christ saved and is saving. A spirit of adoration may change our perception of humankind. We may be able to see the goodness that is around us. Adoration may become the outward movement of our inner desire for the consecration of this world—for a world at peace, for the recognition of human dignity in all people, the construction of a society with justice, for a world enhanced by charity; to be enriched by the Other and to contribute to the Other—that all may become one. The psalmist points us in this direction, writing,

> When I see your heavens, the work of your fingers,
>   the moon and the stars that you set in place—
> What is man that you are mindful of him,
>   and a son of man that you care for him?
> Yet you have made him little less than a god,
>   crowned him with glory and honor. (Ps. 8:4–6)

Trained in eucharistic adoration, the spirit of adoration may elicit a transcendent mystical union with many dimensions of our reality. A spirit of adoration can heighten our awareness of the capacity of the self to take in a universe of awesome scale, dynamism, and beauty. It might enhance the self as the knowing self is encouraged to feel at home in a knowable universe. The spirit of adoration can marvel at a loving person discovering her own lovability from a loving partner. One might be bowled over that the universe cares enough to speak as the inner voice of conscience directing one from destructive habits to life-enhancing actions. Humans enjoy many kinds of transcendent moments that lift us out of ourselves to discover the processions of God's intellect and God's will to us. Sometimes the divine processions seem to come straight toward us. Religious rites may open us to the tendencies of life to fulfill itself.

Explicit religiosity is not compromised and certainly not invalidated by searching for other dimensions of the Christian truth. Expansive religiosity opens our eyes to the truth that God is everywhere. It expresses our desire to unite with God through all that is. Worship of the triune God is its own justification. A transcendent, mystical union with all that is of God, however, can only enhance the experience of worship itself. Sharing in God's glory through a spirit of adoration not only glorifies God but changes our vision and ennobles us.

14

In One, Holy, Catholic, and Apostolic Church

THE FOURTH REPETITION OF "I believe in . . ." feels formulaic. Pastoral ministers, however, might benefit from a meditation on the conditions for belief *in the church*. Belief in an organization led by humans feels different from belief in God, Jesus, and the Holy Spirit. Belief in God is based on God's self-revelation, millennia of reflections on this revelation, and experiences of the divine. The revelation, the deliberations, and the experiences lift belief in God to the supernatural. Because God is infinitely beyond us, our faith is perceived as a wonderful divine gift, uplifting each believer. The church, however, is an organization steeped in history's vicissitudes and subject to humanity's shortcomings.

Even with the dogmas of infallibility and inerrancy, even with the belief in the indwelling of the Holy Spirit, belief in the church needs to account for the vagaries of flawed humans. History records the church's defects. Current headlines expose them. All believers experience them. I don't wish to repeat the litany here, except for one. What saddens me is the number of believers who feel diminished psychologically or spiritually by church ministers even though the ministry of church ministers is to bring the gospel or good news. Too many believers feel marginalized, beat down, and even excluded. I find myself in agreement with Edward Schillebeeckx. He writes, "It is better not to believe in God than to believe in a God who minimizes human beings, holds them under and oppresses them, with a view to a better world."[1] If flawed humans acting as ministers diminish others or beat them down with guilt or shame, all while dangling a future paradise before them, the church becomes impossible to believe. Equally inexcusable is an inability in pastoral ministers to present a positive, aspirational incentive for participating in a Christian community, one that complements the gift of faith itself. Without the positive and aspirational, believers are left to flounder in the negative, in a bleak picture of self and society. Most people I know will opt out of such an organization to discover other paths to the loving God.

The messy state of the church makes it difficult to reflect on *church* as a symbol. But a very human church is where we must begin. Searching for the performatory truth of *church* brings us close to the lived reality where the pushing and shoving and human shortcomings are evident. A performatory truth will not permit an escape into abstraction; a truth that inspires action and life choices needs to include its whole reality. Likewise, a performatory truth cannot permit a whitewashing of problems with piety. I would like to believe in the church because it is one, holy, catholic, and apostolic. The facts are elsewhere. I believe in a church that is sometimes divided, usually flawed, even sinful, sometimes intolerant and exclusive, and sometimes authoritarian. A performatory truth needs to straddle the whole, the theological ideals and the real mess, and the large space in between.

If the whole is included, pastoral ministers and parish leaders will have a lens—a schemata—for an honest assessment of a given community. It takes in data about itself, processes that information, and reforms itself. I think the assessment needs to include these factors:

- theologically based ideals defining the church and the various actions of the church—for example, its worship and sacraments;
- the conditions of possibility for contemporary communal interaction;
- the articulation of a positive vision for ecclesial interaction—for example, being the gifted people of God;
- and an ongoing response to life's contingencies, to sickness, death, privation, and so forth.

---

1. Schillebeeckx, *Church with a Human Face*, 35.

THEOLOGICAL IDEALS

The easiest path to explain the tensions in the church is to blame the world outside the organizational boundaries of the church. The modern world, some claim, is lined up against it. Some even claim the world is at war with the church. The problems within the church, therefore, are explained as the internal struggle over strategies for coping with the external threat. This may contain some truth. But the more impactful forces are within. The church has been changing its self-understanding for some time. The mode of signification is shifting. The pushing and shoving in the church are the internal strife over the identity and meaning of *church*. Four internal factors are moving the transformation:

1. The church is returning to biblical imagery for its self-understanding. Leo XIII recognized the historical-critical study of the Bible in the 1903 encyclical *Providentissimus Deus*. The Modernist Crisis set back such studies. In 1943, Pius XII reaffirmed the necessity of such study in *Divino afflante Spiritu*. And in 1965, the Second Vatican Council promoted these studies in *Dei verbum*, the dogmatic constitution on divine revelation. The Hebrew Scriptures offer the church much that will reshape it. The idea of the *people of God* is reforming the organizational structures. The creation stories and the theological reflections on history direct us to a this-worldly religiosity; both the creation stories and the historical books require consideration of the goodness of the material and temporal world and make us its stewards. Likewise, the prophetic insistence on justice and harmony requires a this-worldly dimension to our ministry. The Christian Scriptures also compel transformations. St. Paul's exploration of the variety of charisms in the body of Christ presents challenges to an ordained minister's relations to the general membership. Of course, Jesus Christ's teaching directly challenges church leaders—that is, the Lord's inclusiveness, his demand for a leadership of service, his rebukes of religious authority that burdens believers, and his vision of equality in the church. Worship of the God of mercy and love redefines authority. The official decrees steer the church away from fundamentalism. With divine guidance, we can lead believers from the flight into faux security. I believe the most important factor in the church's self-understanding is the careful reintroduction of biblical imagery.

2. The Second Vatican Council's understanding of holiness is restructuring our church. The perfection of holiness is no longer conceived as set within a singular hierarchy with the most other-worldly life orientation on the top rung (e.g., cloistered monks and nuns) and a this-worldly life on the bottom (married persons making a livelihood in this world). Instead, the church calls for the perfection of holiness according to one's state in life. Because organizational leadership remains in the hands of celibate priests, tension exists between the leadership and the general membership; one is always at a disadvantage to fully understand the other. The organization is enhanced by a professional class of lay ministers, many of whom are married. But the existence of their positions remains dependent on a celibate priest-pastor's understanding of the ministry.

3. The Second Vatican Council reformed the worship of the church. All members are called to full participation in it. I am concerned here with the performative meaning of our liturgy. The sacraments, including the Eucharist, convey an amazing valuation of each believer. The indwelling of the Spirit, life *in* Christ and through Christ, life *in* the Father, becoming the body of Christ: such New Testament ideals demand a heightened sense of the sacred dignity of each member. When I contemplate this valuation, I cannot help but think about the interaction of the entire membership, the peopling of its ministries and governance, and especially the interaction of the parish ministers and leadership with the community to encourage full participation. Our interaction does not yet reflect our theology. The reform of parish structures does not match the exalted valuation found in Scripture.

4. The Second Vatican's Council's call for ecumenical sensitivity and religious liberty is also transforming the church. Officially, the church sees otherness not as a threat and not as an inferior path to God. Others share in truth and have a role in the sanctification of this world. Social boundaries become porous. If taken on its merits, ecumenism allows Catholics to consider others as contributors to a more complete truth, enriching the truth found in the church.

These factors play on the imagination of all church members, but especially on those in leadership. Combined, they insist on a religiosity that finds goodness in this world and inspires the sanctification of this world. These four major factors working within the church require a ministry that values the multiple states of life within the community. And these factors require a ministry that values pluralism in the community itself and among world religions and cultures. The four internal dynamics make the aspiration for truth more inclusive, welcoming the contributions of various cultures, religions, philosophies, life-orientations, both genders, and contributions from those outside the formal organization of the church. Understandably, time is needed to realize the relatively fresh ideals. For now, the church is in a state of disequilibrium: the ideals and the reality do not yet coincide.

These internal reorientations require a reconsideration of the attributes or marks of the church, the creed's "one, holy, catholic, and apostolic." Oneness cannot mean uniformity. Holy cannot mean only other worldly. Catholicity does not end at the boundary of the organization but requires genuine appreciation of all peoples, cultures, value systems, and religions. Apostolic not only traces authority through the bishops to the twelve apostles but also advances the ministry of all members for the consecration of this world. After reconsideration comes the hard part—the reorganization or restructuring to embody the ideals.

THE CONDITIONS OF POSSIBILITY FOR A CONTEMPORARY COMMUNITY

The performatory truth of the *church* (or the *church* as a symbol) can be imagined around the idea of *community* enhanced by the biblical images of *the people of God* and *the body of Christ*. Before we can explore those images, however, we need some analysis on the nature of a church community. At the risk of over-simplifying history, I think it can be said that the church community is realized between two poles: (1) All gatherings of people require order, structures, discipline, implied or explicit rules and norms. (2) Voluntary gatherings of people rely on attachments evoked from aspirational values. Because we are looking at *community* as a symbol, and because we are imagining a contemporary expression of it, these values today include the active agency of the membership, mutual respect among members, as well as the support for, nurturing of, and *space* for growth, development, and creativity. A church community in contemporary society, a voluntary community, does not have the power to compel obedience and conformity. Even right order becomes aspirational. St. Paul confronted a similar situation. He hoped the church could "preserve unity through the bond of peace" (Eph 4:3). A contemporary church community, therefore, strives for the whole. A church community is animated by its values—mutuality, nurturing, space for agency—all ordered through the bond of peace. The combination is tricky.

Here is a minister's predicament. The church is in transition. Some members wish to live in memory, in the present of past things. The version of the church they imagine seems to enjoy a high degree of certainty and security. The singular purpose—getting one's purified soul to heaven—was definitive. The lines of authority were clean and neat. It seemed well-ordered. The church also has members who live in expectation, in the present of future things. They value the freedom to create, imagine, and change. They can compromise the ordered structures to obtain the desires of heart and soul. They demand their agency to think and act without hierarchical approval. Their purpose may be expressed in terms of the Lord's Prayer, that God's will be done on earth as it is in heaven. These two forms of religiosity do not sit easily together. Pastoral ministers certainly have their own preference. Even so, ministers need to extend kind understanding to all.

Because believers are perplexed over the meaning of *church*, a continuous meditation on the possibilities of belief in *church* is crucial for church ministers. If we take in the whole, the reflection will carry us close to what Charles Taylor calls the *modern imaginary*.[2] As said above, Taylor documents a fundamental change in the juxtaposition of an individual and a collective. In a premodern mindset, an individual is subsumed in the collective. A person can hardly define the self without reference to the collective—one's family, tribe, ethnicity, nationality, and one's religion. The collective used to have a formidable hold on the individual. It could demand obedience and conformity. And it could apply a powerful sanction: expulsion resulting in social death for the expelled member. Without the collective, one loses his/her identity.[3]

The modern world changed the juxtaposition. Theories of unalienable human rights and intrinsic dignity led individuals to be valuated apart from the collective. In addition, the range of values in the contemporary world requires an understanding of the nature of choice.

---

2. Taylor, *Secular Age*, 512.

3. An excellent example of social death occurs when Romeo is exiled from Verona in William Shakespeare's *Romeo and Juliet*. Romeo responds, "There is no world without Verona walls, / But purgatory, torture, hell itself. / Hence-banished is banish'd from the world, / And world's exile is death" (Shakespeare, *Rom.* 3.3.18–23).

The modern person perceives God, the world, and the self through the necessity of choice. In premodern society, pressure from all parts of the social order, including one's associates, family, and friends kept one focused on the one source of ultimacy. In today's society, multiple sources of value exist, and social pressure is minimized, including that of family and friends. The collectivity's role becomes the support for and nurtures one's freely designed self.

A believer's personal spiritual journey becomes essential data for all religious organizations. One's journey is to be welcomed, encouraged, and supported by one's chosen collectivity, one's parish. The church community must learn to include its believers' aspirations and hopes about the self and society. It must come to terms with the efforts at self-creation. Here's the complication. Those living in memory, in the present of past things, are as taken up in the self-creation process as those living in expectation, in the present of future things. Both the traditionalist, conservative members and the progressive, liberal members are self-selecting the forms of worship and piety, the types of parish structures, and the nature of the formation programs they desire to augment the life choices they have made. Unless the ministerial team of a parish is acutely aware of the dynamic of the construction of the self, it is impossible to achieve St. Paul's ideal to become "all things to all" (1 Cor 9:19–23). But on the basis of the construction of self process, the team may be able to offer a variety of experiences to please most members.

In the self-creating process, the honest person knows the self is unfinished, at the very least. A believer is somewhere on the path to goodness and holiness. Because the universe is ultimately mysterious, the believer has an incomplete grasp on the truth concerning God, life, the self, society, and the world. Because few of us live fully the values we have chosen, authenticity remains a challenge. In honest moments, most will admit to being less than the best spouse, parent, worker, citizen, believer, minister. The church community can respond if it embraces an expansive religiosity, the proclamation of gospel values for the contemporary world in all its manifestations. I am certain of this: the church-community could find purpose supporting the process of self-construction, including the study of and a dialogue on what believers have set out to become.

The challenge of the gospel remains acutely felt. Most people understand that an encounter with the divine is demanding. In fact, a believer may find satisfaction knowing that the gospel is "a two-edge sword," penetrating to the core of one's existence (Heb 4:12–13). Without some tension between the self and the belief system, the individual is likely to dismiss the religious body as anemic and unworthy of an investment of time and energy. The goals of a faith—for example, eternal life, life with God—come at a cost. Continuous conversion is expected; the world requires transformation. People will pay the cost if faith enhances their life journey and if the church community is a participant in the consecration of this world. After all, the first sermon Jesus preached was, "Repent, for the kingdom of heaven is at hand" (Matt 4:17).

A believer considering church involvement faces existential questions analogous to the God-question. The questions are as penetrating but concern thoughts and feelings about collective experience and apprehensions about belief *in the church*. The questions differ from the one's leading to God; they involve an individual's thoughts and feeling about collective experience. I can imagine four such questions:

1. What is my need for comfort and solace when the universe seems to turn against me—in other words, how do I deal with my guilt, with others' evil, with betrayal and loneliness, with pain, suffering, and death?

2. What need do I have for a model for my aspirations—Christ's life, the lives of the saints, the perfections of God?

3. Do I have an intellectual need to find a tradition of religious language, God-talk, and a belief system to substantiate my generic faith?

4. Do I have a need to engage in worship, ritual, and adoration when the universe smiles on me—that is, when I feel awestruck by beauty, amazed by the universe's expanse, overwhelmed by human achievement, amused by human sociability, raised up by friendship and intimacy, and delightfully perplexed by the complexity of it all?

In sadness and pain, in awe and pleasure, in wonder and curiosity, in a spirit of adoration, and in a spirit of gratitude, I may discover a desire for a collective experience, a community of fellow believers.

Pastoral ministers need to accept a nonnegotiable condition brought to the experience by believers today: mutual respect. Participation in a collectivity or church community means that one's freely designed life journey is respected, nourished, and supported. And because the believer realizes a need for mutuality, the believer's participation depends on whether the believer can demonstrate respect for others and is given opportunities to interact with the faith life of others. In our times, pastoral ministers need to acknowledge the freedom—read, active agency—of the believer. St. Paul said it like this: "Now the Lord is the Spirit, and where the Spirit of the Lord is, there is freedom" (2 Cor 3:17).

A POSITIVE, ASPIRATIONAL VISION

In our times, the believer asks, What is in it for me? The question is not necessarily narcissistic. With the array of values in contemporary society, the believer is simply asking the church to compete, and more, to demonstrate, the efficacy of the faith for the construction of a good life. So, what does participation in the church do in and for us? My shorthand answer is our faith provides a safe space for building a spiritual home. In a Christian spiritual home, believers should enjoy a feeling that they are part of God's creating and are connected to creation. They should know that their lives are significant, that they are invited to participate in the creating. This means that believers are empowered for the construction of the self, one another, family, society, and their physical and human environment. And they should feel morally responsible for that construction. In our contemporary situation, much space is needed for change, growth, and for conversion because potential and possibility are built into modernity's soul. Because the way of Jesus Christ prioritizes self-giving love, such love will become the standard for all life decisions. Charity should expand ever outward and sometimes be expressed as a critique of the social system and embodied as a movement for peace and justice. In this way, believers will know they are directed to the good and to the true. Then they may experience an inner peace. To arrive at such peace, believers should also be forgiven for their failures, be loved without conditions, be unconditionally loving in return, and, at or near the end of life, be confident of salvation.

The facilitation of the building of a spiritual home might seem like a formidable task for the pastoral minister. Each minister can take solace in this: the active agents in the building process are God and the believer. The church and its ministers, however, are still necessary. The church provides the symbolism and language for the believer's deliberations and meditations. In addition, its symbols provide a sense of connection with the Creator and creation. Through worship and prayer, the church can offer moments of transcendence. Its programming must encourage interaction with others for mutual support and nurturing. Its ministries should exemplify compassion and inspire it in its members. Its teaching should stipulate the conditions for authentic Christianity. And if it is bold enough, the church should arrange for actions that transform this world. Through it all, the active agent is the Holy Spirit working for renewal of the earth and, of course, the believer in Christ making the investment of self for the re-creation (read, the ongoing conversion) of the self and society.

However complex my prescriptions may sound, the insights of a biblically based ecclesiology are even more challenging. The significance of the Second Vatican Council's use of *the people of God* as a definition of the church is well-known. A pastoral meditation on the full participation of believers in the prayer, governance, and ministry of the parish may wish to consider what the author of Hebrews calls the "cloud of witnesses" who participated in salvation history (Heb 12:1). God is always the senior partner in the effort; but the range of junior partners is amazing: patriarchs, their wives and children, the judges of Israel, prophets, monarchs, soldiers, sages, and priests. Matthew included significant women in the Lord's genealogy, including Tamar, Rahab, Ruth, and the wife of Uriah. Luke mentions women who provided for the Lord's apostles, including Mary Magdalene, Joanna, Susanna, "and many others" (Luke 8:2–3). Salvation history passes through less than decorous situations—for example, the brothers of the patriarch Joseph selling him into slavery or David fathering Solomon through an illicit affair with Bathsheba. In the New Testament, the Lord himself offers a challenge to the structuring of the church when he says, "Among those born of women there has been none greater than John the Baptist; yet the least born in the kingdom of heaven is greater than he" (Matt 11:7–15). The least born into God's kingdom echoes the indecorous situations of the Hebrew Scriptures. In the blink of an eye, Simon Peter goes from rock on which the church is built to Satan (Matt 16:13–23); Saul of Tarsus, a Pharisee who persecuted Christians, becomes Paul, the most effective apostle. Every disciple in Mark's Gospel fails the Lord. Even so, the pastoral minister must take stock in what the New Testament proclaims about believers born into God's kingdom. A believer baptized into the Holy Spirit has that Spirit groaning from within (Rom 8:23), making her an adopted child enabled to call God "*Abba*, Father" (Rom 8:15, emphasis added). In addition, a believer who receives the Lord Jesus in the Eucharist lives in the Lord Jesus and the Lord Jesus lives in the believer. Together, they live in the Father (John 6:54–58). One must be amazed at God's dealings with human actors to serve salvation history. Upon reflection, a minister needs to note the valuation of humanity implied in God's interaction with humanity. And all of it must come to bear on a pastoral minister contemplating the structuring of the parish community that peoples its ministries and governing structures today.

Another meditation might take us into the very messy church in the city of Corinth. Consider the gifted people Paul was addressing in that relatively small community.[4] Paul knew that the Spirit gave these gifts: the expression of wisdom, the expression of knowledge, faith, the gift of healing, the ability to perform mighty deeds, prophecy, the discernment of spirits, the ability to speak in tongues, and the ability to interpret tongues (1 Cor 12:7–11). These gifts were distributed to apostles, prophets, teachers, those who did mighty deeds, those with the gift for healing, those who assisted others, the administrators, and those with a variety of tongues. In the end, Paul trumpets this ideal: "You are Christ's body and individually parts of it" (1 Cor 12:27). Paul summarizes his inspired ecclesiology, writing, "There are different kinds of spiritual gifts but the same Spirit; there are different forms of service but the same Lord; there are different workings but the same God who produces all of them *in everyone*" (1 Cor 12:4–6, emphasis added). Paul concludes with these dramatic words: "*To each individual* the manifestation of the Spirit is given for some benefit" (1 Cor 12:7, emphasis added).

Paul found the same situation in the communities in Rome (Rom 12: 3–8) and Ephesus (Eph 4: 1–16). His churches had a variety of gifted persons in different roles and functions, all with the purpose of building up the body of Christ. Paul was holding two socio-logics at one time: one is the logic of right order; the other is the logic of gifted people freely ministering in the way they felt moved by the Spirit. Paul brings these two logics together with one ultimate principle—Christian love, *agape*. He completes his discussion on the Corinthian church with his Ode to Love (1 Cor 13). He does something similar with the church in Rome (Rom 12:9–21). And Paul's ecclesiology in Ephesians is sustained with love: "Living the truth in love, we should grow in every way into him who is the head, Christ" (Eph 4:15–16). All this must weigh on the pastoral leadership.

---

4. Schillebeeckx, *Church with a Human Face*, 59.

A RESPONSE TO LIFE'S CONTINGENCIES

The performatory truth of the last propositions of the creed informs pastoral ministers that an essential feature of the church community is pastoral care. Deutero-Isaiah may have said it best:

> Comfort, give comfort to my people,
>   says your God.
> Speak to the heart of Jerusalem, and proclaim to her
>   that her service has ended,
>   that her guilt is expiated. (Isa 40:1–2)

Believers should experience comfort from their church community.

The doctrine of original sin offers us a symbolic communication to assess the evil in our world. Sin, suffering, and death are part of our reality. I do not think God's people are expected to be paralyzed by evil, however. The remedy for it was divinely planned from the time evil, sin, suffering, and death entered creation. St. Paul offers the framework for a hope-filled outlook: "Where sin increased, grace overflowed all the more" (Rom 5:20). A hope-filled outlook can be fostered when the ministers of the church effectively respond to moments when the impact of evil and sin become palpable to a believer. When a believer becomes burdened by guilt for his personal sins, the church can offer the forgiveness of sin. When the death of family and friends has one staring into the abyss, the church can proclaim life after death—eternal life, heaven. When violence, hatred, and immorality gang up to induce fear, if the church can address evil with charity and compassion, the believer can reestablish hopefulness. In our times, the church can fulfill Isaiah's prophecy to end servitude and to expiate guilt.

Our response to evil conditions imposed upon us is a measurement of authentic humanity. No one escapes pain, suffering, evil, the condition of mortality, and, ultimately, death itself. Our response to our own pain and our empathy for others become the measure of a our character. After all, we never forfeit the divine gift of freedom; our response to sin, evil, and death is our choice. We can always hope and imagine. We can dream of different conditions. We can act. Saints develop what we now call critical thinking. They see through the *ways of the world* to a greater truth, to different conditions, to a new heaven and a new earth.

A Christian response to our condition is never utopian and even less is it magical, even though some preachers and teachers present it as such. Most of all, the Christian dynamic can never become passive acceptance of pain and suffering, even if generations of spiritual directors urge acceptance on believers. Christianity is a religion of salvation. It has no greater truth than *Jesus saves*. Jesus himself expanded that truth when he invited every believer into the work of salvation by taking up the cross.

Jesus taught, "Blessed are they who mourn, for they will be comforted" (Matt 5:4). Blessed mourning is all but oxymoronic. It can be imagined only in light of the cross as the evangelist John describes it. John's Gospel portrays the cross as glory. Jesus saves by willingly entering into the worst of human suffering, even death. The purpose of this act was not to glamorize suffering or even to accept suffering. The cross participates in God's glory because the cross is an act of self-giving love that redeems humankind. John's explanation quotes Jesus, "No one has greater love than this, to lay down one's life for one's friends" (John 15:13). Elsewhere, the same evangelist will tell us that God is love (1 John 4:7–8). Compassionate love is divine. It is why mourning is blessed and the cross is glory. Humankind reaches its highest expression—it touches on divinity—when love moves us to empathetic action.

In his book *Tears and Saints*, Emil Cioran offers us insight into blessed mourning. He tells us that the tears of the saints remind us that "we cry because we long for a lost paradise."[5] Christianity invites its members into the intersection of suffering and salvation. Out of love, Jesus saves by entering the worst of human suffering, even death. Solidarity with Christ is solidarity with suffering humanity, which raises the suffering out of their condition. Empathetic action brings salvation to others. Christians long for, or better, strive for a paradise.

There is a strange feeling when we engage in empathetic action. We do seem to feel one another's pain. But there is also a feeling of satisfaction, of inner peace, a sense of the rightness or goodness in the action. We sense that the embrace of suffering humankind to heal, restore, and comfort ought to be the constant human response to the conditions we all face. It took the death of the Son of God on a cross to teach us this. There is glory in the cross and blessing in mourning. It may be when we are closest to God. We should not deny or belittle this feeling. Emil Cioran writes, "Were heaven and earth to disappear, the saints' tears would still endure. Out of the light and tears, a new world would be born, in which

---

5. Cioran, *Tears and Saints*, 3.

we could heal our memories."[6] Satisfaction is derived at the intersection of suffering and salvation.

To conclude these thoughts on belief in the church, I would like to recall an assertion—better put, perhaps, an unrealized wish I noted years ago from Edward Schillebeeckx's 1985 book *Church with a Human Face*. His is a plea for "humanity in the church." Ministers must adopt a lesson Schillebeeckx takes from Jesus. He writes, "Humanity's cause is God's cause and God's cause is humanity's cause."[7] The conditions for belief in the church are predicated on how well the church embodies that line. I can believe in a messy church—in part, because a messy church is an honest, human church; but I can also believe in a messy church if I can see God's cause being advanced through it. Belief in the church requires a community united to God for the advancement (read, salvation) of humankind. And I can contribute to the ministry in that church if I have the possibility to move humanity's cause ever so slightly toward God's cause.

---

6. Cioran, *Tears and Saints*, 59.
7. Schillebeeckx, *Church with a Human Face*, 41.

Part 3.

Concluding Thoughts

15

Amen

ASKING WHO GOD IS and what God does for us is an issue for systematic theology. In brief, God creates; God sustains; God saves. Of course, it gets far more complex. Because of the limits on our apprehension, the study of God's self-disclosure is divided into bits and pieces—theology's many subdisciplines. Some of them begin with humanity's desire for God and our ability to receive and understand the revelation. The fundamental questions, however, concern God.

Asking what religion is and what religion does for us are different questions altogether. Believers take what is presented as revelation and shape it into a force that defines the times and place and, most importantly, the collective as a people and the individual as a self. Religion is a system of symbols and symbolic acts embedded in a culture, communicating deeply held values for the construction and reconstruction of self, community, and society. Moreover, religion becomes a mode of perception that allows believers to take in, organize, valuate, and act upon the information needed for believers to survive and flourish.

Religiously motivated people make claims about the power at the core of the universe and whether humans can connect to and participate in that power. Christianity identifies the power as benevolent. It invites connection and participation. Not all preachers and teachers present our faith in terms of benevolent power; many think sinful humanity besmudged the whole. I lean in the other direction. God creates in goodness and saves in love. We can know and experience God's presence. As a result, believers can feel comfortable in their own skin and at home in the universe. The goodness at the core of reality allows for a positive valuation of this world, ourselves, and others. And it allows us to shape a response to human fragility that mitigates what could become a paralyzing fear of evil, suffering, and death.

Religion is a collective experience, even if American culture tries to privatize it. A lone individual cannot sustain a belief system, especially when it is challenged by suffering and death. A community of believers is required in those inevitable moments. The temptation to individualize religious experience might be based on the attraction of religious virtuosi, the heroes and heroines of the faith. Saints, prophets, messiahs, and saviors seem to rise above time and place, gaining a supernatural aura. The facts about them, however, are the opposite. These fascinating men and women create charismatic bonds with believers in particular moments and places. They are rooted in their faith, their times, and in their people. The bond they create results from their engagement. They reflect more deeply on their religious and cultural traditions, feel more intensely the predicament of their people, and reshape the traditions in response to their people's troubles. If their solutions succeed over time and adapt to different places, a supernatural aura develops.

This claim may sound over the top: effective pastoral ministers share something with religious virtuosi. Ministers must know and cherish the revelation and traditions. They must understand and feel the situation of the people. And they must articulate the faith in a way that assists believers to navigate the times. At their best, pastoral ministers share a bond with a congregation, an assembly, a people.

A theology for pastoral ministry exists in a space between systematic theology and religious studies. It is about the adaptation of the faith for believers in a particular time and place. This fine tuning may take place when ministers understand that the one truth has multiple dimensions, one of which is a symbolic dimension. In the articulation of a pastoral theology, the truth of the revelation cannot be detached from the deep feelings evoked by a symbol. The articulation of a symbolic system requires an authoritative grounding in the revelation and traditions. Believers must be able to perceive the revelation in what ministers say and do. The communication occurs in homilies and teaching moments and is embodied in the governance of the community, the peopling of its ministries, and the services and programs of the community. If the grounding is not evident, the minister's words and deeds will be dismissed as mere human opinion, a part of the cacophony of pundits and influencers.

A pastoral minister must also empathetically understand the situation of the people s/he serves. While based in the traditions of the community, the ministry is not to and for the past. While building a future, the ministry is not visionary. To expand on a concept from St. Augustine, we minister in the present of memory and of expectation. If believers perceive this grounding, experience the minister's sensitivity to their needs, and are offered wisdom for the times, the communication from the minister will appear as God's will in the here and now.

The essays in chapters 3 through 14 are attempts to think in that space. If the essays have succeeded, two levels of learning may be discerned: first, what it takes to create a pastoral theology; and, second, what the Christian creation of a self, community, and society may look like in the first half of the twenty-first century—at least from my situation in greater Cincinnati, Ohio, USA. The essays may seem abstract, removed a step or two from their communal context. This is inevitable, a price for disseminating these ideas to a larger audience. As I write, however, I am recalling the people I have served since my ordination in 1975. The ideas in this book have been tested from pulpits and in classrooms and vetted by congregations and students.

The primary purpose of this book is the creation of a pastoral theology, the features of which, after struggling with the experimental essays, I can now distill:

1. Before all else, the pastoral minister's art form is evocative. Ministers call forth what is stirring in the minds, hearts, and spirits of believers. In theological terms, God's Spirit is moving believers from within. Pastoral ministers can name the experience, explain that which is perplexing, and ground it in revelation. Ministers can also offer a community to nurture that experience. And ministers can point the believer to the omnipresence of God. Keeping this in mind gives perspective to the minister: God's Spirit is the cause, and the believer is the respondent! As much as the contemporary person is surrounded by entertainment, ministry is not showmanship. As much as the contemporary person is conditioned by consumerism, a minister is not a salesperson. As much as we admire the creative genius, the minister is not an original source. The pastoral minister attends to the movement of the Spirit in the believer. Pastoral ministry is an evocative art.

2. The contemporary person is confronted with an array of value systems. The creation of a coherent self requires choosing from that array and prioritizing the values the self has chosen. Pastoral ministers offer the gospel as the primary value source. If God directs history—as I believe God does—then the minister should not present a situation in which the gospel is set *against* the world, but a situation in which the gospel is working *in* the world. Certainly, there are moments when the times run contrary to Christian morality. On those occasions, a minister may become a prophet. But even in those times, the minister is likely rubbing shoulders with people who have chosen goodness. The crucial issue for pastoral ministry in a culture with such a vast array of choices is the grounding of the ministry itself. Pastoral ministry must be well-grounded in the revelation. Communications from the minister to the people must demonstrate that grounding.

3. The truth of Christianity was lived before the truth was articulated in propositional form and even before the evangelists wrote the Gospels. The same lived truth must be articulated for our communities. I have used the term performatory truth, a dimension of the truth that inspires action. I am most concerned with the action required in the creation of the Christian self and community. I have concluded that an active faith is generated from fundamental moods and motives, schemata for perceiving, valuating, and acting. If the faith percolates from that level, I am convinced Christian discipleship will follow. A believer will participate in the Christian community, follow a Christian way of life, and worship God.

4. Symbols are multivalent, and values migrate. This is a constant challenge to pastoral ministry. A pastoral minister implores believers to apply Christian values to all forms of social interaction—for instance, politics, economics, and family life. The minister must know that values developed in various forms of social interaction seep into the presentation of the gospel, some good—such as human rights and liberation movements—and some bad—such as consumerism. Likewise, the times will make demands that other generations of Christians were not required to face—environmental degradation, for example. The times may be a component in interpreting our truth—*one* God in our times requires us to be inclusive rather than exclusive. A critical approach to the times can develop

if pastoral ministers engage in dialogue with the people they serve, with one another, and with the larger church. Such dialogue may be contentious, but ultimately, it should prove insightful. After all, the ministers of the church work within a sacramental system. They profess that believers are united, through those ritual acts, in the divine. This obliges the pastoral minister to recognize the freedom of each believer and the active agency of believers in their own life journey. The dialogue of believers within community must be valued as sacred. Structures for dialogue are called for by the Second Vatican Council. The church has come a long way on the development of consultative structures. I think we have a long way to go.

5. Religion expresses a desire to connect with and participate in the power at the core of reality. The *Catechism of the Catholic Church* says, "The desire for God is written in the human heart."[1] Pastoral ministry today needs to cultivate transcendent moments that mediate God's presence. We are provided with many starting points for what Bernard Lonergan calls *the eros of the human spirit*: the wonder of creation; humanity's participation in the process of creating—art, music, literature; the record of humanity's pursuit of knowledge, truth, and wisdom; humanity's response to suffering and the degradation of the human person; the satisfaction derived from charity and compassion; humanity's long, hard slog toward freedom and human rights; and all the ways love is lived. All of it needs to be incorporated into the ministry of the Christian community. Anything that draws us out of ourselves toward God should be approached with a spirit of adoration and a spirit of gratitude, and therefore incorporated into Christian worship.

I hope the essays above are built around these premises. I hope these essays allow pastoral ministers to hone their own ability to articulate the lived truth of Jesus Christ.

Before I repeat some insights for the creation of a Christian self, allow me this one absolute truth: my insights are conditioned by my time and place. Lived truth is contingent. This means that my insights are highly debatable. They are open to enrichment by other ministers in different situations. Therefore, I present this summary as a series of questions for further research, reflection, and debate. I apologize to the reader if a listing of questions sounds like an examination of conscience.

1. *Catechism of the Catholic Church*, para. 27.

I intend to present questions that might instigate a dialogue to energize ministry. If I am right about the performative dimension of the truth, a pastoral minister not only proclaims the creeds and Scripture as forming a personal belief system, but s/he also professes them as an agenda for shaping a Christian community in a place and time.

1. How does one say *I believe* in contemporary times? Society does not necessarily support religion. Families have grown tolerant of non-believing relatives. To come to faith, a person is likely to encounter doubt and questioning, have flights of imagination, moments of hope and even creativity—all corollaries of freedom—as s/he envisions newness of life. Should not the ministry celebrate freedom as a gift from the same source as the gift of faith?

2. What does it mean to believe *in one God?* We teach that God is the one in whom we live, and move, and have our being. Can we teach how the divine draws us out of ourselves toward divinity? How would we imagine life connected to and participating in the Creator of all that exists and in the Savior of all humankind? How does proclaiming *one* define our relationships with people who differ from us?

3. What does *Almighty Father* mean? Can we imagine power that does not dominate or coerce but liberates? Can incarnation, *kenosis*, and *agape* define how we imagine God's use of divine power, and, by extension, how we use power?

4. What does *maker of heaven and earth, all things visible and invisible* communicate? William James wrote that religious people perceive an unseen order. Biblical wisdom literature confirms that God's wisdom is woven throughout creation. Can we experience that order? Can our experience of it re-embed us in creation for the sake of life and in the human family for the sake of peace?

5. What does our proclamation of the *Lord Jesus Christ* do for the valuation of our own lives and the lives of others? Can we develop a Christian ethic—the pursuit of a good life—along with Christian morality—a life given to right over against wrong? Can we articulate an aspirational Christianity through which we respond to a vertical pull, what Paul calls "a more excellent way"?

6. Does *incarnation* shape our lives? Does not God-with-us raise our valuation of each other? Can natality join mortality to define a Christian way of life for this world and the next?

7. What does *crucified* do to our perception of power? Jesus Christ was killed by the religious and political powers of his day. Does not the crucifixion offer a foundation for a critique of all power? How should Christians perceive and use power after the cross? Can the cross—in other words, the highest expression of liberating love, *agape*—redefine the exercise of power?

8. How do *resurrection* and *ascension* disrupt our lives? Can we imagine an alternative to the pushing and shoving of everyday life? Can we create lives that reflect the victory over all forces of sin and death?

9. How does *end-time* thinking change our sense of life goals? Can *end* mean fulfillment of life in this world, a fulfillment that anticipates the world to come?

10. What does the *indwelling of the Holy Spirit* mean for the direction of our lives? Should it not make us active agents for the renewal of the face of the earth? How does a church community facilitate the active involvement of inspirited believers for the consecration of this world?

11. Can finite humanity aspire to the perfections of the infinite triune God? We perceive an outward movement of God toward us. Can that movement become the model for our approach to others? Can it shape our valuation of the earth?

12. What does *belief in the church* mean? It is a flawed organization, scarred by the vicissitudes of history. Can we maintain order and encourage an inspirited assembly? Why do we desire a collective experience and do our faith communities reflect that desire? Can the church assist us in creating a spiritual home in this world?

During a liturgical year, we celebrate all the propositions of the creed. Likewise, each liturgical year, an assembly hears most of a Gospel. Pastoral ministry can think in that time frame. The whole of the truth cannot be presented and absorbed at one time—not in one year, perhaps not in a lifetime. Jesus showed great sympathy for his disciples when he allowed his truth to sink in before adding more (John 16:12). All the same, in one year, by addressing fundamental moods and motives, a pastoral minister can assist believers to move closer to discovering life's direction—its end, meaning, and purpose—and to think through and act upon the valuations of self, others, and the world. S/he can help believers understand *agape*, and therefore, the nature of God, as well as their relations with people like themselves and people who differ. And a pastoral minister can promote the construction of self and of a spiritual home in which to dwell in peace.

Bibliography

Alter, Robert, trans. *The Five Books of Moses*. New York: W. W. Norton, 2004.
Aquinas, Thomas. *Summa Theologica*. Translated by the Fathers of the English Dominican Province. New York: Benzinger Brothers, 1947.
Arendt, Hannah. *The Human Condition*. Chicago: University of Chicago Press, 1958.
Assad, Talal. *Genealogies of Religion: Discipline and Reasons of Power in Christianity and Islam*. Baltimore: John Hopkins University Press, 1993.
Augustine. *The Confessions*. Translated by Maria Boulding. Edited by John E. Rotelle. Hyde Park, NY: New City, 1997.
———. *The Trinity*. 2nd ed. Translated by Edmund Hill. Edited by John E. Rotelle. Hyde Park, NY: New City, 2011.
Balthasar, Hans Urs von. *Dare We Hope "That All Men Be Saved"? With a Short Discourse on Hell*. 2nd ed. Translated by David Kipp and Lothar Krauth. San Francisco: Ignatius, 1988.
———. "Vocation." *Communio* 37.1 (Spring 2010) 111–28.
Benedict XVI. "Diakonia of Truth." *Humanum* 2 (2015) 1–6. https://humanum-review.files.svdcdn.com/production/pdfs/Benedict-2015IssueTwo.pdf?dm=1624816932.
———. *Spe salvi*. Encyclical letter. Vatican website. Nov. 30, 2007. https://www.vatican.va/content/benedict-xvi/en/encyclicals/documents/hf_ben-xvi_enc_20071130_spe-salvi.html.
Berger, Peter L. *The Heretical Imperative: Contemporary Possibilities of Religious Affirmation*. New York: Anchor/Doubleday, 1979.
———. *The Many Altars of Modernity: Toward a Paradigm for Religion in a Pluralistic Age*. Boston: De Gruyter, 2014.
Bonanno, George A. *The Other Side of Sadness: What the New Science of Bereavement Tells Us About Life After Loss*. New York: Basic, 2009.
Borg, Marcus J. *Speaking Christian: Why Christian Words Have Lost Their Meaning and Power—and How They Can Be Restored*. New York: HarperCollins, 1989.
Bromiley, Geoffrey W. *Theological Dictionary of the New Testament: Abridged in One Volume*. Edited by Gerhard Kittel and Gerhard Friedrich. Grand Rapids: Eerdmans, 1985.
Brueggemann, Walter. *Theology of the Old Testament: Testimony, Dispute, Advocacy*. Minneapolis: Fortress, 1997.
Burt, Stephanie, and David Mikics, eds. *The Art of the Sonnet*. Cambridge: Belknap, 2010.
Catechism of the Catholic Church. 2nd ed. Libreria Editrice Vaticana, 1997.

Cioran, E. M. *Tears and Saints*. Translated by I. Zarifopol-Johnston. Chicago: University of Chicago Press, 1995.
Code of Canon Law: A Text and Commentary. Edited by James A. Coriden et al. New York: Paulist, 1985.
Cottingham, John. *On the Meaning of Life*. London: Routledge, 2003.
———. *Philosophy and the Good Life: Reason and the Passions in Greek, Cartesian and Psychoanalytic Ethics*. Cambridge: Cambridge University Press, 1998.
———. *The Spiritual Dimension: Religion, Philosophy and Human Value*. Cambridge: Cambridge University Press, 2005.
Crane, Tim. *The Meaning of Belief: Religion from an Atheist's Point of View*. Cambridge: Harvard University Press, 2017.
De Botton, Alain. *Religion for Atheists: A Non-Believer's Guide to the Uses of Religion*. New York: Pantheon, 2012.
Del Noce, Augusto. *The Age of Secularization*. Edited and translated by Carlo Lancellotti. Montreal: McGill-Queen's University Press, 2017.
Donahue, John R., and Daniel J. Harrington. *The Gospel of Mark*. Edited by Daniel J. Harrington. Sacra Pagina 2. Collegeville, MN: Liturgical, 2002.
Durkheim, Emile. *The Elementary Form of the Religious Life*. Translated by Joseph Ward Swain. New York: Free, 1965.
Dworkin, Ronald. *Justice for Hedgehogs*. Cambridge: Belknap, 2011.
———. *Religion Without God*. Cambridge: Harvard University Press, 2013.
Eco, Umberto, and Carlo Maria Martini. *Belief or Unbelief? A Confrontation*. Translated by Minna Proctor. New York: Arcade, 2000.
Edwards, Michael. *The Bible and Poetry*. Translated by Stephen E. Lewis. New York: New York Review Books, 2023.
Falque, Emmanuel. *The Guide to Gethsemane: Anxiety, Suffering, Death*. Translated by George Hughes. Perspectives in Continental Philosophy. New York: Fordham University Press, 2019.
———. *The Metamorphosis of Finitude: An Essay on Birth and Resurrection*. Translated by George Hughes. Perspectives in Continental Philosophy. New York: Fordham University Press, 2012.
Fenn, Richard K. *Beyond Idols: The Shape of a Secular Society*. Oxford: Oxford University Press, 2001.
———. *Toward a Theory of Secularization*. SSSR Monograph Series 1. N.p.: Society for the Scientific Study of Religion, 1978.
Feuerbach, Ludwig. *The Essence of Christianity*. Translated by George Eliot. New York: Cosimo Classics, 2008.
Flannery, Austin, ed. *Apostolicam actuositatem*. In *Vatican Council II: The Conciliar and Post Conciliar Documents*, 776–98. Rev. ed. Collegeville, MN: Liturgical, 1992.
———. *Gaudium et spes*. In *Vatican Council II: The Conciliar and Post Conciliar Documents*, 903–1001. Rev. ed. Collegeville, MN: Liturgical, 1992.
———. *Lumen gentium*. In *Vatican Council II: The Conciliar and Post Conciliar Documents*, 350–426. Rev. ed. Collegeville, MN: Liturgical, 1992.
Fox, Everett, trans. and ed. *The Five Books of Moses: Genesis, Exodus, Leviticus, Numbers, Deuteronomy*. Schocken Bible 1. New York: Schocken, 1983.
Francis. *Veritatis gaudium*. Apostolic constitution. Vatican website. Jan. 29, 2018. https://press.vatican.va/content/salastampa/en/bollettino/pubblico/2018/01/29/180129c.html.

Fuller, John. *Flying to Nowhere*. New York: George Braziller, 1984.
Gauchet, Marcel. *The Disenchantment of the World: A Political History of Religion.* Translated by Oscar Burge. Princeton: Princeton University Press, 1997.
Geertz, Clifford. "Religion as a Cultural System." In *Anthropological Approaches to the Study of Religion*, edited by Michael Banton, 1–46. London: Tavistock, 1966.
Giddens, Anthony. *Modernity and Self-Identity: Self and Society in the Late Modern Age.* Stanford: Stanford University Press, 1991.
Hadot, Pierre. *Philosophy as a Way of Life: Spiritual Exercises from Socrates to Foucault.* Oxford: Blackwell, 1995.
Harrington, Daniel J. *The Gospel of Matthew.* Edited by Daniel J. Harrington. Sacra Pagina 1. Collegeville: Liturgical, 1991.
Harrington, Wilfrid J. *Revelation.* Edited by Daniel J. Harrington. Sacra Pagina 16. Collegeville: Liturgical, 1993.
Hervieu-Leger, Daniele. "Individualism, the Validation of Faith, and the Social Nature of Religion in Modernity." In *The Blackwell Companion to Sociology of Religion*, edited by Richard K. Fenn, 161–75. Malden, MA: Blackwell, 2001.
James, William. *The Varieties of Religious Experience.* Library of America. New York: Vintage, 1990.
Joas, Hans. *Do We Need Religion? On the Experience of Self-Transcendence.* Translated by Alex Skinner. Boulder, CO: Paradigm, 2008.
———. *The Power of the Sacred: An Alternative to the Narrative of Disenchantment.* Translated by Alex Skinner. Oxford: Oxford University Press, 2021.
Kolakowski, Leszek. "Jesus Christ—Prophet and Reformer." In *Is God Happy: Selected Essays.* Translated by Agnieszka Kolakowski, 143–59. New York: Basic, 2013.
Levinas, Emmanuel. *Of God Who Comes to Mind.* Translated by Bettina Bergo. Stanford: Stanford University Press, 1998.
Lifton, Robert Jay. *The Protean Self: Human Resilience in an Age of Fragmentation.* New York: Basic, 1993.
Lindbeck, George A. *The Nature of Doctrine: Religion and Theology in a Postliberal Age.* Louisville: Westminster John Knox, 1984.
Lohfink, Gerhard. *Jesus of Nazareth: What He Wanted, Who He Is.* Translated by Linda M. Maloney. Collegeville, MN: Liturgical, 2012.
———. *The Our Father: A New Reading.* Translated by Linda M. Maloney. Collegeville, MN: Liturgical, 2015.
Lonergan, Bernard. *Method in Theology.* Toronto: University of Toronto Press, 1971.
Martin, David. *The Breaking of the Image: A Sociology of Christian Theory & Practice.* Vancouver: Regent College Publishing, 1979.
———. *A General Theory of Secularization.* New York: Harper & Row, 1978.
———. *On Secularization: Towards a Revised General Theory.* Aldershot, UK: Ashgate, 2005.
Masuzawa, Tomoko. *The Invention of World Religions: Or, How European Universalism Was Preserved in the Language of Pluralism.* Chicago: University of Chicago Press, 2005.
Merton, Thomas. *The Seven Story Mountain.* San Diego: Harcourt Brace, 1948.
The Most Holy Rosary. "First Saturdays Devotion." Last updated May 2020. http://www.themostholyrosary.com/appendix2.htm.
Nogar, Raymond J. *The Lord of the Absurd.* Notre Dame: University of Notre Dame Press, 1998.

Nongbri, Brent. *Before Religion: A History of a Modern Concept.* New Haven: Yale University Press, 2013.
Order of Christian Funerals. Translated by the International Commission on English in the Liturgy. New York: Catholic Book, 1989.
Orsi, Robert A. *History and Presence.* Cambridge: Belknap, 2016.
———. "The Problem of the Holy." In *The Cambridge Companion to Religious Studies*, edited by Robert A. Orsi, 84–105. Cambridge: Cambridge University Press, 2012.
Otto, Rudolf. *The Idea of the Holy: An Inquiry into the Non-Rational Factor in the Idea of the Divine and Its Relation to the Rational.* Translated by John W. Harvey. Oxford: Oxford University Press, 1976.
Pius IX. *Ineffabilis Deus.* Encyclical letter. Papal Encyclicals Online. Dec. 8, 1854. www.papalencyclicals.net.
Pius XII. *Munificentissimus Deus.* Apostolic constitution. Vatican website. Nov. 1, 1950. https://www.vatican.va/content/pius-xii/en/apost_constitutions/documents/hf_p-xii_apc_19501101_munificentissimus-deus.html.
Rahner, Karl. *The Content of the Faith: The Best of Karl Rahner's Theological Writings.* Edited by Karl Lehmann and Albert Raffelt. Translated by Harvey D. Egan. New York: Crossroad, 1994.
———. *Foundations of Christian Faith: An Introduction to the Idea of Christianity.* Translated by William V. Dych. New York: Crossroad, 1994.
———. "Incarnation." In *Encyclopedia of Theology: The Concise Sacramentum Mundi.* Edited by Karl Rahner, 690–99. New York: Crossroad, 1984.
———. *The Practice of the Faith: A Handbook of Contemporary Spirituality.* Edited by Karl Lehmann and Albert Raffelt. New York: Crossroad, 1984.
Robbins, Bruce. "Enchantment? No, Thank You!" In *The Joy of Secularism: 11 Essays for How We Live Now.* Edited by George Levine, 74–94. Princeton: Princeton University Press, 2011.
Roman Missal. 3rd ed. Totowa, NJ: Catholic Book, 2011.
Rorty, Richard, and Gianni Vattimo. *The Future of Religion.* Edited by Santiago Zabala. New York: Columbia University Press, 2005.
Roszak, Theodore. *The Making of a Counter Culture.* Berkeley: University of California Press, 1969.
San Martin, Inés. "Pope Francis Delivers Another Lesson in the 'Theology of Tears.'" *Crux*, May 5, 2016. https://cruxnow.com/church/2016/05/pope-francis-delivers-another-lesson-in-the-theology-of-tears.
Schillebeeckx, Edward. *The Church with a Human Face: A New and Expanded Theology of Ministry.* Translated by John Bowden. New York: Crossroad, 1985.
Schmaus, Michael. "Holy Spirit." In *Encyclopedia of Theology: The Concise Sacramentum Mundi.* Edited by Karl Rahner, 642–50. New York: Crossroad, 1984.
Schmidt, Josef. "A Dialogue in Which There Can Only Be Winners." In *An Awareness of What Is Missing: Faith and Reason in a Post-Secular Age.* Edited by Jurgen Habermas. Translated by Ciaran Cronin, 59–71. Cambridge: Polity, 2010.
Schmitz, Robert E. *A Methodology for a Pastoral Theology.* Morrow, OH: Inspired, 2023.
———. *A Pastor's Thoughts on Secularization.* Morrow, OH: Inspired, 2023.
Searle, John R. *Making the Social World: The Structure of Human Civilization.* Oxford: Oxford University Press, 2010.
Shakespeare, William. *The Tragedy of Romeo and Juliet.* Edited by W. A. Nelson and A. H. Thorndike. The Tudor Shakespeare. New York: Macmillan, 1911.

Sloterdijk, Peter. *God's Zeal: The Battle of the Three Monotheisms*. Translated by Wieland Hoben. Cambridge: Polity, 2009.

———. *You Must Change Your Life: On Anthropotechnics*. Translated by Wieland Hoban. Cambridge: Polity, 2013.

Smith, William Cantwell. *The Meaning and End of Religion: A Revolutionary Approach to the Great Religious Traditions*. New York: Harper & Row, 1978.

Stark, Rodney, and William Sims Bainbridge. *The Future of Religion: Secularization, Revival, and Cult Formation*. Berkeley: University of California Press, 1985.

Sullivan, Harry Stack. *Conceptions of Modern Psychiatry*. New York: Norton, 1953.

Taylor, Charles. "Disenchantment—Reenchantment." In *The Joy of Secularism: 11 Essays for How We Live Now*, edited by George Levine, 57–73. Princeton: Princeton University Press, 2011.

———. *A Secular Age*. Cambridge: Belknap, 2007.

———. *Sources of the Self: The Making of the Modern Identity*. Cambridge: Harvard University Press, 1989.

Taylor, Mark C. *After God*. Chicago: University of Chicago Press, 2007.

Teilhard de Chardin, Pierre. *The Divine Milieu*. New York: Harper Torchbooks, 2001.

Vattimo, Gianni. *After Christianity*. Translated by Luca D'Isanto. New York: Columbia University Press, 2002.

———. *Belief*. Translated by Luca D'Isanto and David Webb. Stanford: Stanford University Press, 1999.

———. *Nihilism and Emancipation: Ethics, Politics, and Law*. Translated by William McCuaig. New York: Columbia University Press, 2004.

Weber, Max. *Economy and Society: An Outline of Interpretive Sociology*. Edited by Guenther Roth and Claus Wittich. Translated by Ephraim Fischoff et al. Berkeley: University of California Press, 1978.

———. "Science as a Vocation." In *From Max Weber: Essays in Sociology*, edited by H. H. Gerth and C. Wright Mills, 129–58. Oxford: Oxford University Press, 1958.

Index

Page numbers followed by "n" and a number indicate a footnote. For example, 77 n16, indicates footnote 16 on page 77.

abba, God as, 56, 66, 148, 152–53, 182
Abraham, 17, 21, 54, 58–60, 103
absolutes, 36–37
abundant life, 19, 35–38, 97
actuality, 157, 164–65
adoption of believers, 56, 66, 148–49, 152
adoration, spirit of, 57, 171–72, 193
afterlife, 17–18, 25, 31–32, 143–44, 146, 184
agape. *See also* love
　overview, 67, 69
　the church and, 68–69
　as command, 59–60
　between Father and Son, 67–68
　Jesus Christ and, 119, 121
　power as, 67, 70
agency. *See also* freedom
　of all humans, 44–45, 149, 159
　of believers, 9, 47, 140, 145, 177–78, 193
Alter, Robert, 156
Annas (chief priest), 100
the Annunciation, 26
Anselm, St., 109, 118
anthropotechnics, 13
apocalyptic literature, 23, 135–40, 147
the Apostles Creed, 71
Apostolicam actuositatem, 168. *See also* the Second Vatican Council
Aquinas, Thomas, St., 146–47, 155, 164–66, 169–70
Arendt, Hannah, 19, 106–7

art and creativity, 26, 28–29, 61, 193
the ascension of Jesus Christ, 23–24, 126, 128, 130–32
askesis, 77
aspirational Christianity, 92–96, 166, 174, 181–83
Assyrian Empire, 103, 129, 135
atheism, 5
atonement, substitutionary, 109–10
Augustine, St., 20–22, 41–42, 171
authenticity, xiv, 21–22, 34, 179
authoritarianism, 6, 91, 174
authority, religious
　correct use of, 113
　crucifixion and, 115–16
　misuse of, 61, 175
　ontological security and, 46–47
　secularization and, 5
autonomy. *See* freedom

Babylonian Empire, 56, 103, 129, 135
Balthasar, Hans Urs von, 43, 73
baptism
　explicit religiosity and, 8
　the Holy Spirit and, 153
　of Jesus Christ, 67, 88
　results of, 18, 31, 35, 53, 110, 123
Barabbas (revolutionary), 64
Bathsheba, wife of Uriah, 182
the Beatitudes, 33
belief. *See* faith

believers. *See also* the church; community, Christian; cross, taking up our; empowerment of believers
  adopted by God, 56, 66, 148–49, 152
  agency of, 9, 47, 140, 145, 177–78, 193 (*See also* freedom)
  communion of, 146–47
  glory of, 59, 68, 69, 91, 163, 170–71
  love of, 59, 68–70, 119, 169–71
  mission of, 57, 59–60, 95–96, 131–34, 162
  resurrection of, 18, 56, 57, 110, 144
Benedict XVI, Pope, xii, 4–5, 104
bereavement/grief, 31–33, 79. *See also* mourning/sorrow
Berger, Peter L., xiii
Bethlehem, 88, 100
the Bible. *See* the Scripture/revelation
blood, meaning of, 110, 118
the body (human)
  care for, 57
  resurrection of, 18, 57
  the soul and, 27, 57, 77, 77 n16
Bonanno, George, 33
Book of Signs (John 1–11), 93
Borg, Marcus, 115, 162
boundaries, social
  the church and, 19, 95, 176
  God's love and, 37, 67
  identity and, 19, 150
  Jesus Christ and, 19–20, 58, 69, 95, 116–17
Bromiley, Geoffrey W., 66, 67

Caesar Augustus, 100
Caiaphas (chief priest), 100
calling, personal, 43, 48–49, 73, 75
Calvin, John, 105
the Canticle of Zechariah, 100
Capernaum, 88
capitalism, 105
Catechism of the Catholic Church
  communion of the saints in, 146–47
  desire for God in, 193
  divine-human partnership in, 24
  doubt in, 47–48
  gifts of the Holy Spirit in, 154

  mission of believers in, 95–96
  transformation of believers in, 89–90
The Catholic University of America, xii
celibacy, 157, 169, 176
the centurion at the cross, 111, 119–20
the centurion requesting cure for servant, 49
Chair of Peter, 47
change
  the church and, 158–59, 175–77
  our lives and, 15, 94, 110, 149
  secularization and, 4
  social systems and, 149
chaos, 45–46, 138–41
children, 112–13
choices/decision making. *See also* agency; freedom
  in culture/society, xiii, 37–38
  faith and, xii, 36–38
  of light or darkness, 144–45
  secularization and, 5–6
  values for, 4, 6
Christianity, aspirational, 92–96, 166, 174, 181–83
Christians. *See* believers
Christmas, 99–103
the church. *See also* community, Christian; participation in the church; power in the church
  assessment of, 174
  biblical imagery of, 18–19, 175
  as the body of Christ, 24, 54, 70, 146–47, 155, 167
  change in, 158–59, 175–77
  comfort in, 29–34, 184–85
  compulsion by, 7
  diversity in, 16–17, 19–20, 37
  ecumenism in, 19, 176
  holiness in, 20, 80–81, 97–98, 169, 176
  mission of, 57, 59–60, 95–96, 131–34, 162
  the Nicene Creed on, 173–86
  problems with, 74, 151, 158, 173–75, 186
  role of, 71–74, 159, 177–78, 180

INDEX

the Second Vatican Council on, 18,
    158, 175, 182
  unity in, 54, 178
Church with a Human Face
    (Schillebeeckx), 186
Cioran, Emil, 33, 34, 185–86
climate change, 55
cognition, xi–xii, 10, 26–27, 53
cognitive interaction, 4
coherent self. *See* self, coherent,
    formation of
comfort, 29–34, 184–85
Communion, Holy. *See* the Eucharist/
    communion
communion of the saints, 146–47
Communist Poland, 5
community, Christian. *See also* the
    church
  overview, 177–81
  assessment of, 174
  bereavement/grief and, 31
  construction of, 16–17, 38
  fight against evil and, 35
  isolationism in, 104
  Jesus Christ and, 125, 140
  necessity of, 190
  pluralism and, 167
  purpose of, 73–74
compulsion by the church, 7
condemnation, 58, 144–45, 148
confession of sin, 25–26, 31, 96–97, 170
The Confessions (Augustine), 20–21, 41
confirmation, 9, 18, 153, 166
control. *See* power in the church:
    misuse of
Corinth, 154–55, 183
Cottingham, John, 75, 76
counterculture, the church as, 3
the creation
  accounts of, 7–8
  our responsibility for, 7, 37, 55–57,
    60, 95
  waiting for the end times, 56, 95, 148
the creation, new
  description of, 57, 95
  Hebrew Scriptures and, 18
  hope for, 56, 148
  prophets on, 57, 126

the Second Coming and, 18
creativity and art, 26, 28–29, 61, 193
Creator, God as, 25, 27, 45, 57, 86–87
creeds, xi–xii, 71, 194. *See also* the
    Nicene Creed
cross, taking up our
  meaning of, 34, 123
  calling to, 121
  consequences of not, 143
  as participation in salvation, 195
  viewed as victimization, 127
the crucifixion/cross, 6, 34, 58–60,
    109–21
crying/tears, 33–34, 185–86
culture/society, xiii–xiv, 3–6, 146

David, King, 182
De Botton, Alain, 25, 30
death. *See also* the crucifixion/cross;
    suffering
  afterlife and, 17–18, 25, 31–32,
    143–44, 146, 184
  bereavement and, 31–33, 79
  freedom from, 56–57, 132–33, 148
  social, 178, 178 n3
decision making/choices. *See* choices/
    decision making
Dei verbum, 18, 175. *See also* the
    Second Vatican Council
democracy, 4, 105
desacralization, 5, 111, 116–17, 149
Descartes, René, 42
the devil/Satan, 23, 112, 136, 139, 182
dignity, human, 75, 93, 107, 176
disabled persons, 80–81
disciples of Jesus
  empowerment of, 23, 126–27,
    130–32, 152
  failure of, 143
  faith and, 24–25, 49
  Jesus Christ's identity and, 112
  love and, 68
  mission of, 131–32
  opposition to, 138
  resurrection and, 124–30
  seeking power, 112–15

205

diversity in the church, 16–17, 19–20, 37. *See also* inclusivity; pluralism
Divine Milieu (Teilhard de Chardin), 55
divinity of Jesus Christ, 89, 118, 120
Divino afflante Spiritu (Pius XII), 18, 175
division, social. *See* boundaries, social
doctrines, 10, 30, 99
domination of others, 3, 6, 51, 63, 104, 119
Donahue, John, 112–14
doubts and questions, 9, 42–49, 72–74
Dworkin, Ronald, 77–78, 78 n18

Eco, Umberto, 17, 36, 137
economics, 4, 5, 95, 149, 166
ecumenism, 19, 176. *See also* diversity in the church
Edwards, Michael, 27
Egypt, 51, 63, 100
Emmanuel, 130
Emmaus, 100, 129
emotions/feelings, 10–11, 81, 110–11
empowerment of believers
  faith as, 49–50
  Holy Spirit and, 131–32, 152, 154
  Jesus Christ and, 23, 131
  religious leaders and, 62, 70
the end times, 34–36, 132–33, 136–37, 147–51. *See also* the Second Coming
enemies, love for, 20, 59, 69, 148, 170
the Enlightenment, 105
the environment, 7, 37, 55–57, 60, 101
Ephesus, 138–39, 183
equality/human rights, 95, 159, 178
eternal life, 17–18, 25, 31–32, 143–44, 146, 184
ethics, xiii, xiii n5, 78, 137, 139–40. *See also* morality
the Eucharist/communion. *See also* rites and sacraments
  adoration of, 171–72
  the cross and, 118–21
  prayers of, 55–56, 106
  preparation for, 25
  results of, 18, 31, 53, 146–47

evil. *See also* sin
  in apocalyptic literature, 23
  Christian response to, 139–40, 145, 184–85
  limits on, 136
  morality and, xiii n5
  our participation in, 30–31, 35, 121, 161
  Satan/the devil and, 23, 112, 136, 139, 182
  sin *vs.*, 96–97
  source of, 153
evolution and science, 4, 8, 157
exclusivity, 7, 19, 20, 192. *See also* boundaries, social; inclusivity
the exodus, 27, 51, 103
expansive religiosity. *See also* aspirational Christianity; explicit religiosity
  content of, 13–14, 159–60
  effects of, 172
  lay participation and, 168–69
  pastoral ministry and, xiii–xiv, 9
  procession of the Jesus Christ as, 168
  transcendence and, 91–92
expectation/hope, 21–22, 56, 89, 135–38, 148, 184
explicit religiosity, 8–9, 91, 157, 159, 172
expulsion from community, 178, 178 n3

failures, 7, 97, 139, 143, 181. *See also* sin
faith. *See also* solitude
  comfort and, 29–34, 184–85
  community and, 16–17
  decision making/choices and, xii, 36–38
  the end times and, 34–36
  expansive *vs.* explicit religiosity and, xiii, 9
  functions of, 15–16
  inclusivity and, 19–20
  life and, 17–19
  perspective and, 24–26
  power of, 49–50
  time and, 20–22
  transcendence and, 26–29
  the world and, 22–24
Falque, Emmanuel, 151, 153, 166

INDEX

fatherhood
    of God, 56, 66, 69, 148
    patriarchal, 20, 65–66, 113
fear, 7, 135–36, 184
feelings/emotions, 10–11, 81, 110–11
Fenn, Richard, 62, 91
Feuerbach, Ludwig, 24, 93
Flying to Nowhere (Fuller), 171
forgiveness. *See also* sin
    Jesus Christ and, 89, 92, 118, 125
    pastoral ministry and, 25–26,
        31–32, 38, 96–97, 170, 184
Foundations of Christian Faith
    (Rahner), 47
Fox, Everett, 156
Francis, Pope, xii, 34
freedom. *See also* agency
    as gift, 37, 45, 48, 119, 149
    Holy Spirit and, 155–56, 158
    Jesus Christ provides, 115–19
    ontological security and, 47–48
    from sin and death, 56–57, 132–33,
        148
    society and, 6
fruit of the Holy Spirit, 53, 59–60, 97, 155
Fuller, John, 171
fundamentalism, 46–47, 175

Gabriel (angel), 26
Galilee, 125–26, 128–29, 132
gap, 77, 78, 79, 87, 158
Gauchet, Marcel, 114
Geertz, Clifford, 11
genealogies of Jesus Christ, 65, 182
Genesis, 10, 56–57
Germany, Nazi, 5
Giddens, Anthony, 45–46
gifts of the Holy Spirit, 69, 153–55, 183
glory
    of believers, 59, 68–69, 91, 163,
        170–71
    of God, 53, 59, 110, 161, 171–72
    of Jesus Christ, 59, 68, 141, 163, 185
God. *See also* the Holy Spirit; Jesus
        Christ
    activity in history (*See* history,
        God's activity in)
    as Creator, 25, 27, 45, 57, 86–87
    as father, 56, 66, 69, 148
    glory of, 53, 59, 110, 161, 171–72
    image of, 41–42, 57, 95
    love of, 23, 37, 53–54, 59, 67–69,
        119
    nature of, 52–53, 71–72
    the Nicene Creed on, 9, 61–70,
        71–87
    objectified image of, 156–57
    omnipresence of, 26–27
    power of, 61–63, 66–68, 114, 117,
        153
    presence of, 26–28
    reconciliation to, 36, 110, 124–25,
        162
    as triune, 60, 69, 161–73
God's Zeal: The Battle of the Three
    Monotheisms (Sloterdijk),
    103–4
the good news/gospel (message)
    content of, 26
    abandonment of, 139
    the incarnation and, 102
    spread of, 57, 125–26
the Gospels (books of the Bible)
    overview, 122
    divinity of Jesus Christ in, 89, 118,
        120
    the end times in, 132–33
    endings of, 130–32
    the Eucharist/communion in, 118,
        120
    faith in, 49
    humanity of Jesus Christ in, 88–89
    identity of Jesus Christ in, 119–20
    Lord as title for Jesus Christ in, 89
    power/greatness in, 63, 112–17
    predictions of Jesus Christ's death
        in, 111–14
    the resurrection in, 122–30
grace of God, 45, 110, 125, 151, 163
gratitude, 17, 193
greatness. *See* power in the church
Greeks, ancient, 76–77, 103, 129, 135
grief/bereavement, 31–33, 79. *See also*
    mourning/sorrow
guards/soldiers at tomb, 125, 127

Hadot, Pierre, 76–77
the Hail Mary, 106
Harrington, Daniel, 112–14, 132, 142
Harrington, Wilfrid, 138–39
heaven, 35, 38, 49, 86–87. *See also* afterlife
the Hebrew Scriptures, 18, 175
Herod, King, 100, 114
history, God's activity in
 gives meaning, 137–38
 Jesus Christ as, 132–33
 major interventions and, 103
 as principal actor, 23
holiness, 20, 80–81, 97–98, 169, 176
the Holiness Code, 20
the Holy Spirit
 overview of, 152–53, 156
 attitude of Christ and, 54
 believers' adoption and, 152
 Christ's body and, 54
 the church and, 152
 at creation, 152
 empowerment by, 131–32, 154
 freedom and, 155–56, 158
 fruit of, 53, 97, 155
 gifts of, 69, 153–55, 183
 indwelling of, 126, 152, 156, 162
 intercession of, 152–53
 love and, 155
 mind of the Lord and, 54
 misappropriation of, 153–54
 the Nicene Creed on, 152–72
 procession of, 165, 169
 as wind, 156
home, spiritual, 7, 9–11, 15–16, 159, 181
hope/expectation, 21–22, 56, 89, 135–38, 148, 184
humanity of Jesus Christ, 88–89
humankind
 agency of, 44–45, 149, 159
 creation of, 57
 dignity of, 75, 93, 107, 176
 in divine-human partnership, 24
 equality/rights of, 95, 159, 178
 image of God in, 41–42, 57, 95
 language and, 10
 role of, 57
hypostatic union, 99–100

iconography, 26, 111
The Idea of the Holy (Otto), 82
identity formation, 19–21, 93–94, 150. *See also* self, coherent, formation of
image of God, 41–42, 57, 95
imagery, biblical, of the church, 18–19, 175
imagination, 9–10, 21–22, 44, 61, 166–67
the incarnation, 23, 88–91, 99–108, 130. *See also kenosis*
inclusivity, 19–20, 117, 126, 177. *See also* diversity in the church; pluralism
individualism, 24, 153–54, 155, 158–59, 190
infallibility, papal, 46–47, 173
interactions, social, 3–6, 91, 107, 192. *See also* community, Christian
Irenaeus, St., 52, 162
Islam, 103
Israel/Israelites
 aggression against, 103, 129, 135
 apocalyptic literature by, 135
 expectations of Messiah in, 112, 132–33
 God's promises to, 103, 171
 the Holiness Code and, 20
 Jesus Christ as king of, 64
 judgment of, 141–42
 leaders of and Jesus Christ, 63, 116

James, son of Zebedee, 113
James, William
 on journey to faith, 45
 on religion, 27, 42, 45, 72, 194
 on tradition of *more,* 29
Jesus Christ. *See also* disciples of Jesus; God; the Holy Spirit
 the ascension of, 23–24, 126, 128, 131–32
 the baptism of, 67, 88
 community and, 125, 140
 the crucifixion/cross of, 6, 34, 58–60, 109–21
 divinity of, 89, 118, 120
 forgiveness and, 89, 92, 118, 125

freedom through, 115–19
genealogies of, 65, 182
glory of, 59, 68, 141, 163, 185
humanity of, 88–89
identity of, 88–89, 112, 119–20
the incarnation of, 23, 88–91, 99–108, 130 (*See also* kenosis)
love of, 38, 59, 67–68, 118–19, 121
the Nicene Creed on, 88–151
as Passover lamb, 116–17
procession of, 165, 168
the resurrection of, 89, 110, 122–34, 128 n2
return of, 18, 132, 140
salvation through, 19, 35, 110, 151
social boundaries and, 19–20, 58, 69, 95, 116–17
the temptations of, 52–53
the transfiguration of, 67
Joanna, 125, 182
Joas, Hans, 79
Job, 25
John, Gospel of. *See* the Gospels (books of the Bible)
John, son of Zebedee, 113
John Paul II, Pope, 4–5
John the baptizer, 88, 116–17, 182
Joseph, husband of Mary, 65, 100
Joseph, son of Jacob, 182
joy
　eternal life and, 146
　faith and, xiii, 92, 119
　as fruit of the Holy Spirit, 97
　sources of, 37, 45
Judaism, 20, 103. *See also* Israel/Israelites
judgment, 141–46, 151. *See also* condemnation
justice, 7, 18, 69, 95, 103, 154, 175
justification, 110

kenosis, 3, 67, 118–19, 121. *See also* the incarnation
knowledge, 5, 26, 70, 85–86, 161
Kolakowski, Leszek, 149–51
Kung, Hans, 36

La Rochefoucauld, François de, 151

language, 10–12, 27, 181
Laodicea, 139
the Last Supper, 53, 68, 116, 118, 119
lay ministry, 17, 168–69, 171, 176. *See also* participation in the church
Leo XIII, Pope, 22–23, 175
Levinas, Emmanuel, 52, 54
life
　eternal, 17–18, 25, 31–32, 143–44, 146, 184
　newness of/abundant, 19, 35–38, 97
　value of, 17–19
light, 56, 92, 103–5, 129, 144–46
Lohfink, Gerhard, 17, 128 n2
Lonergan, Bernard, 10–11, 48, 84–86, 91–92, 193
the Lord's Prayer, 19, 25
Lourdes, 80
love
　of believers, 59, 68–70, 119, 169–71
　for enemies, 20, 59, 69, 148, 170
　of God, 23, 37, 53–54, 59, 67–69, 119
　Holy Spirit as, 155
　of Jesus Christ, 38, 59, 67–68, 118–19, 121
loyalties, 93–96
Luke, Gospel of. *See* the Gospels (books of the Bible)
Lumen gentium, 158, 167. *See also* the Second Vatican Council

the Magnificat, 100
Margaret of Citta di Castello, 80–81
Marion, Jean-Luc, 29, 81
Mark, Gospel of. *See* the Gospels (books of the Bible)
Martini, Cardinal (archbishop of Milan), 17, 36, 136–37, 147
Mary, mother of James, 124, 125
Mary, Virgin
　the Annunciation, 26
　Blessed Virgin at Lourdes, 80
　feasts of, 30
　the Hail Mary, 106
　the Magnificat, 100
　mother of Jesus Christ, 88, 100
　Salve Regina and, 22–23

Mary Magdalene/of Magdala, 124–26, 128–29, 131, 182
the Mass, 25, 106, 111, 120
Matthew (disciple), 59
Matthew, Gospel of. *See* the Gospels (books of the Bible)
mediators, 52, 90–93, 155, 159, 166
Meditations (Descartes), 42
Merton, Thomas, 145–46
ministry, lay, 17, 168–69, 171, 176. *See also* participation in the church
ministry, pastoral. *See also* theology, pastoral
    challenge of, xii–xiv
    Christian values and, 6–7
    comfort through, 29–32
    doubts and questions and, 44
    energizing, 194–96
    explicit *vs.* expansive religiosity in, xiii–xiv, 8–9
    freedom and, 48
    the present and, 21–22
misery. *See* suffering
mission of believers, 57, 59–60, 95–96, 131–34, 162
modernity, 42, 159
monasticism, 104
monotheism, 54
moods and motives, 11–12
morality, xiii, xiii n5, 78, 96, 104. *See also* choices/decision making
more, 79, 81, 87, 92, 93, 96, 97, 158
mortality, 38, 106–7. *See also* death
Moses, 58, 171
mourning/sorrow, 33–34, 185–86. *See also* bereavement/grief

narcissism, 24–25, 52–53, 153–55
natality, 19, 37, 106–7
nationalism, 94–95, 104
the nativity story, 100–101. *See also* the incarnation
Nazareth, 49, 88
Nazi Germany, 5
the new creation. *See* the creation, new
newness of life, 19, 35–38, 97
the Nicene Creed
    about, 70

    "I believe," 9, 41–50
    "in one God," 9, 51–60
    "Father almighty," 9, 61–70
    "maker of heaven and earth, of all things visible and invisible," 71–87
    "Lord Jesus Christ," 88–98
    "incarnate," 99–108
    "crucified," 109–21
    "rose again and ascended," 122–34
    "come again in glory," 135–51
    "in the Holy Spirit, the Lord, the giver of life," 152–60
    "who proceeds from the Father and the Son, adored and glorified," 161–72
    "in one, holy, catholic, and apostolic church," 173–86
Nicodemus, 102, 144, 156
Nietzsche, Friedrich, 13
Nihilism and Emancipation: Ethics, Politics, and Law (Vattimo), 105
nostalgia, 21

Ode to Love (Paul), 68–69, 155, 183
omnipresence of God, 26–27
ontological security, 45–48
Order of Christian Funerals, 31
original sin, 34–35, 37, 184
Orsi, Robert, 28–29, 80–81, 84
Otto, Rudolf, 81–83

papal infallibility, 46–47, 173
parishioners. *See* believers
participation in the church
    explicit religiosity and, 8–9
    pastoral ministry and, 180–81
    reasons for or against, 6–7, 15–16, 180, 181
    the Second Vatican Council on, 17, 167–69, 176, 193
Passover, 9, 63, 64, 116–17
pastoral ministry. *See* ministry, pastoral
patriarchy, 20, 65–66, 113
Paul VI, Pope, xii
Paul/Saul, 126, 182
peace
    in the church, 178

INDEX

God's love and, 37, 69
inner, 7
justice and, 7, 18, 69
in the new creation, 95
through the Messiah, 18, 103
Pentecost, 152, 156
performative truth, xii, 9, 38, 163
Pergamum, 139
perseverance/persistence, 140–41, 145
Persian Empire, 103, 129, 135
perspective, 22–26, 53, 60, 164
Peter (Simon)
    Chair of, 47
    denial of Jesus Christ, 125
    giving up everything, 124
    identity of Jesus Christ and, 112, 119
    the resurrection and, 124–26
    as rock, 182
    as Satan, 112, 182
    walking on water by, 49
Philadelphia, 138
Pilate, Pontius, 63–64, 100, 114, 117
Pius XII, Pope, 18, 175
pluralism. *See also* diversity in the church; inclusivity
    definition of, 107
    benefits of, 16, 95, 106
    difficulties with, 16–17
    pastoral ministry and, 177
Poland, Communist, 5
politics/political structures
    definition of, 4
    Christian involvement in, 94–95, 104–5
    church leaders and, 7
    as human constructs, 5, 149
    interactions in, 73
    Jesus Christ on, 114
popes. *See also* infallibility, papal
    Leo XIII, 22–23, 175
    Pius XII, 18, 175
    Paul VI, xii
    John Paul II, 4–5
    Benedict XVI, xii, 4–5, 104
    Francis, xii, 34
potentiality, 157, 164
power in the church. *See also* empowerment of believers

God as source of, 62, 66–68, 70
    the Holy Spirit and, 153
    Jesus Christ on, 49–50, 63–65, 112–17
    loss of, 3
    misuse of, 3, 25, 61–63, 90, 104
    use of, 61–63
praxis, 77
Prayer of St. Michael (Leo XIII), 22–23
preaching/homilies
    avoidance of expansive religiosity in, 8
    Christian values in, 12
    Jesus Christ in, 102, 134
    misuse of, 24–25, 104–5
presence of God, 26–28
procession of triune God, 164–70
Protestantism, 105
Providentissimus Deus (Leo XIII), 18, 175

questions and doubts, 9, 42–49, 72–74

Rahab, 182
Rahner, Karl
    on coming to God through Jesus Christ, 102
    on freedom to question, 47–48
    on God's nearness, 162–64
    on God's self-communication, 163–64
    on hypostatic union, 99–100
    on knowledge of God, 72
    on original sin, 34–35
    on the resurrection, 133
    on salvation, 86
    on the transcendent, 85–86
ransom, 113–14, 116
reconciliation to God, 36, 110, 124–25, 162
relationship
    with God, 68, 109, 166
    with others, 93–94, 166, 170
religion. *See also* aspirational Christianity; authority, religious; Nietzsche, Friedrich; Sloterdijk, Peter; Geertz, Clifford; Taylor, Mark
    definition of, 189–90
    functions of, 12, 29

religion (continued)
   expansive (*See* expansive religiosity)
   explicit, 8–9, 91, 157, 159, 172
   influence on society and culture, 5, 8
   language of, 10–11
   as morality, 96
   narcissism and, 24–25
   power in, 3, 61–65, 68, 70
resilience, 33
the resurrection
   of believers, 18, 56, 57, 110, 144
   of Jesus Christ, 89, 110, 122–34, 128 n2
the return of Jesus Christ, 18, 132, 140
revelation. *See* the Scripture/revelation
Revelation, Book of, 138–39, 140
rights, human/equality, 95, 159, 178
rites and sacraments, 16, 18, 30–31, 79, 171, 176. *See also various rites and sacraments*
Roman Empire
   crucifixion in, 115
   Jesus Christ and, 19
   oppression by, 112, 116, 129, 142
   power of, 63–65
Rome (city), 126, 183
Romeo and Juliet (Shakespeare), 178 n3
Rorty, Richard, 63 n5
Ruth, 182

the Sabbath, 117, 125
Salome, 124
salvation
   creation and, 56–57
   the Hebrew Scriptures on, 18
   light as symbol of, 56
   participation in, 195
   this-worldly vs. other-worldly, 22–23
   through Jesus Christ, 19, 35, 110, 151
Salve Regina (Leo XIII), 22–23
Samaritans, 49
San Martin, Inés, 34
the Sanhedrin, 64–65, 117
Santner, Eric, 29, 81
Sarah (wife of Abraham), 17, 54, 60
Sardis, 139
Satan/the devil, 23, 112, 136, 139, 182

Saul/Paul, 182
schema/schemata, 12, 94, 95, 101, 108, 156, 164, 167, 174, 192
Schillebeeckx, Edward, 173–74, 186
Schmaus, Michael, 153
science and evolution, 4, 8, 157
the Scripture/revelation
   as authoritative, 21, 111
   the church's need for, 57
   contact with God in, 18–19
   as foundation for pastoral theology, xii, 48, 110, 145, 190
   the Hebrew Scriptures, 18, 175
   Jesus Christ and, 18
   misuse of, 110
   use of story in, 110
the Second Coming, 18, 132, 140
the Second Vatican Council
   on the church, 18, 158, 175, 182
   on culture, 22
   on ecumenism, 19, 176
   on holiness, 97–98, 176
   on lay involvement, 17, 167–69, 176, 193
secularization, 4–6, 8, 104, 149
security, ontological, 45–48
self, coherent, formation of. *See also* spirituality
   overview, 6, 13, 38, 179
   the church and, 14, 17, 192
   doubt and questioning and, 44
   perspective in, 24–26
the Sermon on the Mount
   in the daily lectionary, 92–93
   on faithful and unfaithful servants, 142
   as Jesus Christ's holiness code, 20
   on judgment of the nations, 143
   love and, 59, 69
The Seven Story Mountain (Merton), 145–46
Shakespeare, William, 178 n3
shepherds, 100
Signs, Book of (John 1–11), 93
Simeon, 100
Simon the Zealot, 115
sin. *See also* evil; forgiveness
   confession of, 25–26, 31, 96–97, 170

definition of, 153
freedom from, 56–57
original, 34–35, 37, 184
substitutionary atonement for, 109–10
skepticism, modern, 42
Sloterdijk, Peter, 12–14, 75, 91, 103–4
Smyrna, 138
social boundaries. *See* boundaries, social
social death, 178, 178 n3
social interactions, 3–6, 91, 107, 192. *See also* community, Christian
society/culture, xiii–xiv, 3–6, 146
Socrates, 13, 75, 104
soldiers/guards at tomb, 125, 127
solitude, 42–43, 49–50
Solomon, King, 101, 182
sorrow/mourning, 33–34, 185–86. *See also* bereavement/grief
the soul
    relationship to the body, 27, 57, 77, 77 n16
    religion and, 146
    threefold aspect of, 41–42
    the world and, 146
Sources of the Self (Charles Taylor), 75
Spirit, Holy. *See* the Holy Spirit
spiritual home, 7, 9–11, 15–16, 159, 181
spirituality, 75–78, 78 n18, 87
substitutionary atonement, 109–10
suffering. *See also* death
    comfort in, 29–34
    future glory and, 148
    God's victory over, 23, 184
    Jesus Christ's experience of, 30, 185
    pervasiveness of, 184
    solidarity with, 33–34, 185
    theodicy and, 29, 150–51
the suffering servant, 64, 112
Sullivan, Henry Stack, 46
Susanna, 182
swaddling clothes, 100–101
symbols, 10–11, 164

Tamar, 182

Taylor, Charles, 46–47, 73–74, 75, 158–59, 178
Taylor, Mark, 12, 18, 94–95
Tears and Saints (Cioran), 33, 185
tears/crying, 33–34, 185–86
Teilhard de Chardin, Pierre, 55
the temple, 110, 116, 141–42
the temptations of Jesus Christ, 52–53
the Ten Commandments, 51–52
theodicy. *See* evil
Theological Dictionary of the New Testament (Kittel, abridg. Bromiley), 66
theology, pastoral
    expansive religiosity and, 9
    faith in, xi, xiii, 15
    features of, 191–93
    Jesus Christ in, xii
    questions for, 6
    Scripture and creeds in, xii, 48, 110, 145, 190
    systematic *vs.*, xi, 145, 189–90
theoria, 77
Thomas Aquinas, St., 146–47, 155, 164–66, 169–70
Thyatira, 139
Tiberius Caesar, 100
time, 20–22, 41–42
the tomb, 124–27, 130
traditions
    nostalgia and, 21
    open minds and, 108
    original sin and, 34–35
    as polyvalent, 99
    religion and, 190–91
    social needs and, 99
    spirituality and, 75
transcendence, 26–29, 38, 79–86, 91–92, 172
the transfiguration, 67
The Trinity (Augustine), 41–42
the Trinity (doctrine of), 60, 69, 161–73
truth, xii, 9, 38, 70, 140, 163

unity
    in the church, 54, 178
    with God, 18, 35, 73, 120, 132

universalism, 103–5
Unleavened Bread, feast of, 116

values
    choosing guiding, 4
    Christian, xiii, 6–7, 8, 12, 17, 78, 192
    coherent self and, 24–26, 192
    conflict between, 4
    life and, 17–19
    social boundaries and, 19–20
    time and, 20–22
    vast number of, xiii, 6
    the world and, 22–24
The Varieties of Religious Experience (James), 26–27, 42, 72
Varillon, Francois, 151

Vattimo, Gianni, 62, 63 n5, 66–67, 105–6
Veritatis gaudium (Francis), xii
victimization, 118, 127
Vigil for the Deceased, 31
vine and branches, 53
violence, 94, 139–40
Virgin Mary. *See* Mary, Virgin
von Balthasar, Hans Urs, 43, 73

Weber, Max, 22, 105
wine, new, 3
wisdom, 76–77, 104, 152, 154, 194
women in Scripture, 124–26, 129, 182
the world, 22–24, 102–3, 146

Zealots, 115
Zechariah (priest), 100

www.ingramcontent.com/pod-product-compliance
Lightning Source LLC
Chambersburg PA
CBHW062024220426
43662CB00010B/1461